Migration and International Trade

The US Experience since 1945

Roger White

Franklin & Marshall College, USA

Edward Elgar
Cheltenham, UK • Northampton, MA, USA

Published by
Edward Elgar Publishing Limited
The Lypiatts
15 Lansdown Road
Cheltenham
Glos GL50 2JA
UK

Edward Elgar Publishing, Inc.
William Pratt House
9 Dewey Court
Northampton
Massachusetts 01060
USA

A catalogue record for this book
is available from the British Library

Library of Congress Control Number: 2009940742

Mixed Sources
Product group from well-managed
forests and other controlled sources
www.fsc.org Cert no. SA-COC-1565
© 1996 Forest Stewardship Council

ISBN 978 1 84844 696 0

Printed and bound by MPG Books Group, UK

Contents

Acknowledgements

I am grateful to the Franklin & Marshall College Hackman Scholars program and the John F. Kennedy Presidential Library's Abba P. Schwartz Research Fellowship program for their financial support. A special note of thanks to my frequent co-author, Bedassa Tadesse, whose insight into the immigrant–trade relationship has benefited me immeasurably. Shamma Alam and Fei Wang provided excellent research assistance.

PART I

What is the immigrant–trade link and why it matters

Even though international economic integration is but one facet of a more broadly defined 'globalization' that also involves cultural and political integration, much of the anti-globalization backlash witnessed in recent years has focused on matters related to economics. The debate over the proper pace of globalization and what limits or restrictions, if any, can or should be imposed on the process has spread from advanced post-industrial societies to the developing world. In essence, the debate has 'gone global'.

Those in favor of increased economic integration argue that a more open world improves lives as new products and ideas become universally available and that the removal of trade and investment barriers spurs economic and social development. Such development is said to prompt the emergence of democratic institutions, leading adversaries to become allies and people to become empowered. Opponents express concern over related welfare and distributional consequences, the implications for national sovereignty, worries of cultural homogenization and the environmental impact of economic integration. Unfortunately, those on both sides of the debate often speak with certainty even though their positions frequently are based on incomplete information. Although the topic of globalization is far too vast to be adequately addressed here, this book does examine one aspect of economic integration and, hence, of globalization: the influence that immigrants have on trade between their host and home countries.

Chapter 1 defines the immigrant–trade link, discusses why it is important and presents a roadmap for the remainder of the book. Subsequent chapters offer an expansive treatment of the topic by surveying the related literature, presenting the results of our empirical analysis, and offering thoughts on the corresponding public policy implications.

1. An overview of the immigrant–trade relationship

The increased pace and scope of economic integration has contributed, particularly within developed nations, to the emergence of immigration and international trade as important domestic policy issues. A large body of literature has emerged in recent years to detail the positive influences of immigrants on trade between their host and home countries. These pro-trade influences are thought to result from immigrants' knowledge of host and home country customs and business practices, their language abilities and understanding of informal contracting structures, and their connections to business and social networks that act to reduce trade-related transaction costs. Immigrants are also thought to increase their host countries' imports from their respective home countries if they arrive with preferences for home country goods and find that neither the desired products nor reasonable substitutes are available.

Immigrants may also exert indirect influences on their host country's imports if their consumption exposes native-born residents and immigrants from other countries who reside in the host country to home country products. This may lead to spillover effects as these individuals also begin to consume the home country products. If so, then the host country's imports from the immigrants' home countries will increase further. Additionally, immigrants' remittances may enable individuals in the immigrants' home countries to consume at higher levels than would otherwise be possible. If so, this potentially increases the host country's exports to these home countries. Likewise, if immigrants act to increase foreign direct investment (FDI) between their home and host countries, subsequent corresponding increases in host–home country trade may also occur.

While the literature offers assumed channels through which immigrants exert pro-trade influences, it largely fails to identify an underlying basis for the immigrant–trade link or to indicate the public policy relevance. This book serves to fill the corresponding gaps. By providing detailed coverage of the immigrant–trade relationship and offering a quantitative treatment of the US immigrant–trade relationship, the existence of an immigrant–trade link is verified, factors that are likely to contribute to the presence and magnitude of and variation in the link are explored, and the associated public policy implications are considered and discussed. This augments the existing understanding of the implications of economic integration and, more generally, of the globalization process and, by doing so, provides important information that is relevant for domestic policy formulation. Due to limited data availability the empirical analysis is restricted to the period from 1992 to 2006, but the general focus is on the period since the close of World War II as, during this time, US immigration and trade policies underwent marked changes which facilitated increased integration into the global economy/community.

1.1   RECENT PERIODS OF INTERNATIONAL ECONOMIC INTEGRATION

The US immigrant–trade link is perhaps best understood if considered within the context of US and global economic integration. While many view globalization as a recent phenomenon, there have been several periods during which the processes that are generally associated with globalization have been witnessed. The three most recent periods are particularly relevant for the work undertaken here as each has involved changes in US public policy regarding trade, foreign direct investment and immigration.

The first period spans the years from the end of the US Civil War until the onset of World War I. During this time, international trade, FDI and migration all increased significantly. The value of global exports as a share of world income doubled to 8 per cent with much of this growth preceded by a large-scale international reallocation of factor inputs. Additionally, nearly 10 per cent of the world's population migrated internationally during this period. This included an estimated 60 million individuals arriving in the western hemisphere from Europe. Other relatively land-abundant nations, such as Argentina, Australia and New Zealand, also realized rapid population growth that was primarily due to immigration from European nations. At about the same time, a similar outward migration occurred from the densely populated nations of China and India to neighboring countries such as Myanmar, the Philippines, Sri Lanka, Thailand, and Vietnam (World Bank, 2009b).

The international capital flows that preceded the large-scale migrations of this period were quite impressive. Crafts (2000) notes that estimated FDI stocks as a share of gross global product more than doubled in just three decades: from 6.9 per cent in 1870 to 18.6 per cent in 1900. Afterwards, this share leveled, yet in 1913 it remained equal to 17.5 per cent. The movements of labor and capital led to changes in the levels and compositions of countries' outputs, which subsequently translated to growth in international trade. Also during this period of globalization, trade in primary products (that is, commodities produced by extractive industries such as agriculture, fishing, forestry, mining and/or quarrying) roughly tripled, while trade in manufactured products more than doubled, with the majority of this growth being realized after 1895 (League of Nations, 1945).

The onset of World War I brought this period of economic integration to a close, and an era of economic protectionism that led to increases in import tariffs and the adoption of many non-tariff trade barriers coincided with the war's conclusion. The erection of trade barriers led world economic growth first to slow and then to stagnate. Global exports as a share of world income soon declined to the 4 per cent level observed in 1870 (World Bank, 2009b). Like many of its trading partners, the US economy withdrew behind a wall of protectionism. In 1917, the average US tariff on dutiable imports was 38 per cent. By 1931, this value had increased to 55 per cent (Milanovic, 2002). These increases in import tariffs were largely due to two pieces of legislation: the Fordney–McCumber Act of 1922 and the Hawley–Smoot Act of 1930.

In an attempt to promote economic self-sufficiency, the Fordney–McCumber Act imposed tariffs to restrict imports in hopes of expanding domestic firms' production and their market shares. Passage of the Hawley–Smoot Act further limited imports. Once again, the justification was that higher tariffs on imported goods would discourage domestic consumers from importing foreign goods and, with fewer imports entering the US economy, there would be an increase in domestic production. The Hawley–Smoot Act, however, was not passed to promote economic self-sufficiency so much as to increase domestic employment by 'exporting' US unemployment to its principal trading partners. A 'beggar-thy-neighbor' policy, the Hawley–Smoot Act raised tariffs for more than 20 000 imported goods to record levels. In response to both measures, the major trading partners of the US retaliated by imposing tariffs on US exports. Not surprisingly, the volume of US trade (that is, the combined value of US imports and exports as a share of gross domestic product (GDP)) decreased from roughly 12 per cent at the beginning of World War I to 8 per cent at the outset of World War II (Baldwin and Martin, 1999). Coinciding with this decrease in trade intensity, FDI stocks as a share of gross global product, which were equal to 17.5 per cent in 1913, declined sharply to 8.4 per cent by 1930 (Crafts, 2000).

Pre-dating these legislative attempts to restrict international trade, a movement towards influencing the demographic composition of US immigrant inflows began in the latter decades of the nineteenth century. This involved targeted reductions or, in certain instances, the cessation of non-European immigration to the US. The experience of the Chinese is illustrative. A large inflow of Asians, particularly Chinese, to the western US began shortly before the California Gold Rush. In total, an estimated 300 000 Chinese immigrants, predominantly male, arrived between 1843 and 1880. Initially, as there was a need for low-wage labor, the Chinese immigrants were accepted, although begrudgingly in some instances. In the 1850s, however, as the Gold Rush came to a close, efforts were undertaken to limit the inflow of Asians. The State of California passed the Foreign Miners' Tax in 1852 which, although usually enforced for immigrants from China and Mexico, was reportedly often waived for European immigrants. Poll taxes and laundry license fees were also imposed on Chinese immigrants and, to further encumber Chinese immigrants, schools were segregated. Anti-Chinese sentiment was exacerbated by the onset of the 'Long Depression' (1873–9), culminating in 1882 with the passage of the Chinese Exclusion Act. Initially, the Act imposed a ten-year ban on Chinese immigration and banned inter-racial marriage in order to restrict Chinese immigrants from becoming US citizens. The Geary Act (1892) extended the ban for an additional ten years. The Extension of the Exclusion Act (1902) extended the ban once more, and passage of the Exclusion Act of 1904 finally made the ban permanent.

The Chinese Exclusion Act was not the first overt anti-immigrant statute enacted by the US government. That distinction belongs to the Naturalization Act of 1790 which, although it did not restrict immigration per se, discouraged non-European migration by limiting naturalization to only 'free white persons with good moral character'. The Chinese Exclusion Act, however, marked the beginning of a decades-long episode during which US immigration policy was purposefully structured, by and large, to afford sustained entry preference to immigrants from European nations.

Even though legislative efforts banned or limited immigrant inflows from certain countries or regions, the US immigration rate (per 1000 residents) increased from 6.4 in 1870 to 10.4 in 1910 (Crafts, 2000). This enabled the foreign-born share of the US population to increase slightly from 14.4 per cent to 14.7 per cent during the 1870–1910 period (Briggs, 2003). The Immigration Act of 1917 broadened the Chinese Exclusion Act to exclude immigrants from most of Asia. Specifically, the Act required immigrants to pass a literacy test and created the Asiatic Barred Zone. Passed against President Wilson's veto, the Act of 1917 excluded immigration from Afghanistan, Arabia, the East Indies, India, Indochina, Polynesia, and the portion of Russia that lies in Asia. The combined effect of increased migration and the imposition of limits on Asian migration was that the US population continued to be predominantly of European descent.

The Johnson Quota Act of 1921 (the Emergency Quota Act) and the Johnson–Reed Act of 1924 (the Immigration Act of 1924) further codified this preference for European immigrants. The Emergency Quota Act imposed a system under which total annual immigrant inflows were capped at 3 per cent of the 1910 US foreign-born population, and country-specific quotas were implemented such that the composition of subsequent immigrant inflows mirrored the foreign-born population of the US in 1910. The Immigration Act of 1924 is also often referred to as the Japanese Exclusion Act. The Act, which went into effect in 1929, banned Japanese immigration to the US and amended the Emergency Quota Act such that the total annual inflow was adjusted downward to equal only 2 per cent of the 1890 US foreign-born population. Further, country-specific immigrant entry quotas were determined based on the demographic composition of the US foreign-born population in 1890. Due in part to these stringent restrictions, the US immigration rate (again, per 1000 residents) declined from 10.4 in 1910 to 3.5 in 1930 (Crafts, 2000) and, by 1940, the foreign-born population as a share of the US population had decreased to only 8.8 per cent (Briggs, 2003).

Passage of the Magnuson Act in 1943 (the Chinese Exclusion Repeal Act), the Displaced Persons Acts of 1948, 1950 and 1951, and the McCarren–Walter Act of 1952 (which changed the laws governing the naturalization of immigrants and removed the ban on Japanese immigration) marked the beginnings of a shift in US immigration policy that would culminate with the Hart–Cellar Act of 1965. This Act is more commonly known as the Immigration and Nationality Act of 1965 or, more simply, as the Immigration Act of 1965. For the purposes of understanding the US immigrant–trade link, it is important to note that although there were significant changes in the source regions/countries of immigrant arrivals following the July 1968 implementation of the Act of 1965, the policy change was made possible by the legislative changes that began following the end of World War II.

The changes in immigration policy that occurred in the years after World War II coincided with shifts in US trade policy and the creation of several international institutions that were charged with the responsibility of fostering greater economic interaction between nations. The Reciprocal Tariff Act of 1934 marked the beginning of a movement towards increased trade openness by giving the Executive branch of the US government the authority to negotiate bilateral tariff reductions, essentially reversing the effects of the Fordney–McCumber Act and the Hawley–Smoot Act. Even so, the dismantling of trade barriers was hindered by the prolonged duration of the Great Depression, World War II, and general protectionist sentiment. The volume of US trade decreased from 9.2 per cent of GDP in 1929 to 6.9 per cent in 1939 and was only 4.8 per cent in 1945 (FRBSL, 2009a; 2009b and 2009c). In July 1944, however, representatives of the 44 Allied nations met at the United Nations Monetary and Financial Conference (more commonly known as the Bretton Woods Conference) to discuss the post-war international financial architecture. The results were the establishment of the International Monetary Fund (IMF), the International Bank for Reconstruction and Development (IBRD), which is now part of the World Bank Group, and the General Agreement on Tariffs and Trade (GATT), which remained in operation until it was replaced, in 1995, by the World Trade Organization (WTO).

The establishment of the IMF, the IBRD and the GATT, coupled with the relaxation of US immigration policy, generally corresponds with the start of a second period of globalization that emerged at the close of World War II and lasted until roughly 1980. During these decades, the developed economies of Europe, North America and Japan restored trade relations through a series of multilateral liberalizations. Technological advances continued to result in lower transport costs, and the noted multilateral negotiations led to reductions in tariffs and non-tariff barriers. This led to increases in the volume of US trade; however, the sum of exports and imports did not reach the 1929 level of 9.2 per cent of GDP until 1969, and in 1980 the US volume of trade was only equal to 12.3 per cent of GDP (FRBSL, 2009a; 2009b and 2009c).

While other developed countries, such as Australia and New Zealand, shared in the post-World War II trading boom, much of the developing world chose to maintain high barriers on many imports. Often, these bar-riers existed for the purpose of generating government revenue; however, in a number of instances, the governments of developing nations sought to limit imports in order to promote domestic production of comparable goods. The result of these 'import substitution' and/or 'infant industry' policies was that, while trade between developed economies flourished, developing countries continued to face substantial barriers to trade in most products other than primary commodities. The restrictions, main-tained on developing countries' exports by developed countries and on developed countries' exports by most developing countries, led developing nations to trade, on average, less intensively than developed countries and less in general than would be expected in the absence of such barriers.

The Immigration Act of 1965 replaced the quota system that had first been implemented by the Emergency Quota Act of 1921, and that had been later modified by the McCarren–Walter Act of 1952, with a system that granted priority to immigrants based on three principles: family reunification, filling vacancies in the labor market, and the entrance of refugees and asylum-seekers. The policy change soon produced a shift in the source countries/regions of US immigrant inflows. After the Act was implemented in July 1968, the principal departure regions of immigrant arrivals quickly changed from Europe, Canada and, to a much lesser extent, Australia and New Zealand, to Asia, the Caribbean Basin, Mexico and Central America. This led, in subsequent decades, to a decrease in the proportion of the US immigrant population that was born in Europe and increases in the shares that were born in Latin America (that is, Mexico and Central America) and the Caribbean Basin and in Asia. More specifically, in 1960, 74.5 per cent of all US immigrants had been born in Europe; however, by 2000, that figure had declined to 15.8 per cent. Similarly, between 1960 and 2000, the proportion of the US immigrant population that had been born in Asia increased from 5 per cent to 26.4 per cent, while the proportion of the population born in Latin America increased from 9.3 per cent to 51.7 per cent (Briggs, 2003; US Census, 2003).

The current period of globalization began roughly in 1980 when a number of then-developing countries (for example, Bangladesh, China, India, Indonesia, Mexico, Morocco, the Philippines, Sri Lanka and Turkey) began to enact policies that would increase their participation in global markets. As this occurred, the US volume of trade more than doubled from its 1980 value of 12.3 per cent to 29.3 per cent in 2008 (FRBSL, 2009a; 2009b and 2009c). This 17 percentage point increase in the intensity of US trade is particularly striking when one considers that the value increased by only 3.1 percentage points during the more than five decades from 1929 until 1980. Inclusion of a large portion of the developing world made the globalization process much more global in scope. As with prior periods, transport costs have decreased in part due to technological advances but also because greater trade in services has decreased the average weight of traded products. This reduction in 'trade weight' is to some degree a distinct characteristic of the current period (IOM, 2008).

As mentioned, in conjunction with the developing world's general opening to the global economy, the US has realized large and sustained increases in the number of immigrant arrivals from many developing countries. The most notable example is that of Mexico. The 1970 Census counted approximately 760 000 Mexican-born individuals in the US. Three decades later, in 2000, that number had increased more than tenfold, as the Census counted 7.8 million Mexican-born US residents. While undocumented immigrants may well participate in the US census, it is likely that some (and perhaps many) would seek to avoid inclusion. Of the estimated 8.5 million unauthorized immigrants in the US in 2000, 4.68 million were thought to be from Mexico (US DHS, 2007a). This places the Mexican-born population of the US in 2000 at upwards of 13.2 million persons, a proportional increase from the 1970 Census count of more than 1600 per cent.

In total, the 1970 Census counted 9.6 million foreign-born residents in the US. The 2000 Census estimated the nation's foreign-born population at slightly more than 31 million persons. Although Mexico accounts for a very large portion of the increase in the US foreign-born population, it is hardly the lone contributor. In 1970, for example, the US was home to fewer than 200000 individuals from each of China, the Dominican Republic, El Salvador, India, the Philippines, South Korea and Vietnam; however, in 2000, the US was home to 765000 immigrants from El Salvador and 692000 immigrants from the Dominican Republic. Even larger increases were observed in the numbers of immigrants from several Asian nations: China (1.4 million immigrants in the US in 2000), the Philippines (1.2 million), India (1 million), Vietnam (863000) and South Korea (701000).

As the US foreign-born population has increased, so too have FDI flow, and trade flows; offering evidence of the extent to which economic integration has developed in recent decades. In 2007, global FDI inflows reached $1.83 trillion, a value that was equal to slightly more than 3.3 per cent of gross global product. This figure dwarfed the $58 billion of global FDI flows (0.5 per cent of gross global product) witnessed a mere quarter of a century earlier (UNCTAD, 2008). During this same period, global exports of goods and non-factor services increased from 19.8 per cent to 31.4 per cent of world income (UNCTAD, 2008). The US experienced increases in FDI flows and trade flows largely comparable to those witnessed globally. The sum of US FDI inflows and outflows increased from 0.5 per cent to 4.1 per cent of GDP (US BEA, 2008a and 2008b), while the US trade volume more than doubled. Just as the US experience with respect to FDI flows and trade flows largely mirrored corresponding global changes, between 1980 and 2006 the US foreign-born population nearly tripled, increasing from 14.1 million persons to 37.5 million persons (US Census, 2008 and 2006), while the estimated number of immigrants worldwide doubled during the period to approximately 200 million persons (UN, 2005; IOM, 2008).

The depth of global economic integration, as measured by trade- and FDI-to-GDP ratios and by increases in international migration, has been echoed by increased interconnectedness among individuals and greater international engagement by national governments. In recent decades, sustained and significant increases have been realized in international tourism and overseas telephone traffic. More recently, Internet access/usage has become more common although this is, admittedly, largely driven by technological innovation and general economic development. Nonetheless, nearly all national governments have expressed a desire for greater inter-connectedness with other nations and have acted to increase the degrees to which they are engaged with other governments and international organizations. Even so, the absolute extent to which economies are integrated, that individuals are connected, and to which governments are engaged to their respective international counterparts remains somewhat limited as compared to the possibilities. This suggests that the process of economic integration as a component of a larger globalization will continue, and will remain an important topic of public and political debate.

1.2 WHY THE IMMIGRANT–TRADE LINK MATTERS

While it is reasonable to expect periodic ebb and flow in the integration of the US economy into the global economy, the immense benefits that economic integration has conferred and the potential gains it promises ensure that the process will not be abandoned. To be sure, there are negatives that accompany this process; however, the net effect on social welfare has largely been viewed as positive. The corresponding gains, however, often appear to be less than fully acknowledged by the public or by elected officials who are charged with the responsibility of formulating public policy. Frequently, it appears that US immigration policy and, to a considerably lesser extent, trade policy are structured to minimize associated costs rather than to maximize the corresponding net social benefits. In short, the public and political debates surrounding these policies are frequently framed such that the discussion becomes 'how many immigrants (or imports) can we afford to let enter the country?' rather than 'what policy maximizes the net social benefits of immigration (or trade)?' By not fully considering the beneficial aspects of immigrants or of trade, policymakers are restricted to formulate and implement sub-optimal public policies.

The views held by the public are important as they may influence policymakers either through the electoral process or via a formal lobbying process. To provide a deeper understanding of public opinion on issues relating to globalization, Scheve and Slaughter (2001) review responses to a large number of US public opinion polls that were conducted between 1988 and 2000. Offering important and detailed insights, the authors conclude that survey respondents generally acknowledge the benefits conferred by international trade such as lower product prices, greater product variety, technology transfers and incentives for domestic producers to innovate. However, a majority of respondents also worry that increased trade liberalization contributes to job loss and places downward pressure on wages for American workers. A telling finding is that, when asked questions that offered a choice between the benefits and costs of international trade, respondents generally chose the answer that emphasized costs. One such example is from an October 1999 Program on International Policy Attitudes survey. Respondents were asked which of the following two statements best reflects their views:

Statement A: Foreign trade has been good for the US economy, because demand for US products abroad has resulted in economic growth and jobs for Americans here at home.

Statement B: Foreign trade has been bad for the US economy, because cheap imports from abroad have hurt wages and cost jobs here at home.

Thirty-two per cent of respondents chose Statement A, while 58 per cent chose Statement B.[1] While this is only one example, it is largely emblematic of the responses to similar survey questions during the period.

More recent opinion polls offer similar evidence:[2]

- Two NBC News/Wall Street Journal polls, conducted in December 2007 and in March 2008, found 58 per cent of respondents believed increased globalization had been bad for the American economy 'because it has subjected American companies and employees to unfair competition and cheap labor'. Only 25 per cent and 28 per cent of respondents, respectively, believed that increased globalization was beneficial 'because it has opened up new markets for American products and resulted in more jobs'.
- A separate NBC News/Wall Street Journal poll, conducted in March 2007, found that 48 per cent of respondents believe the US 'is being harmed by the global economy', while 25 per cent believe the US 'is benefiting from the global economy'. Likewise, two *Los Angeles Times*/Bloomberg polls (November 2007 and May 2008) found that 44 per cent and 50 per cent, respectively, of respondents believed that free trade has hurt the US economy, while only 26 per cent and 27 per cent of respondents, respectively, were of the opinion that free trade has been beneficial for the economy.
- An April 2006 *USA Today*/Gallup poll found that 65 per cent of respondents believed that trade 'mostly hurts American workers' while only 30 per cent believe it 'mostly helps American workers'. An interesting follow-up question asked whether or not American companies were mostly helped or hurt by increased trade: 50 per cent of the respondents believed that trade mostly hurts American

firms and 44 per cent of those surveyed reported believing that trade mostly helps.

- Indicative of both the cleavage in public opinion regarding trade and the extent to which the public is uncomfortable with the potential effects of trade, eight Gallup Poll surveys conducted between 2001 and 2009 asked the question: 'What do you think foreign trade means for America? Do you see foreign trade more as an opportunity for economic growth through increased US exports or a threat to the economy from foreign imports?'

  A large proportion of respondents, slightly less than 45 per cent, on average, considered trade to be a threat, while slightly more than 46 per cent of respondents considered trade to be an opportunity for economic growth. This near-even split in public opinion was persistent across the eight polls, as the share of respondents who believed trade to be a threat ranged from 37 per cent to 52 per cent, while the share who believed trade to be an opportunity for growth ranged from 41 per cent to 52 per cent.

Members of the American public who favor maintaining current immigrant inflow levels or who advocate a more liberal immigration policy include the business lobby, which is comprised of those who hope to gain access to immigrant labor. In recent years, union leaders have also expressed support for expanded legal migration and for amnesty for illegal immigrants. This has been viewed as an attempt to increase union presence/ power through expanded union membership. Unlike their leaders, union members generally oppose a more liberal immigration policy and prefer reducing current inflow levels. Environmentalists fall on both sides of the issue. Those favoring increased immigration argue that by having immigrants in the US, where environmental protection may be more stringent as compared to their home countries, less strain is placed on the environment worldwide. Environmentalists opposed to a more lax immigration policy and/or that prefer reducing current inflow levels contend that having the immigrants in the US places an undue strain on local ecosystems. In general, opposition also includes worries that immigration leads to an expansion of the welfare state, dilutes American culture and may even pose a threat to national security (Daniels, 2003; Tichenor, 2002). A final basis for opposition is the argument that immigrants adversely affect public finances and, in doing so, represent a net tax burden to the native-born (Borjas and Hilton, 1996; Borjas, 1999; Fix and Passel, 2002; Zimmerman and Tumlin, 1999; Smith and Edmonston, 1997). In short, the issue is divisive and there is no shortage of competing perspectives or opinions.

Since the US economy usually creates more jobs than can be filled by native-born workers, one benefit of immigration is the increase in aggregate output that results when immigrants fill vacancies in the domestic labor market. For example, new immigrants accounted for more than half of the employment growth witnessed during the 1990s (Sum et al., 2002) and this certainly contributed to overall economic growth. Similarly, since American colleges and universities commonly graduate too few native-born science and engineering students relative to the growth in labor demand for workers in possession of such skills, domestic firms gain in terms of their competitiveness by employing high-skilled immigrant workers. Immigrants are also more likely than members of the native-born population to be self-employed or business owners (Batalova and Dixon, 2005). Thus, it is likely that immigrants also create employment opportunities. In addition to labor market-related benefits, immigrants add cultural diversity to the US population, and immigration is an important aspect of US foreign policy in the sense that immigrants, through their interactions with family, friends and colleagues in their home countries, convey information regarding the values and culture of the US. In spite of these benefits, poll respondents frequently express worry regarding immigrants' labor market effects. In fact, the results of several polls indicate the public prefers either holding constant the number of immigrants admitted to the US each year or allowing fewer immigrants to enter.

- A series of National Election Studies surveys, conducted in 1992, 1994 and 1996, asked respondents: 'Do you think the number of immigrants from foreign countries who are permitted to come to the US to live should be increased a little, increased a lot, decreased a little, decreased a lot, or left the same as it is now?'

  In 1992, a plurality of respondents (46.9 per cent) answered that they would prefer a decrease (either by a little or a lot) in the number of immigrant arrivals. This figure increased to majorities in 1994 and 1996 as 62.9 per cent and 51 per cent, respectively, favored decreasing the number of immigrants admitted. In each of the three surveys, fewer than one in ten respondents expressed a preference for increasing the number of immigrant arrivals, with the remaining responses in favor of holding inflow levels constant.

A cursory review of more recent public opinion polls provides equally interesting responses.

- A series of Gallup polls (conducted each June from 2002 to 2008, with the exception of 2004) posed the following question: 'On the whole, do you think immigration is a good thing or a bad thing for this country today?'

In each poll, the majority of respondents (ranging from 52 per cent in 2002 to 67 per cent in 2006) were of the opinion that immigration was a good thing for the country. Further, other than the 2002 poll, when the gap between the shares of respondents answering 'good' or 'bad' was 10 per cent, the margin of 'good' over 'bad' was not less than 27 per cent. While this would suggest that a majority of the public holds a favorable opinion of immigrants, the results of five NBC News/*Wall Street Journal* polls, conducted between April 2006 and December 2007, asked respondents: 'Would you say that immigration helps the United States more than it hurts it, or immigration hurts the United States more than it helps it?'

The responses show no clear overall opinion, as the share of respondents answering that immigration 'helps more' ranged from 39 per cent to 46 per cent, and the share of respondents answering that immigration 'hurts more' ranged from 42 per cent to 52 per cent.

- Two NBC News/*Wall Street Journal* polls, conducted in March 2005 and December 2007, respectively, found that 46 per cent and 40 per cent of respondents viewed immigration as a benefit 'because immigrant workers fulfill jobs in America that citizens either do not want or cannot do', while 45 per cent and 43 per cent viewed immigration as a threat 'because immigrant workers take jobs that would otherwise be fulfilled by American citizens'.

- Asked the question 'In your view, should immigration be kept at its present level, increased or decreased?', respondents to a dozen Gallup Polls that were conducted between March 2001 and June 2008 consistently reported preferences for either holding migration at its current level or decreasing the number of immigrant arrivals. On average, only 14 per cent of respondents favored allowing more immigrants to enter each year; however, more than 46 per cent favored decreasing the number of arrivals, and slightly more than 36 per cent favored holding the number of arrivals constant. The public's views on this topic were quite stable over time. The share of respondents who favored increased immigration ranged from 8 per cent to 18 per cent, while the share who favored decreasing immigration ranged from 39 per cent to 58 per cent.

Scheve and Slaughter (2001) conclude that the opinions of the American public regarding these facets of globalization are linked to uncertainty, characterized by a discernible level of risk aversion, and marked by an overall lack of information pertaining to the issues at hand. Further, the authors argue that the anti-globalization sentiment indicated by responses to public opinion polls reveals skepticism regarding the benefits of globalization and, in particular, worries about the domestic labor market consequences of increased economic integration. As the results of more recent opinion polls are aligned with the results of earlier polls that were examined by Scheve and Slaughter (2001), it appears that US public opinion on these topics has not fundamentally changed in recent years.

It may appear contradictory for the public both to recognize the benefits associated with international trade and immigration while also offering tepid support for these forms of integration. These views, however, are entirely reasonable if we consider that the American public may be risk-averse with respect to migration and trade. This would lead individuals who are aware that they will probably gain from economic integration to oppose integration and be willing to forgo associated benefits because they believe that their opposition may reduce the likelihood they will experience an adverse outcome. Generally speaking, such risk aversion is rooted in a desire to avoid losses. This means that individuals are willing to pay, in the form of forgone benefits, to reduce the likelihood that they will suffer a loss. In such a scenario, the tendency to strongly prefer avoiding losses provides an explanation for observed public opinion relating to the topics of immigration and trade. In Chapter 11 we discuss risk-averse preferences for immigration as they have implications for public policy formulation.

1.3   WHAT WE ARE DOING IN THIS BOOK (AND HOW WE DO IT)

The tensions reflected in the polling data appear to signal uncertainty, seemingly attributable to limited or incomplete information, regarding the expected outcomes of greater integration of the US economy into the global economy. With respect to both trade and immigration, there appears to be a considerable lack of information among the public in terms of the specifics of the issues. For example, it is quite likely that the perceived risk of experiencing an adverse labor market outcome is in excess of the actual risk and/or that the extent of benefits to be received is understated when individuals formulate their opinions regarding immigration and trade. The intent of this work is, in part, to confer information that results in a better-informed public, more efficient public policy formulation and, hence, a greater likelihood that the potential gains of global economic integration will be garnered. Creation of a US immigration policy that confers the greatest benefits to the largest number of citizens while minimizing the associated costs requires as accurate an accounting of the related benefits and costs, both real and perceived, as is possible. The immigrant–trade relationship is examined in detail to confirm and explore this source of benefits. In doing so, this work contributes to a better understanding of how the immigrant–trade link operates which, in turn, provides for a deeper and more precise understanding of the globalization process.

This book contains four parts. We begin by providing an overview of the immigrant–trade relationship and the general theoretical intuition/framework upon which the examination of the US immigrant–trade link is based. The first part also contains a review of the relevant literature. From this, a series of testable hypotheses regarding the immigrant–trade relationship is generated. The second part discusses the underlying factors that are thought to affect the operability of the US immigrant–trade link. The third part presents the data, the empirical strategy/framework and a discussion of the corresponding results as they relate to the hypotheses presented in the first part. Finally, the book concludes with a discussion of the associated policy implications, final thoughts and possible avenues for future research.

The remainder of this introductory part begins, in Chapter 2, by considering whether the theoretical relationship between immigrants and trade is one of complements or of substitutes. Factor-endowment models of trade (that is, the Heckscher–Ohlin model and the Specific-Factors model) generally hold that migration and trade are substitutes; however, under certain conditions, factor-endowment models predict a complementary relationship. Similarly, models of trade based on New Trade Theory treat migration and trade as potentially complementary activities. As a complementary relationship between migration and trade is agnostic in terms of the direction of causality, the chapter elaborates on the channels via which immigrants are thought to influence host–home country trade. This is followed in Chapter 3 by a review of the relevant literature. The expectations garnered from the conclusions of prior studies provide testable hypotheses that are addressed as part of our empirical analysis.

Chapters 4 to 7 focus on possible factors that may underlie or 'explain' the US immigrant–trade relationship. Quotation marks are used in the preceding sentence because it is the conditions that may prove conducive for immigrants to exert pro-trade influences that are explored rather than the immigrant–trade relationship necessarily being explained in any strict sense of the word. More specifically, Chapter 4 provides an overview of US immigration history, emphasizing the shift in US immigration policy that began during World War II and which culminated with passage of the Immigration and Nationality Act of 1965. As noted, in the years after World War II, European immigration to the US slowed considerably. This decline occurred in conjunction with an increase in the flows of immigrants from Asia, Latin America and the Caribbean Basin. In fact, immigrant inflows from these latter regions accelerated sufficiently that they emerged as the primary sources for recent immigrant inflows. This history is important as it provides a basis for variation in the immigrant–trade relationship across immigrants' home countries.

The concepts of primacy effects and recency effects are introduced in Chapter 5. Compared to what may be described as more traditional source countries of US immigrant inflows, the home countries of recent arrivals are typically lacking in terms of the presence and quality of requisite trade-facilitating infrastructure. Chapter 6 discusses how immigrants from relatively infrastructure-poor countries potentially face greater opportunities to influence trade relative to immigrants from countries that tend to have more or better infrastructure. Chapter 7 introduces a measure of the cultural differences between the US and each of its trading partners. Greater cultural differences are thought to coincide with variation in preferences across native-born and immigrant populations. Such differences are also thought to correspond with product- and market-related information asymmetries and with US–home country institutional dissimilarity. As a result, cultural differences may affect trade in a number of ways. For example, the findings of several studies suggest that cultural distance inhibits trade by increasing related transaction costs. Immigrants have been found to offset, at least in part, this trade-inhibiting influence; however, similar to variation in preferences, variation in US–home country cultural and/or institutional (dis)similarity is likely to generate differences in immigrants' opportunities, and hence their abilities, to affect trade.

Chapters 8 to 10 present our empirical examination. Chapter 8 presents the data and econometric specifications. Chapter 9 verifies the pro-trade effect of immigrants and examines variation in the US immigrant–trade link across a number of immigrant characteristics and in relation to US–home country cultural distance. Chapter 10 considers the extent to which the link is explained by variables controlling for what are termed 'primacy' and 'recency' effects and how these effects relate to US–home country cultural distance. We also explore the effects of immigrants on disaggregated measures of trade to gain further insights into the trade-intensification effects of immigrants as well as discerning their trade-initiation effects.

Finally, Chapter 11 discusses asymmetric information and risk-averse preferences as explanations for observed public opinion on the topics of migration and trade. It also summarizes the findings of the analysis presented in Chapters 8 to 10 and considers the implications of the immigrant–trade link for US immigration policy. In Chapter 12, we conclude by revisiting the central theme of understanding the immigrant–trade relationship and its relation to the broader topic of globalization, summarizing our findings, discussing the corresponding policy implications and suggesting possible extensions to the literature.

NOTES

1. Due to additional responses being offered by interviewers or other responses offered voluntarily by respondents, poll numbers generally do not sum to 100 per cent. For example, for this poll, the remaining respondents answered either 'Some of both' (6 per cent) or 'Unsure' (4 per cent).
2. Unless noted as being from Scheve and Slaughter (2001), information related to polls conducted since 2000 are from Polling Report (2009a and 2009b).

2. What are the channels through which immigrants affect trade?

There are several channels through which immigrants are thought to affect trade between their host and home countries. The direct channels include a 'preference effect' and an 'information bridge' effect. Greenaway et al. (2008) suggest that this latter effect consists of separate 'cultural bridge' and 'enforcement bridge' effects. First, due to their preferences for home country products, immigrants potentially increase their host country's imports from their home country. Second, immigrants may have the ability to act in various capacities as de facto trade intermediaries that resolve information asymmetries which contribute to higher trade-related transaction costs and, hence, that hinder trade. If so, then both the host country's imports from and exports to the immigrants' home countries would potentially increase. Likewise, immigrants may be connected to business and/or social networks in their host and home countries that aid in the matching of buyers and sellers and in ensuring the enforcement of informal contracts.

Indirect effects include the possibility that immigrants' consumption of home country goods exposes other host country residents to such products. Thus, there is the potential that these individuals' preferences will be altered such that they too demand home country products. This, of course, would act to further increase the host country's imports from the immigrants' home countries. Additionally, immigrants often send remittances to individuals in their home countries and may also act to increase host–home country FDI flows. If remittances are allocated towards consumption, then the exports of the host country may increase as a result. Similarly, greater FDI flows may lead to subsequent increases in the host country's exports to and/or imports from the immigrants' home countries.

Before entering into a more detailed discussion of these channels, we provide a cursory overview of trade theory as it relates to the question of whether migration and trade are viewed as complements or substitutes. Addressing this foundational question buttresses our analysis by providing a theoretical expectation for a positive immigrant–trade link.

2.1 ARE MIGRATION AND TRADE COMPLEMENTS OR SUBSTITUTES?

In recent years, a large body of literature has emerged that firmly establishes a positive statistical relationship between migration and host–home country trade flows. Whether theory predicts a complementary relationship or whether the two are considered likely substitutes depends on the model of trade considered. Under standard assumptions, the Heckscher–Ohlin (H-O) model and its short-run variant, the Specific-Factors (SF) model, suggest that migration and trade are substitutes. These factor endowment-based models predict that trade will lead to the equalization of product prices across trading partners and, under the assumption of competitive factor markets, result in an equalization of factor prices. With respect to labor, the corresponding decrease in wage and income differentials across trading partners reduces the incentive to migrate. In other words, in an 'H-O world' trade substitutes for migration in the sense that an increase in the former is expected to decrease the latter. However, as we examine the assumptions that underlie the standard H-O and SF models, the appropriateness of these models in terms of evaluating the expected relationship between migration and trade becomes questionable.

The most basic version of the H-O model employs a $2 \times 2 \times 2$ framework. That is, there are two countries, which can be referred to, for simplicity, as home and foreign. Each country produces two goods (which we will call X and Y) using two factor inputs (labor and capital, denoted by L and K, respectively). The model assumes differences in the endowments of L and K across the two countries. In this regard, the H-O framework departs from the standard Ricardian model of comparative advantage which posits that differences in production technologies across the home and foreign countries determine comparative advantages and the pattern of trade. The Ricardian framework illustrates that Pareto improvements can result from specialization and trade if undertaken in accordance with the Law of Comparative Advantage. The H-O model offers differences in factor endowments as an explanation for the existence of comparative advantage while the Ricardian model, by assuming differences in productive technologies but not explaining the reason for these differences, assumes the basis for comparative advantage. This should not be taken as a critique of the Ricardian framework. Ricardo's aim was to illustrate the potential gains from specialization and trade rather than to explain the underlying basis for the existence of the potential gains.

The H-O model assumes that firms will act to maximize their profits while consumers will act to maximize their utilities. Additionally, the home and foreign countries are assumed to have identical production technologies. This means that, given identical factor input combinations in the home and foreign countries, the same output levels could be achieved. Good X and good Y are also assumed to be identical (that is, homogeneous) across the two countries. In other words, a unit of good X produced in the home country cannot be distinguished from a unit of good X produced in the foreign country. The same applies for good Y. Production of good X and good Y, in both the home and foreign countries, is described by standard Cobb–Douglas production functions that exhibit constant returns to scale. This is to say that, in both countries, the output of good X will increase proportionally to an increase in the amounts of L and K employed in the production process. The same, of course, holds for good Y. Although identical output levels could be achieved in the home and foreign countries, because factor endowments differ it would be inefficient for profit-maximizing firms to produce at such levels. This follows from variation in factor endowments that lead to differences across the two countries in terms of relative factor prices. Thus, the assumed differences in factor endowments dictate that profit-maximizing firms in the home country will employ different production technologies than will be employed by their counterparts in the foreign country.

Regarding the mobility (or immobility) of factor inputs, L and K are assumed to be perfectly mobile within each country but perfectly immobile between the two. The assumption of perfect internal mobility follows from the H-O model being a long-run model of trade. Since in the long-run all factor inputs are variable, the assumption that L and K can be costlessly reallocated between the production of goods X and Y is certainly reasonable. The assumption of factors being perfectly immobile between the two countries is analogous to saying there is no international migration or international capital flows. This assumption of factor immobility is important in terms of the model's appropriateness in identifying the relationship between migration and trade as being one of complements or of substitutes.

Perfect internal competition is assumed in both product and factor markets. This assumption implies, among other things, perfect information. However, imperfect external competition is also assumed. There are no tariffs or non-tariff trade barriers that would hinder trade. Likewise, there are no exchange controls or transportation costs. In essence, the Law of One Price holds, and there is nothing permitted in the model that would lead consumers in either country to favor the output of a local producer over that of a foreign supplier or that would favor the foreign supplier over the local producer.

From the general description of the H-O model provided here, we can state that the predictions of standard factor endowment-based models of trade, with respect to migration, are related to the likelihood that an individual will choose to migrate. The predictions are not related to the influence someone who has migrated may have on trade between their host and home countries. This emphasis on the effect of increased trade on the decision to migrate diminishes the usefulness of these models in terms of predicting the effects that immigrants may have on trade subsequent to having migrated. Nevertheless, working through a simple version of the model is illustrative as it provides information regarding the expected effects of trade on output, consumption and employment levels, the pattern of trade, social welfare and, most important for our purposes, the prices of goods X and Y in each country and, accordingly, wages and incomes.

In autarky, consumption of good X and of good Y is constrained by each country's production capacity. Beginning with a scenario under which both the home and foreign countries produce and consume some amount of each good, the relative prices of the two goods vary across the countries because of the differences in factor endowments between the two. Assuming that the home country is capital-abundant relative to the foreign country, the foreign country must be labor-abundant relative to the home country. Further, if good Y is capital-intensive, then the home country will hold the comparative advantage in the production of good Y, while the foreign country will hold the comparative advantage in good X, the labor-intensive good. Using asterisks to denote the foreign country, from this it follows that in autarky $P_X > P_X^*$ and that $P_Y^* > P_Y$.

It is these initial differences in relative prices that serve as the impetus for trade. The variation in product prices reflects the relative abundance of L and K in the two countries. Reflective of K being relatively abundant in the home country and L being relatively abundant in the foreign country, we have that $K/L > K^*/L^*$. Since factor markets are assumed to be competitive, the implication follows that relative factor returns (that is, the wage rate received by labor, w, and the rental rate of capital, r) are such that $w/r > w^*/r^*$.

As the two countries open to trade, firms that produce good Y in the home country will realize $P_Y^* > P_Y$. Likewise, firms that produce good X in the foreign country will see that $P_X > P_X^*$. These price differentials will lead to shifts in the composition of output in each country towards the good for which they hold the comparative advantage in production and away from the good for which they do not hold the comparative advantage. They will subsequently export the good for which they hold the comparative advantage in exchange for the good for which they do not. Consumers in the home country, seeking to maximize their utilities, will purchase additional units of good X as long as the expected marginal utility derived from the consumption of good X is greater than the expected marginal utility gained from consuming good Y. Given that good X cannot be distinguished from good X^*, as long as consumers are rational and their budgets are constrained to be finite they will choose to purchase the lower-priced good X^* rather than the more expensive good X. Likewise, consumers in the foreign country will purchase Y instead of Y^*. Simply put, the capital-abundant nation will produce and export the capital-intensive good to the labor-abundant nation in exchange for the labor-intensive good. Similarly, the labor-abundant nation will produce and export the labor-intensive good to the capital-abundant nation in exchange for the capital-intensive good. In the example presented thus far, being relatively K-abundant, the home country will produce good Y, the K-intensive good, and export it to foreign, the relatively L-abundant country, in exchange for the L-intensive good X. This prediction regarding the pattern of trade follows directly from the H-O framework and is known formally as the Heckscher–Ohlin Theorem.

The movement from autarky to free trade enhances both individual and social welfare in both countries. Specialization and trade increase each country's set of consumption possibilities and make it possible that the consumption of both good X and good Y increase in both the home country and in the foreign country. These aggregate gains are the result of increases in production and consumption efficiency. Global production efficiency rises due to each country's output mix shifting towards what they produce best and away from the good they are relatively inefficient at producing. Consumption efficiency is increased due to consumers facing a more pleasing set of choices and prices.

Because units of each factor input are assumed to be homogeneous within each country, they can be reallocated without cost between the production of the two goods. Thus, L and K will be reallocated towards the sector that produces good Y in the home country and towards the sector that produces good X in the foreign country. Being a long-run model, full employment is assumed. That is, the increase in the home country's production of the capital-intensive good, Y, necessitates a decrease in their production of good X. Similarly, the foreign country will produce more of the labor-intensive good, X, and less of good Y. This reallocation of factor inputs towards the goods for which comparative advantage is held will lead to a decrease in employment in the sector which produces good X in the home country and in the sector which produces good Y in the foreign country. As these factor reallocations and changes in output mixes occur, the price of good X rises in the foreign country and falls in the home country, and the price of good Y rises in the home country and falls in the foreign country. The implications for associated factor returns are predicted by the Stolper–Samuelson Theorem which states that a rise in the relative price of a good will lead to a rise in the return received by the factor used most intensively in the production of the good, and conversely, to a fall in the return to the other factor.

If conditions regarding factor endowments and factor intensities are as they have been assumed, then initially $P_X > P_X^*$ and $P_Y^* > P_Y$. Because labor markets are assumed to be competitive, it follows that $w_X > w_X^*$ and $w_Y^* > w_Y$, where the subscripts X and Y denote whether labor is employed in the production of good X or of good Y. As explained above, trade in good X and good Y will have implications for product prices and, hence, for factor returns. Real wages and incomes increase in both the home country and the foreign country as nominal wages rise in proportion to the increases in the prices of goods for which comparative advantage is held and imported goods are priced lower than they were under autarky. Because there are no barriers to trade and no transaction costs, with incomplete specialization this process will continue until $P_X = P_X^*$ and $P_Y = P_Y^*$ and $w_X = w_X^*$ and $w^*_Y = w_Y$. That is, the wage rate paid to workers engaged in the production of good X and who produce good Y^* will fall, while the wage rate paid to workers who produce good Y and good X^* will rise. It is this trade-induced narrowing of the wage differentials, known as Factor Price Equalization, which would act to discourage migration if, in fact, the model were to allow for the international movement of labor.

The Factor Price Equalization Theorem predicts that trade leads to an inevitable equalization of goods prices across trading partners and that, with shared production technology and competitive goods and factor markets, results in the prices of the productive factors (that is, L and K in this example) also equalizing across countries. As mentioned, since the H-O framework is a long-run model, perfect competition prevails. In perfectly competitive factor markets, returns depend upon the values of the factors' marginal productivities. The marginal productivity of labor, for example, is the additional output gained, all else equal, when an additional unit of L is used in the production process. The marginal product of labor depends on the amount of labor being used in the production process as well as the amount of capital being used. The level of K acts as a scalar. Given the assumption of constant returns to scale and two productive factors, if more of a factor is employed then the marginal productivity of that factor will decline. The value of each factor's marginal productivity, however, also depends on the market price of the good being produced. As with the level of K employed, the market price of the good also acts as a scalar. A higher market price, all else equal, results in a higher value of marginal productivity for the employed factors.

As noted, under autarky, the prices for good X and good Y are expected to differ across the home and foreign countries. Even if two firms, one located in the home country and the other in the foreign country, produce the same good using the same combination of L and K, the difference in the prices of the goods is sufficient to produce variation in factor returns across the countries. In the H-O model, as it is a variable proportions model, differences in factor returns affect the firms' decisions as to how much L and K should be employed in the production process. Under autarky, factor returns should be expected to vary considerably across trading partners for a number of reasons. With trade, however, there is an expected equalization of product prices across the home and foreign countries, and the identical production technologies in the two countries imply that home and foreign share the same marginal productivity relationships. As prices equalize, so too do factor returns. Because home and foreign are assumed to have different factor endowments, they will produce using the same relative amounts of L and K yet will use different absolute amounts of each factor and thus will produce different quantities of good X and good Y.

A final theorem provided by the H-O model, the Rybczynski Theorem, is very much applicable to our discussion of trade and factor returns. The theorem states that, if the full-employment condition is satisfied, increasing the available quantity of a factor will increase the output of the good that uses that factor intensively and will decrease the output of the other good. In the example provided here, the home country is K-abundant relative to the foreign country and it specializes in the production of the capital-intensive good Y and exports that good to the foreign country in exchange for the labor-intensive good X. If we assume that trade is taking place between the home and foreign countries and labor chooses to migrate from the foreign country to the home country, then the implication from the Rybczynski Theorem is that the foreign country's production of good X will decrease and its production of good Y will increase. In the home country, there will be an expected decrease in the production of good Y and a corresponding increase in its output of good X. Since the pattern of trade was that of the home country exporting good Y to the foreign country in exchange for good X, the migration-induced changes in output compositions lead to less trade as each country begins to produce more of what it was initially importing and less of what it had been exporting.

The example immediately above assumes migration of the foreign country's abundant factor to the home country where it is added to the stock of the home country's scarce factor. Another way of saying this is that, to a certain degree, the foreign country's relative factor abundance is diminished as the migration caused the home country's factor scarcity to subside. If, on the other hand, labor (being scarce in the home country) were to migrate to the foreign country (where, again, it is abundant in relative terms), the outcome in terms of the expected influence on trade is different. Under such a scenario, the home country would produce less of good X and more of good Y, while the foreign country would produce more of good X and less of good Y. This, in turn, would induce more trade between the two countries. Thus, the implication is that migration of the scarce factor is consistent with a complementary migration–trade relationship even in the standard H-O framework.

Further modification of the assumptions which underlie the H-O model yields theoretical predictions of migration and trade being complementary activities. Markusen (1983), for example, shows that if trading partners possess identical factor endowments then relaxing the assumptions of constant returns to scale in production, identical technologies across trading partners, perfectly competitive markets or of no domestic distortions leads migration and trade to be potentially complementary activities. Gould (1994) also notes, as is shown above, that the standard factor endowment-based model of trade can be consistent with a complementary relationship between migration and trade if the host country is labor-abundant. Since the US tends to be capital-abundant relative to the typical immigrant home country, particularly so for the majority of immigrant arrivals during recent decades, such an outcome is largely irrelevant. Variants of the standard model that allow for industry-specific increasing returns to scale in production or human capital-type externalities are also consistent with a complementary immigrant–trade relationship. Such extensions and modifications, however, represent a movement away from the standard factor-endowment framework and a movement towards the assumptions that underlie models based on New Trade Theory (NTT).

The Specific-Factors (SF) model is a close theoretical variant to the H-O model. Known as a short-run version of the H-O model, the SF model allows for intersectoral mobility of factor inputs; however, at all times at least one factor is immobile and, as a result, is said to be sector-specific. Venables (1999) allows for the existence of differences in factor endowments across trade partners and considers the implications of movements by both the mobile and the sector-specific factors. It is shown that under certain conditions – for example, when scarce factors migrate (as indicated above in regards to the Rybczynski Theorem) – it is possible for migration and trade to be complements in the SF framework. However, the general result remains that migration and trade are substitutes. Mundell (1957), Svensson (1984), Markusen and Svensson (1985), Ethier and Svensson (1986) and Wong (1986) also examine the question of whether factor movements and trade are, from a theoretical perspective, complements or substitutes and conclude that the two can be complements or substitutes depending on the assumptions of the model being considered.

Contrary to factor endowment-based models of trade, models based on NTT allow for increasing returns to scale in production, international factor reallocation, monopolistic competition, the presence of transaction costs, and of other agglomeration forces. Monopolistic competition is a key element with respect to the immigrant–trade relationship as it implies imperfect competition, incomplete information and product differentiation. These principal differences, relative to the factor-endowment frameworks, result in theoretical modeling that is conducive to the examination of the influences of factor movements on host–home country trade flows. Generally speaking, unlike basic versions of the H-O and SF models, NTT-based models suggest a complementary relationship between migration and trade.

Increasing returns to scale in production can be internal or external. External increasing returns occur at the industry level, while internal increasing returns are specific to individual firms. Beginning with a scenario in which increasing returns to scale are external to the firm, the standard model of NTT consists of two countries (home and foreign), two goods (X and Y) and two factors of production (labor (L) and capital (K)). As with the factor-endowment models discussed earlier in this chapter, this basic version follows the $2 \times 2 \times 2$ framework. Because each firm is assumed to be small, markets are assumed to be competitive. If trade occurs, then the presence of external increasing returns leads firms in each country to specialize in order to garner the associated gains. The reward received by the intensively-used factor of production will rise. This provides an incentive for international factor reallocation to occur. If factors do migrate, then because of the presence of increasing returns to scale in production there will be a subsequent increase in output in both countries. This facilitates a corresponding increase in trade.

Increasing returns to scale in production may, on the other hand, be internal to the firm or to the sector. A standard example would assume that one of the two sectors is characterized by constant returns to scale in production while the other sector has internal increasing returns to scale. More specifically, we can assume that production in the sector which produces good X exhibits constant returns to scale, while the sector which produces good Y exhibits increasing returns to scale. Further, we can assume that the home country is relatively large as compared to the foreign country. This assumption has no bearing on the model's theoretical predictions except for determining the direction of factor flows. In the presence of monopolistic competition and internal increasing returns to scale in production, the larger economy (that is, the home country in this example) will be a net exporter of good Y, which is produced by the monopolistically-competitive sector. The real return to labor will be higher in the home country, which will spur migration from the foreign country to the home country. This will lead the home country and the foreign country to become more unequal in terms of their labor endowments. This, in turn, increases the basis for trade. As a result, the relationship between factor movements and trade is one of complements.

It is important to note, however, that while models of trade that are based on New Trade Theory suggest a positive relationship between migration and trade, the mechanism through which trade is enhanced is that of increased production that, in the example of monopolistic competition provided here, is facilitated by inward labor migration. In short, it is a production-based story of increased output that is attributable to increased factor inputs which facilitates subsequent increases in trade. More complex models of trade that account for additional factors, such as immigrants' potential abilities to resolve information asymmetries, not only offer migration and trade as likely complementary activities but suggest that migration increases *bilateral* trade, specifically with the immigrants' respective home countries. Having provided a cursory review of trade theory, inasmuch as it relates to the immigrant–trade relationship, we now can consider, in greater detail, the specific channels through which immigrants are thought to increase host–home country trade.

2.2 HOW DO IMMIGRANTS AFFECT TRADE FLOWS?

The influences of immigrants on trade between their host and home countries may be direct or indirect. As noted in the introduction, the direct channels are described, broadly, as *preference* effects and *information bridge* effects. These latter effects include *cultural bridge* effects and/or *enforcement bridge* effects. Indirect effects include *consumption spillover* effects and *FDI-related* and *remittance-funded* effects. Table 2.1 categorizes these effects, and the remainder of this section discusses each in turn.

2.2.1 Preference Effects and Consumption Spillover Effects

Beginning with immigrants' preferences for home country products, such an effect may increase the host country's imports from the immigrants' respective home countries if immigrants arrive in the host country to find that desired products or reasonable substitutes are unavailable. This influence is referred to by White (2007a) as *transplanted home bias*, a play on the term *home bias* which was first used with respect to trade flows by McCallum (1995). Examining trade between Canadian provinces and US

Table 2.1   Channels via which immigrants affect host–home country trade

	Direct	Indirect
Increases host country imports only	Preference effects	Consumption spillover effects
Increases host country exports only	----	Remittance-funded effects
Increases imports and/or exports	Information bridge effects (Cultural bridge effects and/or Enforcement bridge effects	FDI-related effects

states, McCallum shows that there tends to be more internal trade and less external trade than would be predicted by theory even once factors that may impede international trade are accounted for. McCallum coined the term to indicate that, once other factors that may determine trade flows have been accounted for, domestic residents have what appears to be a preference for goods that are produced in their home country, that is, a bias for home country products. White extended the term to a setting in which immigrants carry their preferences for home country products (that is, their home bias) to their new host country.

A related, indirect influence of immigrants on host country imports involves shifts in domestic residents' preferences towards goods from the immigrants' home countries. This may occur as domestic residents are exposed to home country goods through immigrants' consumption activities. All else equal, if a discernible number of domestic residents are influenced such that they alter their consumption behavior then a measurable increase in the host country's imports from the home country would appear in the trade data. This potential indirect relationship can be thought of as a *consumption spillover* effect.

An interesting aspect underlying the preference effect is that, in order for immigrants' preferences to yield discernible increases in imports from their home countries, the desired home country goods (or reasonable substitutes) must: 1) not be readily available in the host country or, if available, only so in inadequate quantities; and/or 2) the varieties of host country-available substitutes must be sufficiently expensive as compared to home country variants of the good; or 3) the host country-available versions of the home country goods must be deemed insufficiently substitutable by the immigrants.

If these effects are present, it follows that preferences are shaped, to some degree, by the individual's internal response to external factors. For example, an individual's preferences may be likely to be influenced by their personal experiences and interactions as well as the culture and environment in which they have been raised and/or have lived as an adult. This potentially leads immigrants' preferences to be dissimilar from those of host country residents who are not from the immigrants' home country. Clearly, this also applies to consumption spillover effects, since the preferences of home country residents would need to be sufficiently pliable as to be altered by exposure to products from the immigrants' home countries.

Differences in individual consumer preferences are relevant for the immigrant–trade relationship to the extent that variation in preferences across individuals, if common to a certain degree, perhaps due to a common culture, would potentially explain immigrants from different home countries holding seemingly different preferences from the native-born residents of their host countries and from immigrants who migrated from other countries/cultures. Without such differences in preferences, there still exists the potential for a pro-import immigrant effect; however, it would not be attributable to a preference effect. For example, differences in the composition of output between an immigrant's home and host countries that result from differences in resources, climates, technology levels, factor endowments, and so on may create conditions that are conducive to the existence of a pro-import immigrant effect. However, that differences in preferences are likely to exist across host and home country residents corresponds with an increased probability that immigrants affect trade.

Related to preferences, a common topic in the immigration policy debate is that of immigrants' assimilation to the cultures of their host countries. Assimilation is a complex process that involves, to varying degrees, adoption of the predominant (or national) language and adherence to commonly-held social expectations. Assimilation may require immigrants to give up long-practiced traditions or to abandon practices (for example, religious practices and/or social conventions) that are common to their home countries. It certainly would not be surprising to find social pressures encouraging immigrants to assimilate, but assimilation also involves voluntary changes in individuals' views, practices and preferences. As a consequence, we can consider that changes in preferences are the result of the individual's internal response to external factors. Again, the pliability of preferences comes into play. When considered in relation to consumption, immigrants who more readily/easily assimilate may be less likely to exert a preference effect on imports or, more simply, to exert such an effect for a shorter period of time after migrating. To the contrary, immigrants who are less able or less willing to assimilate may be more likely to exert a positive influence on their host country's imports from their home country and for this effect to persist for a relatively lengthier period of time. In general, however, one would expect the cumulative influences of preference effects and consumption spillover effects to wane, although perhaps not entirely, with the passage of time.

To the extent that preferences are determined in response to immigrants' exposure to the culture of their home country, those from home countries that, generally speaking, are more similar culturally to their host country would be expected to exert relatively weaker or, perhaps, no preference effects on their host country's imports. Conversely, immigrants from countries that are more culturally dissimilar relative to their host country would be expected to exert stronger effects on home country imports. Considered in relation to the preference channel, the former would correspond with a greater likelihood that host country-available goods are sufficient substitutes for desired home country goods, while the latter may result from a lack of home country products or of sufficient substitutes in the host country.

2.2.2　Information Bridge Effects

Immigrants may also increase both their host country's imports from and/ or exports to their home countries if they arrive in the host country with knowledge of home country customs and expected business practices or if they are connected to business and/or social networks in their home country that, if successfully utilized, serve to decrease trade-related transaction costs. Such knowledge may range from language abilities to the understanding of complex informal contracting structures or it may be useful in overcoming information asymmetries associated with cultural differences. Similarly, immigrants may arrive with established connections to home country business networks that serve to transmit information regarding future business opportunities, assist in the matching of potential buyers and sellers, or that act to deter opportunistic behavior through a form of reputation-enforcement (Rauch and Watson, 2002; Rauch and Trindade, 2002; Rauch, 2001; 1999). Although the information bridge effect can be described as a combination of a cultural bridge effect and an enforcement bridge effect, we use the term 'information bridge' here with the understanding that this channel is broadly defined to include the cultural, enforcement and general information 'bridging' abilities of immigrants.

Asymmetric information regarding products, markets or the expected/ anticipated behavior associated with formal or informal contracting procedures would be expected to correspond with increased transaction costs. Likewise, difficulties in matching buyers and sellers across markets may entail significant search costs. Immigrants may possess the ability to ameliorate costs that result from the information asymmetry problem or that are associated with protracted search, either fully or in part, by acting as trade-intermediaries of sorts. If so, then immigrants would potentially exert positive influences on both their host country's exports to and imports from their home countries.

An example of product-related asymmetric information is that of differentiated products. That variations of products are found both within and across countries and markets and that information regarding these variants may be scarce, provides immigrants with opportunities to convey information regarding home country products and the preferences of home country residents to individuals and firms in their host countries and to relay similar types of information regarding their host countries to individuals and firms in their home countries. This would decrease the extent to which information is asymmetric and, accordingly, would decrease related transaction costs. In a similar vein, immigrants can utilize their connections to business and/or social networks in either their host or their home countries to decrease transaction costs by matching potential trade partners, assisting in contract negotiations and/or aiding in the enforcement of contracts. This would be especially pertinent in instances where formal judiciary avenues to remedy contract disputes are lacking and/or where informal contracting is common. In each of these instances, the exploitation of network connections potentially leads to a reduction in trade-related transaction costs, which would be expected, all else equal, to increase trade between the host and home countries.

Finally, immigrants' language abilities, if from a nation where English (since the analysis undertaken here involves the US as the host country) is not commonly used, may aid in the writing and interpretation of contracts. Further, as the number of immigrants from any home country who reside in the US rises, one would expect an increase to occur in the likelihood that their native language becomes known or becomes more frequently used by host country residents. The increased prominence of Spanish in certain parts of the US which has been witnessed in recent decades is one example of this. This would decrease associated communications-related barriers to trade. Additionally, as language embodies culture (Lazear, 1999; Boisso and Ferrantino, 1997), increased language commonality may correspond, over time, with decreased cultural differences. A number of studies have employed various measures of language commonality as a proxy variable for cultural similarity when estimating the determinants of trade flows, while others have used specific measures of host–home country cultural differences. In nearly all cases, a negative relationship is reported between trade flows and cultural dissimilarity.

While cultural differences would correspond with asymmetric information, incomplete information would surely exist even if there were no
cultural differences between trading partners. This follows, as noted, from
product differentiation and from differences in market structures, laws,
regulations, and so on. It is reasonable to expect that immigrants would
affect trade in differentiated goods to a greater extent than they would
affect trade in more homogeneous goods. At an extreme, trade in goods
that are generally homogeneous – for example, trade in raw materials –
are likely to be unaffected by immigrants, or affected to a lesser extent,
simply because the lack of unknown product- and market-related information would limit the ability of immigrants to ameliorate information
asymmetries. In short, we would anticipate that, at the aggregated level,
immigrants would exert a more pronounced effect on trade in differentiated goods as both market- and product-specific information asymmetries
would exist, while only the former would apply to trade in homogeneous
products.

2.2.3   FDI-related Effects and Remittance-funded Effects

The extent of FDI-related trade is difficult to determine as firms generally
are reluctant to divulge such information. One piece of information is provided by Graham and Krugman (1995) who note that, in 1990, roughly 23
per cent of US merchandise exports were sold by US affiliates of foreign-
owned parent groups and that just over 40 per cent of these exports were
sold directly to the parent groups. Similarly, in the same year, 36 per cent
of US merchandise imports were purchased by US affiliates of foreign-
owned parent groups, with roughly 75 per cent of these imports being
sold to the affiliates by the parent groups. This gives some indication of
the scale to which FDI affects US trade flows: approximately 9.2 per cent
of total US merchandise exports and 27 per cent of total US merchandise
imports in 1990 occurred between foreign-owned affiliates in the US and
their overseas parent groups. Just as it is likely that immigrants may utilize
connections to business networks in their home countries to enhance host–
home country trade flows, they may also act to increase FDI flows between
their host and home countries. If so, then subsequent host country imports
from and exports to the immigrants' home countries that are attributable
to the immigrant-induced FDI would be indirect immigrant-trade effects.

In 2001, worldwide remittances were equal to $111 billion, with nearly
two-thirds of these remittances being sent to developing countries. This
figure represents about 1.3 per cent of these countries' collective GDP
during 2001; however, certain countries are significantly more dependent upon remittances than others. For example, the total amount of

remittances received by individuals in Haiti in 2001 was equal to 24.2 per cent of GDP. Similarly, remittances to Jordan in that year were equivalent to 22.8 per cent of GDP. Nicaragua (16.2 per cent), El Salvador (14 per cent) and Jamaica (13.6 per cent) are other nations where remittance values exceeded one-tenth of their GDP in 2001 (MPI, 2003). Most immigrants' remittances that originate in the US flow to countries in Latin America and the Caribbean Basin. While exact figures are unknown, countries in this region receive nearly one-third of the world's remittances with over three-quarters of these remittances originating in the US. This means that, in total, the region received approximately $27.5 billion in remittances from the US in 2001. If any portion of these funds are used to finance recipients' consumption and if a share of the increased consumption is in the form of imports, then it is quite possible that there would be a resulting increase in the level of US exports.

2.3 WHAT ARE THE WELFARE IMPLICATIONS FOR THE HOST COUNTRY?

The gains from trade fall into three broad categories. First, countries can gain by exploiting their comparative advantages. Since each country is different from all others, by specializing their production in accordance with the Law of Comparative Advantage and trading for those items for which they do not hold a comparative advantage, countries can benefit in terms of both greater production and consumption efficiencies. Second, if increasing returns to scale in production are present, trade permits countries to produce a more narrow range of products. This allows firms to produce on a larger scale, which also leads to efficiency gains. Third, trade contributes directly to increased competition. By expanding the scope of competition, any monopoly power that large firms may enjoy is countered.

Trade is not, however, without some costs. For example, the Stolper-Samuelson Theorem (mentioned earlier in this chapter) offers a clear prediction regarding changes in factor returns that are attributable to increased trade. A number of studies provide evidence that greater import competition (as measured by decreases in import price indexes, increases in import penetration rates, and so on) correlates with domestic job loss while increased exports correlate with job creation. Much of this literature examines the US experience during the past few decades.[1] While there is some evidence that trade adversely affects the domestic labor market, there is also evidence of beneficial effects. The net effect has generally been estimated to be rather negligible, and whether the overall effect of trade is positive or negative is dependent on the characteristics of the industry or the time period examined. This is important in that it suggests that the results of public opinion polls, such as those discussed in the first chapter, may indicate that individuals overestimate the probability that they will experience an adverse trade-induced labor market outcome when they formulate their opinions of trade.

Related to the potential overestimation of potential losses attributable to trade is the likelihood that benefits from trade will be under-counted. For example, an additional benefit of increased trade stems from what Krugman (1980) referred to as a 'love of variety' effect. This effect relates to the preference effect and the consumption spillover effect that were mentioned earlier. Immigrants' demand for home country goods may increase the variety of products available in host country markets. The increase in variety could be due to new products being introduced or may result from home country-produced goods acting as imperfect substitutes for host country goods. In either instance, both immigrants and host country residents are able to allocate their consumption over a broader selection of products, thus increasing utility for the individual and, hence, raising aggregate social welfare.

The welfare implications of an operable immigrant–trade link for the host economy depend on which of the two broadly-defined channels – the *preference* effect or the *information bridge* effect – is considered (Bryant et al., 2004). Since the preference effect would be expected to increase host country imports but have no effect on host country exports, it is analogous with changes in domestic demand that result from changes in consumer preferences. Standard welfare economics cannot label this as being either good or bad. Nevertheless, since trade is generally considered to be welfare-improving, on net, it may be reasonable to expect that the overall pro-trade effect attributable to immigrants' preferences is positive for host country residents. Information bridge effects, on the other hand, would be expected to increase both host country imports from and exports to the immigrants' home countries. As this effect involves reductions in trade-related transaction costs, it is essentially equivalent to a reduction in shipping costs that results from, say, technological innovation. As such, it permits both home and host country residents to benefit more from international trade and cannot be considered as anything other than welfare-enhancing.

NOTE

1. See Feenstra (2000) and Kletzer (2001 and 2002) for more information on the topic of trade and wages/employment.

3. Lessons from prior studies of the immigrant–trade link

This chapter discusses the key findings of a number of prior studies of the immigrant–trade relationship. The literature, in general, is comprised of empirical examinations, and augmented gravity equations have typically been the econometric specifications of choice. A variety of estimation techniques have been employed to examine the immigrant–trade relationship for a considerable number of host countries, various home country cohorts, several product types/classifications, and many time periods. Reviewing the literature provides information that allows for the formulation of a series of testable hypotheses. The individual facets of the immigrant–trade relationship provide information that deepens our understanding of the topic and this, in turn, allows for the formulation of a richer set of expectations regarding the US immigrant–trade link. These hypotheses are examined as part of the quantitative analysis presented in Chapters 8 to 10. The review begins with a detailed discussion of Gould's (1994) paper and then proceeds to discuss a number of more recent studies.

3.1 IDENTIFICATION OF THE IMMIGRANT–TRADE RELATIONSHIP

Examining annual data for the US and 47 immigrant home countries that span the period 1970–86, Gould (1994) utilized regression analysis to answer the principal question: do immigrants enhance host–home country trade flows? Secondary questions related to the effect that the duration of the average immigrant's stay in the US may have on US–home country trade, whether the skill composition of immigrant populations influences trade, by how much an additional immigrant contributes annually to exports and to imports, whether the immigrant–trade relationship is robust to different empirical specifications, and whether host countries' immigration policies should encourage diversity or be passive in this respect.

The analytical model employed by Gould is a modification of Bergstrand's (1985) microeconomic foundations of the gravity equation, the essential change being the introduction of endogenous transaction costs. As discussed in Chapter 2, immigrants are thought to increase trade if they are able to decrease related transaction costs. The framework used by Gould assumes that these costs decline as immigrants provide host country residents with information relating to their home country's markets, and home country residents with information relating to their host country's markets.

Prior to Gould's study, models of immigration generally treated immigrants as having the same economic impact on their host countries as would be realized from an increase in the number of native-born individuals. This approach ignored what Gould referred to as 'a beneficial human capital-type externality' that is related to the potential pro-trade influences of immigrants. The associated benefits that accrue to non-immigrants in both the host and home countries include production and trading opportunities as well as utility-increasing consumption opportunities. Motivated by the works of Light (1985), Light and Bonacich (1988), Min (1990) and Razin (1990), Gould's work was seminal in that it was the first study to suggest that immigrants influence bilateral trade flows and that the means by which this occurs involves their preferences for home country goods and/or their abilities to decrease related transaction costs.

Gould's analysis revealed a positive immigrant influence for both US exports to and imports from their home countries. Estimated coefficients on the immigrant information variables were equal to 4.96 when aggregate exports were used as the dependent variable and were 1.93 in the case where aggregate imports were used. To facilitate comparison of the coefficients reported by Gould to those of more recent studies, Wagner et al. (2002) computed corresponding elasticity estimates of 0.02 with respect to exports and 0.01 for imports. Elasticity estimates indicate the expected proportional changes in the dependent variable (for example, aggregate bilateral exports or imports) that result from a marginal increase in the corresponding explanatory variable (here, the immigrant stock) with all else held constant. This means the interpretation of Gould's results is that a hypothetical 10 per cent increase in the immigrant stock from a given country is expected to increase US exports to and imports from that country by 0.2 and 0.1 per cent, respectively.

Table 3.1 summarizes the estimated export- and import-elasticities of immigrants that have been reported by researchers who have examined the US immigrant–trade relationship. Differences in sample composition, reference periods, dependent variable choice, econometric technique and the functional forms of the econometric specifications employed in the analyses all limit comparison across studies. Nevertheless, the results do indicate a positive statistical association between immigrant stocks and US–home country trade flows.

Panel A of Table 3.1 summarizes estimates from studies that have

Table 3.1 Estimated immigrant stock elasticities, studies of the US immigrant–trade link

Study	Sample Description	Estimated elasticities	
		Exports	Imports
Panel A: Studies involving aggregate exports and imports			
Gould (1994)[1]	47 trade partners; 1970–1986	0.02	0.01
Dunlevy and Hutchinson (1999, 2001)	17 trade partners; 1870–1910	0.08	0.29
Mundra (2005)[2]	47 trade partners; 1973–1980	n.a.	n.a.
White (2007a)[3]	73 trade partners; 1980–2001	0.15	0.47
White and Tadesse (2008a)	54 trade partners; 1997–2004	0.10	0.17
Tadesse and White (2009)[4]	Tourism services exports to 86 trade partners; 1995–2004	0.14	n.a.
White (2009a)[5]	70 trade partners; 1980–1997	0.33	0.43
White and Tadesse (2009b)	US + 8 other OECD members and 67 trade partners; 1996–2001	0.21	0.30
White and Tadesse (2009c)	59 trade partners; 1996–2001	0.27	0.13
Panel B: Intra-industry trade and state-level exports studies			
White (2008)[6]	Intra-industry trade with 62 trading partners; 1989–2001	0.26 (IIT); 0.19 – 0.22 (vertical IIT); 0.39 – 0.45 (horizontal IIT)	
Bardhan and Guhathakurta (2004)	East/west region exports to 51 trade partners; 1994–1996	0.24 – 0.26 (west coast); 0.06 – 0.09 (east coast)	n.a.
Co et al. (2004)	28 trade partners; 1993	0.29 (OECD members); 0.27 (non-OECD members)	n.a.

Table 3.1 (continued)

Study	Sample Description	Estimated elasticities	
		Exports	Imports
Herander and Saavedra (2005)	36 trade partners; 1993–1996	0.18	n.a.
Dunlevy (2006)	87 trade partners; 1990–1992	0.24 – 0.47	n.a.
Bandyopadhyay et al. (2008)	29 trade partners; 1990–1992	0.27	n.a.
Tadesse and White (2008a)	75 trade partners; 2000	0.11	n.a.
Tadesse and White (2008b)	75 trade partners; 2000	0.05	n.a.
White and Tadesse (2008b)	75 trade partners; 2000	0.05 – 0.09	n.a.
White (2009b)	28 trade partners; 1993	0.12 (OECD members); 0.33 (non-OECD members); 0.14 (high HDI countries); 0.36 (medium HDI countries); --- (high income countries); 0.20 (upper middle income countries); 0.31 (lower middle income countries); 0.52 (low income countries)	n.a.

Notes
1. Elasticities calculated for 1986 immigration levels
2. Not estimated
3. Coefficients from 'low income home country' sample
4. Tourism exports employed as the dependent variable, negative binomial regression technique employed: elasticity based on incidental ratio
5. Coefficients from 'low income home country' sample with differentiated products employed as the dependent variable
6. Logarithmic transformations of the Grubel-Lloyd Index employed as dependent variables.

considered the influence of immigrants on aggregate exports and/or imports. Panel B provides a summary of estimates from studies of the influences of immigrants on US state-level exports and those from a study that considers the extent to which immigrants affect the level of US intra-industry trade. Across all studies for which elasticities are esti-mated, immigrants are found to exert positive and significant influences. As noted, however, there is considerable variation in the magnitudes of reported immigrant effects. The elasticities generated from the coef-ficients reported by Gould are considerably lower than those reported in subsequent studies. Wagner et al. (2002) attribute this to the econometric specification and estimation method that Gould employed.

Of the proportional immigrant influences reported for aggregate US exports, the largest is 0.33 (White, 2009a). The same study also reported the second largest influence of immigrants on aggregate US imports (0.43); however, these values reflect the estimated influences of immigrants from low-income home countries on US trade in differentiated products. Differentiated products would be likely to be characterized by greater information asym-metries and low-income home countries would be likely to have less trade-facilitating infrastructure or infrastructure that is of lesser quality as compared to higher-income trading partners. In both instances, immigrants may face greater opportunities to exert pro-trade influences. Thus, it seems reasonable that these coefficients are of greater magnitude. The largest import elasticity, 0.47, is reported by White (2007a). Similar to the findings reported in White (2009a), this estimate was obtained when aggregate US imports from low-income home countries were used as the dependent variable.

Comparing across the remaining studies, estimated export and import elasticities range from low yet significant values to elasticities as high as 0.30. Of course, as noted, differences in sample composition, reference periods, econometric specifications, and so on all contribute to variation in estimates. That being acknowledged, the consistent finding of a positive and significant immigrant–trade relationship leads to the first two hypoth-eses that we will examine:

H₁: Immigrants exert positive influences on their host countries' aggregate exports to and aggregate imports from their respective home countries.

H₂: The magnitudes of the estimated proportional influences of immigrants on their host countries' aggregate trade with their home countries (that is, the export- and import-elasticities) range from roughly 0.05 to 0.30.

As with studies that have considered the influences of immigrants on aggregate US–home country trade, immigrants consistently exert positive influences on state-level exports and were found to increase the level of intra-industry trade (IIT). The finding with respect to state-level exports is particularly important in the sense that if no significant relationship were found between immigrants and exports at the state-level then findings from studies that report a positive relationship using aggregate trade data would be called into question.

The single study to date regarding immigrants and US IIT (White, 2008) reveals a positive relationship for overall levels of IIT, measured using the Grubel–Lloyd Index, and for both horizontal and vertical IIT (Grubel and Lloyd, 1975). Vertical IIT is characterized as intra-industry trade in goods that are at different stages of production, while horizontal IIT involves intra-industry trade in goods that are at similar stages of production. Thus, horizontal IIT is more likely to involve trade in differentiated products. This would help to explain the larger estimated immigrant influences for horizontal IIT relative to vertical IIT which are reported in Table 3.1.

The immigrant–IIT relationship has also been examined for Spain (Blanes, 2003; Blanes and Martín-Montaner, 2006), Bolivia (Bacarreza et al., 2006) and Portugal (Faustino and Leitão, 2008). The corresponding elasticity estimates are presented in panel B of Table 3.2. As before, due to differences in sample composition, time periods and econometric specifications, the results of these studies are not directly comparable. With the exception of Blanes and Martín-Montaner (2006), who employ Brulhart's marginal IIT 'A' Index, each of these studies utilizes the Grubel–Lloyd Index as the measure of intra-industry trade.[1] However, Bacarreza et al. (2006) do not employ a logarithmic transformation of the Grubel–Lloyd Index. As noted in Balassa (1986), the fact that the Index is bounded between 0 and 100 requires a logarithmic transformation to be made in order to ensure unbiased coefficients. This means that the elasticities of 0.26, 0.21–0.40, and 0.75, which are reported by White (2008), Blanes (2003) and Faustino and Leitão (2008), respectively, while obtained using different samples, time periods, and so on, are more comparable in the sense that they have employed the same necessary transformation to the dependent variable series. It is noteworthy that Blanes and Martín-Montaner (2006), who also perform the logarithmic transformation, report a comparable elasticity, while that reported in Bacarreza et al. (2006), although significant, is nearly zero.

Panel A of Table 3.2 summarizes elasticity estimates reported in studies of the immigrant–trade relationship which consider immigrants' potential effects on aggregate exports and imports for host countries other than the US. Generally speaking, the estimated coefficients are similar to those reported for the US. A crude comparison of the average export- and import-elasticities reveals respective mean values for the US of 0.16 and 0.26 for exports to and imports from immigrants' home countries. Corresponding

Table 3.2 Estimated immigrant stock elasticities, studies of non-US immigrant–trade links

Study	Sample Description	Estimated elasticities	
		Exports	Imports
Panel A: Studies involving aggregate exports and imports			
Helliwell (1997)[1]	9 Canadian provinces and 49 US states; 1990	----	0.22 – 0.24
Head and Ries (1998)	Canada and 136 trade partners; 1980–1992	0.10	0.31
Ching and Chen (2000)[2]	Canada and Taiwan; 1980–1995	0.30	0.30
Girma and Yu (2002)[3]	UK and 48 trade partners; 1981–1993	0.16	0.10
Rauch and Trindade (2002)[4]	63 countries (all considered as host and home countries); 1980 and 1990	0.21 (differentiated products); 0.47 (homogeneous products)	
Wagner et al. (2002)	Canada: 5 regions and 160 trade partners; 1992–1995	0.08	0.25
Blanes (2003)	Spain and 40 trade partners; 1991–1998	0.23	----
Piperakis et al. (2003)	Greece and 60 trade partners; 1981–1991	0.20	–0.04
Bryant et al. (2004)	New Zealand and 170 trade partners; 1981–2001	0.05	0.19
Combes et al. (2005)	Intra-France trade: 94 departments; 1993	0.25	0.14
Kandogen (2005)[5]	Switzerland and 164 trade partners; 1990–2002	0.31	0.24
Parsons (2005)	EU-15 and 15 EU expansion countries; 1994–2001	0.12	0.14
Bacarreza et al. (2006)	Bolivia and 30 trade partners; 1990–2003	0.08 (immigrants); 0.03 (emigrants)	0.09 (immigrants); 0.04 (emigrants)
Blanes (2006)	Spain and 83 trade partners; 1995–2003	0.35	0.23
Hong and Santhapparaj (2006)[6]	Malaysia and 16 trade partners; 1998–2004	0.53	0.88
Lewer (2006)	Intra-OECD trade between 16 member countries; 1991–2000	0.14 (aggregate bilateral trade flows)	

Table 3.2 (continued)

Study	Sample Description	Estimated elasticities	
		Exports	Imports
Murat and Pistoresi (2006)	Italy and 51 trade partners; 1990–2005	--- (immigrants); 0.13 (emigrants)	−0.10 (immigrants); 0.12 (emigrants)
Jiang (2007)[7]	Canada and 125 trade partners; 1988–2004	0.08	0.17
Tadesse and White (2007b)	Australia and 101 trade partners; 1990–2000	0.50	0.20
Tai (2007)	Switzerland and 105 trade partners; 1995–2000	0.27	0.30
White (2007b)[8]	Denmark and 170 trade partners; 1980–2000	0.23 – 0.57	0.19 – 0.34
White and Tadesse (2007)	Australia and 101 trade partners; 1989–2000	0.46	0.18
Dolman (2008)[9]	27 OECD members + US and 162 trading partners; 2000	0.18	0.15
Faustino and Leitão (2008)	Portugal and EU-15 countries; 1995–2003	0.60	0.56
Ivanov (2008)[10]	German regions' exports to 27 trade partners; 1997–1998	0.13 – 0.15	n.a.
Morgenroth and O'Brien (2008)	26 countries' trade with 179 home countries; 1999–2003	0.57	0.68
Qian (2008)	New Zealand and 190 trade partners; 1980–2005	0.04	0.17
White and Tadesse (2009a)	Italy and 68 trade partners; 1996–2001	0.08	----
White and Tadesse (2009b)	8 OECD members + US and 67 trade partners; 1996–2001		
	Australia	0.35	0.27
	Canada	0.19	0.27
	Denmark	0.12	0.12
	Germany	0.25	0.25
	Italy	0.24	0.21

Netherlands	0.16	---	0.23
Norway	---		0.12
Sweden	0.20		0.19

Panel B: Intra-Industry Trade studies

Blanes (2005)	Spain and 42 trading partners; 1991–1998	0.21 – 0.40
Bacarreza et al. (2006)	Bolivia and 30 trade partners; 1990–2003	0.01 (immigrants); 0.04 (emigrants)
Blanes and Martin-Montaner (2006)	Spain and 48 non-EU member trading partners; 1988–1999	0.47
Faustino and Leitão (2008)	Portugal and EU-15 countries; 1995–2003	0.75 (IIT); 1.12 (horizontal IIT); 0.53 (vertical IIT)

Notes

--- indicates no significant effect reported.
1. Results obtained from 'full sample' estimations (i.e., combined inter-province and provine–state trade)
2. Effect of Taiwanese emigrants on Canada's trade with Taiwan
3. Estimated effect of immigrants to UK on trade with non-commonwealth countries
4. Calculated for trade in differentiated products in 1990
5. Estimated elasticity for 'permanent resident' immigrant variable
6. Only effects of skilled immigrants considered
7. Estimated effect on the number of products traded rather than the level of trade occurring
8. Elasticity values vary across home country income classifications and across product classifications
9. Only country pairs for which both immigration and emigration rates were available are included in the data
10. Range of coefficient estimates applies to alternative specifications which examine the effects of all immigrants on regional exports.

45

mean values from the set of studies that have examined host countries other than the US are 0.23 for exports and 0.25 for imports. As with the values presented for the US, the variation observed across studies involving countries other than the US corresponds with differences in the time periods studied, econometric specifications and estimation techniques, product classifications considered and/or the home country cohorts examined.

3.2   VARIATION IN THE IMMIGRANT–TRADE RELATIONSHIP ACROSS PRODUCT CLASSIFICATIONS

Gould reports similar immigrant influences for US exports of both consumer and producer goods; however, while immigrants are found to exert significant and positive influences on US imports of consumer goods, no significant influence is found for imports of producer goods. Gould suggests that the generally weaker influence of immigrants on trade in producer goods relative to consumer goods is due to the former being more likely to be homogeneous and, thus, less likely to be affected by immigrants' preferences or to be characterized by incomplete or asymmetric information. This finding is consistent with a number of subsequent studies, including that of Mundra (2005) who employs a semi-parametric estimation strategy and finds a positive immigrant effect on US imports at the aggregate level and for imports of both producer and consumer goods. For exports, Mundra reports a positive immigrant influence only for consumer goods. Echoing the conclusions reported by Gould, Mundra takes this finding of an immigrant–trade relationship for differentiated goods but not for homogeneous goods as indicative of immigrants acting to offset asymmetric information.

Several studies have considered the influences of immigrants on trade for different types of products. In a number of instances, the Rauch (1999) classification system has been used to categorize 4-digit SITC (Standard International Trade Classification) industries as generally producing either differentiated or homogeneous (reference-priced and organized exchange) goods. Rauch and Trindade (2002) explored the potential influences of ethnic Chinese networks on bilateral trade flows. Trade in products characterized by higher levels of differentiation appear more reliant on networks as compared to trade in homogeneous products. The studies that use Rauch product classifications to consider variation in the US immigrant–trade relationship (for example, Hutchinson, 2002; White, 2009a; 2009b) confirm the general findings of Rauch and Trindade (2002). Also using Rauch product classifications, White (2007b) examines the Danish immigrant–trade relationship, and White and Tadesse (2007) and Tadesse and White (2007b) examine the relationship for Australia. Again, stronger immigrant–trade links are reported for trade in differentiated goods as compared to the effects of immigrants on trade in homogeneous goods.

Additional studies that have explored variation in the immigrant–trade relationship across product types include that of Dunlevy and Hutchinson (2001) which considers the influences of immigrants on US exports of crude foodstuffs, processed foodstuffs, crude materials, semi-manufactures and manufactures for consumption during the 1870–1910 period. Semi-manufactures is the only product classification for which immigrants were found to exert a positive and significant pro-export effect. As with the differentiated and homogeneous product classifications mentioned earlier, relative to foodstuffs and crude materials, the semi-manufactures classification appears more likely to include products for which information asymmetries exist. Further supporting these findings, Bryant et al. (2004) examines the immigrant–trade relationship for New Zealand using data for 170 home countries during the 1981–2001 period. The authors exclude likely homogeneous goods from their data to estimate immigrants' influences on trade when a more differentiated set of goods are considered. Specifically, the estimated export-elasticity increases from 0.05 in the benchmark case (that is, when all product types are considered) to 0.10 when agricultural products are excluded. Similarly, the import-elasticity rises from 0.19 to 0.23 when oil is excluded.

Taken collectively, the results of these studies suggest the existence of variation in the immigrant–trade relationship across product classifications. Such variation would correspond with immigrants being better able to exert pro-trade influences due to an expected positive relationship between product differentiation and the extent to which information is asymmetric. This produces the third hypothesis that we examine:

H_3: *The immigrant–trade link varies across product classifications, with proportional magnitudes of the link increasing with the extent to which information is asymmetric. That is, immigrant–trade effects are larger for differentiated and consumer products as compared to homogeneous and producer products.*

3.3 THE INFLUENCES OF IMMIGRANT CHARACTERISTICS AND ATTRIBUTES

In addition to product characteristics, one may anticipate that immigrant-related factors such as the amount of time that immigrants have been in the US or their skill and/or education levels are related to their abilities to exert pro-trade influences. Gould introduced a variable that measured, for each home country, the average length of time, in years, since each immigrant's arrival in the US. The corresponding elasticity estimates were negative and marginally significant when imports of producer products were used as the dependent variable, but were insignificant in all other specifications. Acknowledging that the influence of an immigrant's stay with respect to trade flows may be non-linear, Gould also included the squared value of this variable in his econometric specifications. Regardless of specification, estimated coefficients on the squared variable were negative but not significantly different from zero. Still, Gould interpreted the estimation results as suggestive of immigrants exerting pro-trade effects only after having been in the US for 3.8 years. The lag between an immigrant's arrival and a discernible effect on US–home country trade is described as a period during which immigrants integrate and gain knowledge about the US. This knowledge is eventually combined with information related to the home country and/or is transmitted to business contacts in the home country. Once the immigrant–trade link is formed, pro-trade immigrant influences are observed; however, as mentioned, the influence is found to wane with the passing of time. Gould suggests this is reflective of preferences for home country goods that diminish as immigrants assimilate to the US and as information regarding the home country becomes more widely known.

As more highly-skilled immigrants may be expected to exert stronger influences on US–home country trade, Gould also includes a variable, constructed based on immigrants' stated occupations at the time of entry to the US, to represent the skill composition of immigrant populations. The estimated elasticities obtained by Gould for this variable yield mixed results. When consumer exports and producer exports are used as the dependent variables, the estimated elasticities are equal to -0.058 and -0.099, respectively. When producer imports are used as the dependent variable, the elasticity estimate is positive and significant (0.14); however, it is insignificant when producer exports are used as the dependent variable. Mimicking this approach, Herander and Saavedra (2005) include variables that represent the duration of the average immigrant's stay in the US, its squared term and the ratio of skilled-to-unskilled immigrants which, as in Gould, is calculated based on the occupations listed by immigrants at their time of entry. Considering US state-level exports, the authors report positive relationships between state-level exports and both the immigrant stay and the skilled/unskilled ratio variables, and a negative and significant relationship for the squared value of the immigrant stay variable. Mundra (2005) also reports a positive coefficient on the variable representing the skill composition of immigrant inflows but does not find a significant effect for the variable which measures the average duration of stay in the US or its squared term.

When examining Spain's immigrant–trade relationship, Blanes (2006) also considered occupations as a proxy for immigrants' skill levels and included separate measures of the immigrant stocks for each of three broad occupational categorizations. Positive influences on both aggregate exports and imports were reported for 'managers or employers and managers without employees', a pro-export effect was reported for the 'others' classification, yet no significant influences on either exports or imports were reported for the 'employees' classification. As an alternative measure, Blanes considered educational attainment as a proxy for skill levels and classified immigrants into one of four categories: no education; primary education; secondary education; and tertiary education (that is, university degree or more). For both exports and imports, no significant effect on trade was found for the 'no education' immigrant class; however, Blanes reported weak but negative influences of tertiary educated immigrants when either aggregate export or imports were employed as the dependent variable. Immigrants who had completed their primary education were found to exert a positive influence on exports while those who had completed their secondary education were found to exert the strongest influences for both exports and imports. This leads to the fourth and fifth hypotheses we examine, both of which are related to immigrant characteristics:

H_4: *Immigrants' influences on trade diminish as the time spent in the host country increases.*

H_5: *The proportional influences of skilled immigrants on US–home country trade are greater than the corresponding effects of unskilled immigrants.*

To consider whether the pro-trade influences of immigrants vary by the immigrant's entry classification, Head and Ries (1998) augmented their specification with separate variables that reflect whether immigrants were categorized upon their arrival in Canada as 'family immigrants', as 'refugees' or as 'independent' immigrants. The results indicated that the pro-trade influences of independent immigrants were the greatest, that the influences of refugees were weakest, and the influences of family immigrants were in the middle. Head and Ries noted that independent immigrants are, in general, more skilled than immigrants in other entry classifications. This is to be expected since they are selected using a point system that considers the individual's level of educational attainment.

Thus, in this instance, as was the case in Blanes (2006), entry classification is potentially indicative of immigrants' skill levels.

Head and Ries (1998) found that refugees have the weakest effect on Canada–home country trade. This seems to follow from such immigrants having relatively weak, or perhaps no, ties to their home country. Many refugees spend considerable time in third countries between when they depart their home countries and when they arrive in the host country. During this time, preferences for home country products may weaken, particularly if the immigrants are exposed to a different culture and/or product selection. Additionally, due to fears of persecution in their home countries, refugees may be less willing to engage home country business connections and may trade less in general.

A similar undertaking is provided by White and Tadesse (2009c). Using US data, the authors considered the influence of refugees and asylum-seekers on US–home country trade relative to the influences of non-refugees/non-asylees (that is, all other entry classes). Refugees/asylees were found to exert relatively weak, yet positive, influences on trade. Much stronger influences were reported for non-refugee/non-asylee immigrants. This finding was taken as being consistent with the notion of refugees, being less connected to or less able to exploit, build and/or maintain connections with potential trading partners or with business and social networks in their home countries. The results of these studies lead to the sixth hypothesis that we consider:

H_6: *The immigrant–trade relationship varies across immigrant entry classifications, with refugees and asylum-seeking immigrants contributing less to US–home country trade than do other immigrants.*

3.4   WHY HOST COUNTRY IMMIGRATION POLICIES MATTER

While it is evident that much was contributed by Gould's (1994) study, subsequent research efforts extended the literature in a number of important and interesting directions. One such study that has already been mentioned is that of Head and Ries (1998). Employing data for 135 trading partners, the authors examined Canada's immigrant–trade relationship during the 1980–92 period. In addition to considering whether the relationship varies across immigrants' entry classifications, the authors confirmed a general immigrant–trade relationship and examined whether changes in Canada's immigration policy corresponded with changes in the immigrant–trade relationship.

Because transaction costs, as noted by McCallum (1995), inhibit Canada's trade, Head and Ries suggested that immigrants, if able to decrease transaction costs, increase trade by serving as intermediaries. Following the precedent set by Gould, an augmented gravity specification was estimated. Unlike Gould, however, who only considered immigrant population stocks, Head and Ries utilized two separate measures of Canada's immigrant population. The first measure ($IMMI^A$) was the cumulative sum of immigrant inflows from each trading partner since 1970. The second measure ($IMMI^B$) was a series of annual immigrant stock estimates that were constructed from a combination of census data and annual inflow data. For both aggregate exports and imports, the estimated elasticities for the $IMMI^A$ variables were greater in magnitude (0.13 and 0.39, respectively) than those estimated for the $IMMI^B$ variable (0.10 for exports and 0.31 for imports).

The fact that the coefficients on the $IMMI^A$ variables were greater in magnitude than the coefficients on the $IMMI^B$ variables regardless of whether exports or imports were employed as the dependent variable was taken to indicate that the pro-trade influences of immigrants who arrived after 1970 were stronger than the influences of immigrants who arrived in earlier years. This is consistent with Gould's finding that the immigrant–trade link weakens as immigrants spend more time in the host country. Although the two immigrant stock measures were highly correlated, immigrant inflows after 1970 were comprised of relatively more immigrants from Asia and fewer immigrants from Europe. This is to say that, similar to the US, the composition of Canada's immigrant inflows has changed in recent decades. Estimation of an auxiliary specification that considered variation across home regions in terms of immigrant–trade links indicated that immigrants from South American and East Asian nations exerted the largest proportional influences on trade. From this, the authors concluded that East Asian immigrants, having comprised a larger share of the post-1970 immigrant inflows, exerted the strongest pro-trade influences. The implication which follows is that Canada's immigration policy, by shaping the demographic composition of the country's immigrant population, had exerted a strong indirect influence on the country's exports and imports.

White and Tadesse (2007) considered, perhaps more directly, the possibility that national immigration policy can affect a nation's trade patterns if it is sufficiently influential in terms of affecting the cultural diversity of the population. The authors examined Australia as it provided a natural experiment of sorts. Prior to the close of World War II, Australia's immigration policy – which was openly referred to as the White Australia policy – afforded entry preference to British citizens. This resulted in the Australian population being, at the close of the war, overwhelmingly of

British descent. In fact, in 1947, 89.8 per cent of the Australian population was either British or were descendants of British immigrants (Price, 1996). As an additional 5.7 per cent of the population was from other northern or western European nations and 1.5 per cent was from southern Europe, 97 per cent of the Australian population in 1947 was either from Europe or were the descendants of European immigrants. In that same year, seeking labor for post-war reconstruction and national defense, Australia adopted annual immigrant inflow targets equal to 1 per cent of the population with a desired ratio of ten British immigrants to every one non-British immigrant (Castles, 2000). However, like Australia, Great Britain faced manpower shortages, and between 1945 and 1960 only 60 per cent of Australia's 1.6 million immigrant arrivals were British (Bouscaren, 1963). This led Australia, beginning in the 1950s, to relax the White Australia policy by formally agreeing to provide preference to emigrants from 11 other European nations.[2]

The composition of post-war immigrant inflows, being 'less British' than the Australian population had been at the end of the war, led to increased ethnic and cultural diversity. In 1973, the Australian government formally announced that the White Australia policy would be replaced by a new policy that would emphasize and promote multiculturalism. As recently as 1999, however, persons of British descent accounted for 69.9 per cent of Australia's ethnic composition. This share increases to 83.8 per cent when you add immigrants from and descendants of immigrants from continental Europe (Price, 1999). This indicates that, although there has been a movement towards greater ethnic and cultural diversity, demographic shifts often occur quite slowly. As a result, Australia remains very much culturally akin to the United Kingdom and to other European nations. It also indicates that, due to the changes in Australian immigration policy, more recent immigrant arrivals often have been from nations that are culturally distinct from Europe and, hence, from Australia. Specifically, 80.1 per cent of the increase in Australia's foreign-born population during the 1990s was due to immigrant arrivals from nations located in Asia and among the Pacific Islands (Price, 1996). White and Tadesse (2007) hypothesized that the greater cultural differences between Australia and the home countries of these more recent immigrants may have led immigrants from nations not afforded preference under the White Australia policy to exert stronger influences on trade between Australia and their respective home countries as compared to the pro-trade influences of immigrants from nations that were afforded preference historically. This follows from the notion that cultural dissimilarities between trading partners are positively related to the presence of asymmetric information which may afford immigrants greater opportunities to exert pro-trade influences.

Classifying immigrants' home countries based on whether or not they were afforded entry preference under the White Australia policy and using data for 101 trading partners that span the years 1989–2000, White and Tadesse (2007) examined potential variation in pro-trade immigrant effects across home country cohorts. Immigrants from nations that were afforded entry preference were found to exert greater proportional influences on Australian imports from their respective home countries than did immigrants from nations not afforded such preference. Immigrants from this latter cohort, however, were found to exert stronger influences on Australian exports to their home countries. The findings were taken to indicate that cultural diversity, if affected by immigration policy, is likely to be relevant to a nation's trade patterns.

White and Tadesse (2007) also reported significant variation in the Australian immigrant–trade relationship across differentiated and homogeneous product classifications, non-manufactured and manufactured product classifications and across 1-digit SITC sectors. The authors concluded that the observed variation in the existence and magnitudes of the immigrant–trade link results from differences in immigrants' abilities in terms of influencing exports and/or imports that are driven by historic entry preferences and, given existing host–home country (dis)similarities, by differences in immigrants' abilities to take advantage of the opportunities afforded. This leads to our seventh hypothesis:

H₇: *Immigration policy can affect the extent to which immigrants influence host–home country trade flows if it is sufficiently influential as to affect the population's demographic composition and, hence, its cultural diversity.*

3.5 HOW HOME COUNTRY CHARACTERISTICS AFFECT THE IMMIGRANT–TRADE RELATIONSHIP

A number of studies have considered variation across home country-specific attributes in terms of the influence of immigrants on trade. For example, Bardhan and Guhathakurta (2004), in considering the link between immigrants and US state-level exports, stratified their sample into east and west coast regions. The authors reported large and significant positive effects of immigrants on the exports from the west coast of the US but found a relatively weak relationship for the east coast. The difference in estimated immigrant–trade influences was attributed to the trade-orientation of immigrants in the two regions; immigrants residing in the western US are more likely to be from China, El Salvador, Mexico, the

Philippines, South Korea or Vietnam, while those residing in the eastern US are primarily from Canada, the Dominican Republic, Germany, Italy or Jamaica. The findings suggest that home country characteristics do matter in so far as whether an immigrant–trade link exists and, if so, the magnitudes of such links.

Both Gould (1994) and Head and Ries (1998) modeled the influence of immigrants on host–home country trade flows as being constant across trading partners. While both studies did allow for differences in the influence of immigrants across measures of trade, immigrant characteristics or entry classifications, neither study explicitly allowed for the possibility that estimated immigrant–trade links varied according to the characteristics of the home country. Gould did estimate per-immigrant effects for each country in his sample; however, these effects were generated using elasticity estimates that were common across the full sample of home countries.

Head and Ries (1998) allowed for differences in the immigrant–trade link across home country regions and reported that immigrants from South American and East Asian countries exerted stronger pro-trade influences than immigrants from other regions. Gould mentioned this possibility, but did not test for expected differences in the immigrant–trade link across home countries' levels of economic development. The thinking behind this is that a relative absence of formal contracting in developing countries corresponds with conditions under which immigrants may prove valuable in terms of facilitating trade. The implication is that trade between the US and developed countries that are characterized by the existence of mature and well-functioning trade-facilitating institutions is potentially less likely, as compared to US trade with developing countries, to be affected by immigrants' pro-trade influences.

The third of the principal papers that we review is that of Girma and Yu (2002) who, while testing for the presence of a UK immigrant–trade link, sought to explain the mechanisms underlying such a relationship. Classifying trading partners as either commonwealth or non-commonwealth nations based on their historical ties to the UK, the authors focused on the abilities of immigrants to decrease trade-related transaction costs. Girma and Yu categorized transaction cost reductions into two mechanisms. The first mechanism is referred to as an 'individual-specific effect'. This effect is said to be 'universal' in that any immigrant, regardless of home country, may act to decrease transaction costs through business or personal contacts with their home country. The second effect is referred to as a 'non-individual-specific effect'. This effect is 'non-universal' in the sense that immigrants reduce trade-related transaction costs by providing knowledge about foreign markets and different social institutions.

In short, the presence and magnitude of this latter effect depends on differences between host and home country political and social institutions. If institutions are similar, then the effect is expected to be weaker than if the institutions are different.

Girma and Yu (2002) hypothesized that, due to their colonial pasts, commonwealth countries are much more similar to the UK in terms of their political and social institutions. This led to the expectation that the pro-trade influences of immigrants from non-commonwealth countries are proportionally greater than those of immigrants from commonwealth countries. Girma and Yu, following the leads of Gould (1994) and of Head and Ries (1998), employed an augmented gravity specification. Unlike earlier studies, however, the authors adapted their empirical specification to allow for variation in the pro-trade influences of immigrants across the commonwealth and non-commonwealth cohorts. The authors reported that the effect of immigrants from commonwealth countries was quite different from that of immigrants from non-commonwealth countries. A significant pro-trade effect was found for immigrants from non-commonwealth countries. Specifically, an assumed 10 per cent increase in the immigrant stock from a non-commonwealth country was estimated to increase UK exports to and imports from the country by 1.6 per cent and 1 per cent, respectively. To the contrary, a like increase in the immigrant stock from a commonwealth country had no significant influence on UK exports to that country and is estimated to decrease UK imports from the country by 1 per cent. Girma and Yu suggested that this latter effect was representative of an immigrant-induced import-substitution effect.

The finding of variation across commonwealth/non-commonwealth cohorts was taken as support for the notion of a non-individual-specific mechanism underlying the immigrant–trade relationship. This conclusion is based on the assumption that personal contacts and connections to business and/or social networks are, in fact, equally applicable to immigrants from all countries. Further, the absence of a pro-trade effect for immigrants from commonwealth nations was assumed to result from commonwealth home countries having legal norms and judicial systems similar to those of the UK. Finally, dovetailing on the notion of variation in the immigrant–trade relationship across developing and developed trading partners that was suggested by Gould (1994) and confirmed by White (2007a and 2009b), Girma and Yu (2002) pointed to expected differences between commonwealth and non-commonwealth countries in terms of communications and formal/informal contracting structures. This led the authors to conclude that the institutional differences between the UK and the non-commonwealth countries in their sample were conducive to the existence of conditions under which immigrants might act to increase

UK–home country trade flows. This brings us to the eighth hypothesis we will consider:

H_8: *Greater institutional dissimilarity between trading partners affords immigrants greater opportunities to exert pro-trade influences and, thus, immigrants from more dissimilar home countries exert stronger influences on US trade with their home countries.*

3.6   CULTURAL DIFFERENCES AND THE INFLUENCES OF IMMIGRANTS ON HOST–HOME COUNTRY TRADE

A number of recent studies have explored the relationships between immigrants, cultural differences and host–home country trade. White and Tadesse (2008a) defined a nation's culture as 'an amalgam of its population's shared habits and traditions, learned beliefs and customs, attitudes, norms and values'. Suggesting that cultural differences correspond with social and/or institutional dissimilarity, the authors posited that such dissimilarity may serve as a catalyst for an operable immigrant–trade link. To garner a deeper and more detailed understanding of the immigrant–trade relationship, White and Tadesse augmented their empirical specification with a composite measure of the cultural differences between the US and the trading partners in their data sample. Data from the World Values Surveys (WVS) and the European Values Surveys (EVS) (Inglehart et al., 2004; Hagenaars et al., 2003) were used to calculate estimates of US–home country cultural distances. The Values Surveys, conducted between 1998 and 2001, provide standardized data from representative national samples for a broad and varying set of topics that relate to economics, politics, religion, sexual behavior, gender roles, family values, communal identities, civic engagement, ethical concerns, environmental protection, and scientific and technological progress. Factor analysis results in classification of respondents along two dimensions of culture: 1) Traditional authority vs. Secular-Rational authority (*TSR*) and 2) Survival values vs. Self-Expression values (*SSE*) (Inglehart et al., 2004).

Employing data that span the years 1997–2004, White and Tadesse began by examining the influence of immigrants and cultural distance on US trade with 54 home countries. They then decomposed their measure of cultural distance to examine the relative influences of the *TSR* and *SSE* dimensions of culture on trade flows between the US and the immigrants' home countries. Cultural distance generally inhibits trade flows; however, as expected, immigrants exert pro-trade influences that partially offset the influence of cultural distance. Further, differences in the *TSR* dimension of culture were found to inhibit trade between the US and immigrants' home countries, while differences in the *SSE* dimension appeared to reduce US imports while increasing US exports. While immigrants offset, at least in part, the trade-inhibiting influences of cultural distance – whether measured in a composite fashion or along separate dimensions – they appear to counter the trade-inhibiting effects of the *TSR* dimension in terms of increasing US exports to a greater extent. This leads to our ninth hypothesis:

H_9: *US–home country cultural distance diminishes trade flows and, by doing so, affords immigrants greater opportunities to enhance trade. Thus, immigrants act to offset the expected trade-inhibiting influences of cultural distance.*

3.7   ESTIMATED PER-IMMIGRANT EFFECTS

A number of studies have calculated per-immigrant effects using observed trade flows and coefficient estimates obtained from their econometric analyses. Table 3.3 summarizes these estimates. Gould (1994) calculates the expected marginal effect of an additional immigrant on annual US trade with each of the 47 countries included in his data sample. Across all trading partners, average estimated marginal effects on US exports to and imports from their home country are $2719 and $3161, respectively. While these estimates are comparable to those offered by other research-ers, the mean values mask considerable variation across trading partners. Specifically, Gould estimates that the marginal immigrant from Singapore increases US exports by $47708 and US imports by $29359, while the marginal immigrant from the Philippines increases exports by $4 and imports by $6. Median values for the estimated marginal effects are much lower: $593 for US exports to and $446 for US imports from the immi-grants' home countries.

Several studies estimate per-immigrant effects for different home country groupings, product types and, even, immigrant attributes/types. Most important for our purposes, a typical pattern is found across home country classifications. Dunlevy and Hutchinson (2001), Co et al. (2004) and White (2009b) each report greater per-immigrant effects on trade for immigrants from relatively developed home countries. The methods of categorizing home countries in these studies vary from listing home coun-tries as being part of (old or new) Europe or as non-European countries (with the former expected to be more developed, on average, than the

Table 3.3   Estimated per-immigrant effects on host country trade flows

Study	Host	Export effect	Import effect
Panel A: Studies involving the US immigrant–trade link			
Gould (1994)[1]	US	$2719	$3161
Dunlevy and Hutchinson (2001)[2]	US	$191 (overall); $2574 (old Europe); $1496 (new Europe); $678 (non-Europe)	----
Co et al. (2004)[3,4]	US	$11 458 – $22 999 (developed countries); $1468 – $4139 (developing countries)	n.a.
White (2007a)[5]	US	$2967	$9102
Tadesse and White (2008a)[3]	US	$2975 (all products)	n.a.
		$64.28 (cultural products)	n.a.
		$2938 (non-cultural products)	n.a.
White and Tadesse (2008a)	US	$607 – $814	$1122 – $1571
White and Tadesse (2009c)[6]	US	452 (all immigrants)	176 (all immigrants)
		---- (refugees/asylum-seekers)	2 – 312 (refugees/asylum-seekers)
		2 – 319 (non-refugees/asylum-seekers)	20 – 382 (non-refugees/asylum-seekers)
White (2009b)[3,7]	US	$10 517 (OECD member countries)	n.a.
		$13 636 (non-OECD member countries)	n.a.
		$13 310 (high HDI countries)[8]	n.a.
		$7105 (medium HDI countries)[8]	n.a.

58

Panel B: Studies involving host countries other than the US

Study	Host country		
Head and Ries (1998)	Canada	$8000	$8785 (middle income countries)[9]
			$14814 (upper middle income countries)[9]
			$7572 (lower middle income countries)[9]
			$9203 (low income countries)[9]
			n.a.
			n.a.
			n.a.
			n.a.
Wagner, Head and Ries (2002)	Canada	$312	$944
			$3000
White (2007b)	Denmark	$50 (low income home countries)[9] – $1429 (high income home countries)[9] $477 (aggregate)	$72 (low income home countries) – $1778 (high income home countries) ---- (aggregate)
White and Tadesse (2007)	Australia	$138 – $1756	$134 – $569
White and Tadesse (2009a)[10]	Italy	$563	$503

Notes

---- indicates no significant effect reported.
1. Average of home country-specific effects
2. Converted from 1913 US dollars to 2000 US dollars
3. US state-level exports employed as dependent variables
4. OECD membership used to categorize home countries as developed or developing
5. Estimates apply to 'low income home country' sample
6. Estimated geodesic distance (in meters) between US and home country that average immigrant offsets
7. Average estimated values across home countries in each indicated cohort
8. Home countries classified based on UN Human Development Index values
9. Home countries grouped according to World Bank income classifications
10. Estimates apply to exports and imports of manufactured products.

latter), whether or not they are members of the Organisation for Economic Co-operation and Development (OECD), their United Nations Human Development Index (HDI) scores and their World Bank income classifications. The observed relationship leads us to our final hypothesis:

H_{10}: *Estimated per-immigrant effects on aggregate trade flows are greater for immigrants from countries that are less culturally distant/institutionally dissimilar.*

The literature in general, and particularly the studies discussed in greatest detail here, provides a number of expectations regarding the influences of immigrants on host–home country trade. First, immigrants are expected to exert positive influences on host country exports to and imports from their home countries. Second, this effect is expected to be stronger with respect to trade in differentiated goods as compared to trade in homogeneous goods. Third, differences in immigrant characteristics (for example, length of stay, skill-level, and entry classification) are expected to correspond with variation in the influences of immigrants on host–home country trade flows. Fourth, shifts in national immigration policies, if sufficiently marked to alter the composition of immigrant inflows, are expected to influence the presence and magnitudes of immigrant–trade links across home country cohorts. Fifth, immigrant–trade links are expected to be stronger if the host and home countries are dissimilar in terms of institutions. Sixth, the proportional influence of immigrants on host–home country trade flows is anticipated to be greater if the home country is culturally different from the host country. These anticipated relationships provide the basis for the empirical analysis presented in Chapters 8 to 10.

NOTES

1. Brulhart's marginal IIT 'A' Index is analogous to the Grubel–Lloyd Index but, rather than measuring levels of IIT, it is constructed using observed changes in trade flows.
2. The 11 nations were Austria, Denmark, Finland, Germany, Greece, Italy, the Netherlands, Norway, Spain, Sweden and Switzerland. These nations, along with the United Kingdom and New Zealand, were included in the cohort of home countries for which entry preference was extended.

PART II

What factors may underlie the US immigrant–trade link

Chapter 3 reviews a number of studies that have examined the influence of immigrants on host–home country trade flows. Among the general conclusions from this literature, immigrants are found to exert pro-trade effects and these effects appear to vary in both their existence and their magnitudes across a number of facets that include product types, industries and sectors, host and home country attributes, and immigrants' characteristics and entry classifications.

In the following chapter, two factors are introduced that potentially underlie the US immigrant–trade relationship. Chapter 4 reviews the history of US immigration. This allows for the introduction, in Chapter 5, of the concepts of primacy effects and recency effects as they apply to the immigrant–trade relationship. Related to these effects, variation across home country cohorts in terms of the existence and quality of trade-facilitating infrastructure is discussed in Chapter 6 as is what this difference implies for immigrants' potential abilities to exert pro-trade influences. In Chapter 7, cultural differences between the US and immigrants' home countries are discussed as a basis for variation in consumer preferences and as a proxy variable that represents product- and market-related asymmetric information. Since imperfect information would correspond with increased transaction costs and act as an impediment to trade, the presence of asymmetric information potentially provides immigrants with the opportunity to exert pro-trade influences. Chapter 7 also introduces a measure of US–home country cultural distance. This pair of possible explanations for the existence of and observed variation in the US immigrant–trade link serves as the focus of the analysis that is presented in Chapters 8 to 10.

4. A brief review of US immigration history

To better facilitate review, the history of US immigration is partitioned into five waves.[1] The first four waves primarily involved migration to the US from European nations. The predominance of immigrant arrivals from Europe was fostered, in large part, by US immigration policy. For example, as early as 1790, the US Congress passed legislation which discouraged immigration from non-European countries. Subsequent policy changes led to the provision of additional incentives for European migration and disincentives for non-Europeans to migrate. As a result, the overwhelming majority of US immigrant arrivals prior to 1968 were from Europe and Canada. Implementation of the Immigration Act of 1965 in July 1968 led to a sustained and pronounced shift in the source countries/regions of immigrant inflows with, in recent decades, Asia and Latin America and the Caribbean Basin having emerged as the principal source regions.

A consequence of US immigration policy is that the composition of immigrant inflows led the culture and institutions of the US to evolve such that they are, broadly speaking, more similar to the cultures and institutions of European nations and of non-European nations that were largely settled by Europeans (that is, Australia, Canada and New Zealand) than to the varied cultures and institutions that characterize much of the rest of the world. Additionally, the sustained entry preference afforded to immigrants from European nations contributed to the development and strengthening of business ties and trade channels between individuals and firms in the US and in Europe. Cultural and institutional similarities coupled with the forging and refinement of trade-related institutions (for example, trade associations and legal and judicial frameworks) have historically acted to facilitate trade. This suggests that the legislative history that pertains to US immigration policy and the timing and composition of immigrant inflows, in terms of source countries/regions, are relevant for understanding the factors that may underlie the existence and operability of the US immigrant–trade relationship.[2]

4.1   WAVE I: 1565–1802

The founding of St Augustine by the Spanish in 1565 and the establishment of the Jamestown settlement and the Plymouth Colony by the
English in 1607 and 1620, respectively, marked the beginnings of sustained
European migration to what would eventually become the US. Indicative
both of the difficulties involved with settlement and the scale of migration,
it is estimated that only 8000 English immigrants made their way to the
Virginia and Massachusetts colonies between 1607 and 1630, and that
fewer than 5000 English colonists lived on the North American mainland
in 1630.[3] This number increased to nearly 70 000 during the subsequent
30-year period, known as the Great Migration, when nearly one of every
25 residents of England left the country. Although slightly more than half
of these individuals migrated to Bermuda and the West Indies, nearly
a third migrated to New England (approximately 25 000 arrivals) and
to the Chesapeake region (50 000 arrivals). This large inflow of English
immigrants accounted for nearly all migration to New England and for
nearly half of all migration to the Chesapeake region during the seventeenth century. In total, roughly 168 000 Europeans migrated during the
seventeenth century to what is now the US. More than 90 per cent of these
arrivals departed from either England or Wales (Purvis, 1997).

By 1700, the 'white population' of the English colonies numbered
approximately 223 000 persons. During the eighteenth century, the predominant source countries of US immigrant arrivals shifted from England
and Wales to include Germany, Ireland and Scotland. In total, an estimated
636 000 immigrants arrived in the English colonies during the eighteenth
century, of which about 468 000, or nearly three of every four arrivals, were
from Europe. Nearly one-third of these European immigrants were Irish.
German immigrants accounted for one-fifth of the inflow, as did immigrants from England and Wales, collectively, and Ulster Scots and Scots
combined to account for yet another one-fifth. The remaining immigrants
were either Haitian colonists, French, or in the cases of approximately
2000 immigrants, from various other countries (Purvis, 1997).

The influence of the eighteenth century's predominantly European
immigrant inflow is magnified when one considers that by 1800 these
immigrants had produced an estimated 4.3 million descendents (Purvis,
1997). As a result, the first decennial US census, conducted in 1790,
reported a population of slightly more than 5 million persons. Nearly
900 000 of these individuals were slaves, and 60.6 per cent of the approximately 4.1 million free persons within the population were either British
or of British descent. Other home countries broadly represented in the
census were France (1.4 per cent), Germany (7 per cent), Ireland (2.9

per cent), The Netherlands (2.5 per cent) and Sweden (0.5 per cent) – all European countries (Heer, 1996).[4]

The Articles of Confederation (1778) and the Constitution (1789) included the first US laws regarding immigration. The Articles of Confederation granted each state the authority to maintain its own citizenship and naturalization procedures and requirements. It also put forth that citizens of each state were citizens of all other states. Not surprisingly, this arrangement led to much confusion as different naturalization standards applied across the states. The confusion was remedied, to a degree, when the Constitution granted the federal government control over immigration.

As the Articles of Confederation and the Constitution established jurisdiction over immigration policy, legislation was passed soon thereafter to implicitly encourage migration of some groups while discouraging that of others. The Tonnage Act of 1789 was, ostensibly, legislation aimed to generate public revenues and to promote the US shipbuilding industry. The Act imposed per-ton fees of 50 cents for foreign ships entering US ports, 30 cents for American-built but foreign-occupied ships, and 6 cents for American ships. While the Act encouraged trade between US states and expansion of the domestic shipbuilding industry, it also made it more expensive for foreign ships to transport immigrants as well as goods. It did not, however, explicitly restrict immigration. It merely discouraged immigration by those with limited financial means.

The Naturalization Act of 1790 was the first federal legislation that specifically governed the naturalization and citizenship process. The Act limited naturalization to 'free white persons who were of good moral character'. The Civil Rights Act of 1866 granted citizenship to all persons born in the US, and the Citizenship Clause of the 14th Amendment to the US Constitution (1868) specifically extended the right to citizenship to African-Americans. Nevertheless, in 1882, immigrants from China were formally excluded from entering the US and those already in the US were made ineligible for citizenship. In 1917, this ban was expanded to encompass immigration from most of Asia.

Although the Act of 1790 restricted naturalization to free whites, it was somewhat radical in the sense that Catholics and Jews were able to gain US citizenship. In Great Britain, it was not until the mid-nineteenth century that Catholic immigrants were eligible for citizenship. Similarly, France did not afford Jewish immigrants the opportunity to become citizens until after the French Revolution. This may have encouraged Catholics and Jews in European nations to migrate to the US, further increasing the number of arrivals in the US from such countries.

The Naturalization Acts of 1795 and 1798 further tightened the laws governing naturalization. The 1795 Act extended the required period of residency in the US from two years to five years and stipulated that those intending to become citizens inform their local court at least three years prior to their application. As part of the Alien and Sedition Acts, the 1798 Act increased the required residency period to 14 years and made immigrants from countries deemed to be enemy powers ineligible for naturalization. The Naturalization Act of 1802 restored the five-year residency period. None of these Acts, however, altered or removed the restriction that barred non-whites from acquiring citizenship. Effectively, US naturalization law afforded preferential treatment to immigrants from Europe (particularly northern and western Europe), and the demographic composition of subsequent immigrant inflows, in terms of sources countries/ region, followed in accordance.

4.2   WAVE II: 1803–68

During roughly the first three-quarters of the nineteenth century, the US maintained a quasi-open immigration policy. While there were no legal restrictions limiting entry to the country, the demographic composition of immigrant inflows was influenced by the laws governing naturalization. These laws encouraged the migration of free white persons; however, the Napoleonic Wars (1789–1815) considerably reduced immigration to the US from continental Europe. Further decreasing inflows, in 1788 the British Parliament banned the emigration of skilled artisans from Ireland, and in 1803 an Act was passed that limited the number of passengers that ships could carry. In 1825, these laws were repealed; however, the effect of the wars and the Acts on immigration to the US was that between 1800 and 1820 only about 184000 immigrants arrived in the US, with most of these immigrants having departed from the British Isles (Heer, 1996). From 1820 to 1860, slightly more than 5 million Europeans migrated to the US (Purvis, 1997). The increase in immigration was facilitated by technological advances that reduced travel costs. Improvements in sailing ship design, navigational equipment and ocean maps all contributed to lower the cost of migration. Similarly, the Great Famine in Ireland led almost 800000 Irish to emigrate to the US during the 1840s and another 914000 to do so during the 1850s (Heer, 1996). An additional 4 million persons entered the US between 1861 and 1875 (Purvis, 1997). While these later arrivals were predominantly from European nations, a large number of Chinese immigrants began to arrive in California during the early 1840s.

The Steerage Act of 1819 required ship captains to keep detailed passenger records and to provide more humane conditions for those on board.

The openness of the immigration policy pursued by the US for most of the nineteenth century is highlighted by the fact that, along with making the slave trade illegal in 1808, the Steerage Act and the Homestead Act (1862) were the most aggressive actions taken by Congress regarding immigration prior to 1882. The influence and effect of this policy stance is evident when one considers that, in 1860, immigrants accounted for 13 per cent of the US population. The 1860 Census describes these individuals as generally English-speaking (59 per cent) and from western Europe: 39 per cent were Irish, 31 per cent German, 14 per cent British, 3 per cent French, 2 per cent Scandinavian and 6 per cent Canadian (Purvis, 1997). As with the first wave of US immigration, Western Europe (namely Ireland, England and Germany) was the principal departure region.

Providing incentives for Europeans to migrate to the US while offering no such incentives to individuals in much of the rest of the world was common practice during the first two waves of US immigration. For example, westward expansion enabled the US to absorb a regular supply of immigrants. These new arrivals frequently occupied the newly-formed territories that would eventually become states. Encouraging such settlement, the Homestead Act offered land grants to citizens and those who intended to become citizens. Because the naturalization restrictions that were in place limited citizenship to free whites, this Act further encouraged European migration to the US. Similarly, while labor force shortages following the Civil War further induced migration to the US, due to the naturalization restrictions in place, once again it was European immigrants who were best able to benefit from migration and, thus, who comprised the majority of immigrant inflows.

Chinese immigration accelerated greatly following the discovery of gold in California in 1848. Perhaps not surprisingly, these immigrants – typically, male laborers who did not intend to stay in the US – were frequently met with prejudice. Chinese immigrants were not eligible for naturalization until after the US Civil War, could not own land or file mining claims, were not permitted to join labor unions, testify in court, hold public office or to vote, and were often required to pay extra taxes or to hold special licenses to operate businesses. In 1860, Chinese children were forbidden from attending public schools in San Francisco and in 1862 the State of California passed the Anti-Coolie Act. (The term 'Coolie' itself was a derogatory term used to describe low-skilled Asian workers.) The Act imposed a monthly 'tax', in the form of a work permit fee of $2.50, on most adult workers of the 'Mongolian Race'. Workers were exempt if they were involved in the production or manufacturing of coffee, rice, sugar or tea (UCB, 2009). As the California Gold Rush wound down in the mid-1850s, anti-Chinese sentiment grew stronger. Illustrating the tensions of the time, in February 1867, a mob comprised of 400 white men attacked Chinese railway workers in San Francisco. At least 12 persons were injured, property was damaged and several shanties and sheds at the railway workers' work site were destroyed by arson. During the same month, similar although less extreme disturbances occurred in Kansas City, Missouri and in Dayton, Ohio (Gilje, 1996).

In spite of the growing anti-Chinese sentiment, the governments of the US and China renegotiated the Treaty of Tientsin (1858), which had been signed at the end of the first part of the Second Opium War, to produce the Burlingame Treaty (1868). The treaty restricted the US and China from imposing limits on immigrants' travel, places of residence and abilities to study. Both nations also agreed to allow unlimited immigration from the other. As a consequence, the Burlingame Treaty ensured the US a continued source of inexpensive labor.

4.3 WAVE III: 1869–1917

The third wave of US immigration was characterized by large, sustained immigrant inflows and a movement away from passive Federal immigration policy. Economic uncertainty that accompanied the Long Depression (October 1873–March 1879) further fueled anti-immigrant sentiment. This third wave differed from the first two in that, although the number of immigrant arrivals from Asia was much smaller than the inflow from Europe, nearly 1 million Asian laborers settled in the western US during the period. The total number of arrivals would surely have been much greater; however, anti-Chinese sentiment led to the passage of legislation which banned immigration from China entirely. At the time, China was the predominant source of Asian immigrants to the US. Even with the restriction placed on Chinese immigration, approximately 25 million persons entered the US during this period, making it by far the heaviest of the first four waves. By the beginning of World War I, which curtailed immigrant inflows, the annual inflow had peaked at roughly 1.2 million persons.

In 1880, an estimated 104 000 Chinese immigrants resided in the US (US Census, 2001). While many other immigrant groups, including those from eastern and southern Europe, were also subjected to discrimination, perhaps no group faced the extreme prejudice encountered by the Chinese. Indicative of the sentiment of the period, an 1879 referendum revealed that over 150 000 California voters opposed Chinese immigration and fewer than 1000 voters favored it (Heer, 1996). Similarly, a *New York Times* article dated February 26, 1880 and titled 'The Chinese Must Go' reads in part:

There is every reason to believe that within a few days a San Francisco mob will make an attack on the Chinamen. The preparations for this attack are in open progress, and Mr. Dennis Kearney, the eminent California statesman whom Mr. Hayes once honored with a long interview at the White House, is now appealing to his followers to furnish money for erecting a neat and serviceable gallows on the Sand Lots whereon to hang the wretches who are guilty of the crime of being Chinamen. As the Mayor of the city is the ally and tool of Kearney, no protection will be given by him to the Chinese, and the fate of these unhappy heathen, in case the anticipated riot takes place, can easily be imagined.

Practical men are growing tired of the foolish sentimentality which is talked in Eastern cities concerning the Chinese. We are told that because the United States has made a treaty with China guaranteeing protection to Chinese residing in this country, it is a disgraceful breach of faith to permit the San Francisco Chinamen to be persecuted and massacred. Suppose it is. What of it? Can China compel us to keep a treaty, and if not, can we be expected to keep it?

Of course, it would be possible to put an end to lawless persecution of the Chinese, provided it were popular to do so, but it so happens that it would be unpopular. Which great political party is foolish enough to risk losing the votes of the Pacific States by undertaking to do justice to the Chinese? What if it is morally right to do justice even to yellow heathen? Politicians do not make a practice of doing right because it is right. They are practical men, and their rule of conduct is to do what will secure votes.

The sooner the Chinamen are exterminated the sooner San Francisco will be at peace.

The article conveys a sense of the public's anti-Chinese sentiment but also projects immediacy with respect to the heightened state of emotions associated with the issue. Perhaps most telling is the acknowledgement that the persecution is lawless and that it could be ended but, in doing so, the cost may well be the Pacific states in the 1880 election. Two years later, in May 1882, the Chinese Exclusion Act was passed by the US Congress. The Act imposed a ten-year ban on Chinese immigration, that was extended for an additional ten years when, in 1892, the Geary Act was passed, was extended once more when the Extension of the Exclusion Act was passed in 1902, and finally made permanent in 1904 when the Exclusion Act was passed.

The Chinese Exclusion Act, along with the Immigration Act of 1882, marked the end of the US government's passive stance towards immigration. The Immigration Act of 1882 sought to stem the growing inflows of immigrants from eastern and southern Europe. Specifically, the Act imposed a poll tax of 50 cents for all immigrants entering the US and banned the entry of those deemed to be lunatics, criminals or who were otherwise unable to provide for themselves. This poll tax was increased by the passage of the Immigration Act of 1907, which also restricted Japanese immigration that had increased significantly following the turn of the century.

When annual immigrant inflows began to average more than 1 million persons (1910–14), concerns were raised over whether the US could continually absorb so many new arrivals and whether immigrants from eastern and southern Europe, in particular, posed special problems in terms of being assimilated to American culture (Purvis, 1997). While the outbreak of World War I curtailed immigrant inflows, a fear that post-war immigration would mirror pre-war levels led Congress to pass legislation to limit the annual inflow of immigrants and to further influence the demographic composition of future immigrant inflows. The Immigration Act of 1917 broadened the Chinese Exclusion Act to exclude immigration from most of Asia. Specifically, the Act required immigrants to pass a literacy test and created the Asiatic Barred Zone that excluded immigrants from Afghanistan, Arabia, the East Indies, India, Indochina, Polynesia, and the portion of Russia that is in Asia. Perhaps indicative of how immigrants from Asia were generally viewed at this time in US history, illiterates, men and women entering for immoral reasons, alcoholics, and vagrants were also on the exclusion list.

What is seen, during this third wave, is a shift from a passive US immigration policy to one that was considerably active. This movement of the Federal government to become more active in setting immigration policy followed relaxation of the prohibition established in 1790 that limited naturalization to free white persons. Once this restriction was removed by the Civil Rights Act of 1866 and the 14th Amendment to the Constitution in 1868, and it was revealed that a continued passive policy stance would result in a shift in the source countries/regions of immigrant inflows, engineering future inflows that were demographically similar to prior immigrant inflows required the Federal government to pass specific legislation that restricted inflows from certain regions (for example, southern and eastern Europe and Asia) while encouraging/privileging potential inflows from other regions, namely northern and western Europe.

4.4   WAVE IV: 1918–68

The fourth wave of immigration (1918–68) spans a transformational period in US immigration history. It began in earnest with passage of the Emergency Quota Act in 1921 and the Immigration Act of 1924. The Act of 1924 amended the Emergency Quota Act which had established quotas for immigration from each foreign nation such that the sum of all quotas was equal to 3 per cent of the 1910 US foreign-born population. The 1924 Act set forth that no persons ineligible for citizenship (such as the Chinese, the Japanese and those from numerous other Asian nations) were allowed to enter. It also revised downward the quotas established by the 1921 Act to just 2 per cent of the 1890 foreign-born population. To place this into context, at the time of the 1890 census there were approximately 9.2 million foreign-born residents in the US. Of these individuals, 86.9 per cent were from Europe, 10.6 per cent from North America (that is, Bermuda and Canada), 1.2 per cent each from Asia and from Latin America and the Caribbean Basin, and 0.1 per cent from Australia and New Zealand. In total, 97.6 per cent of the 1890 US foreign-born population was either from Europe or from nations that had largely been settled by Europeans (namely, Australia, New Zealand and Canada) (Briggs, 2003). The Act of 1924 prescribed that future immigrant inflows would be limited to about 184000 per year, with more than 179500 of these arrivals coming from Europe (nearly 160000 immigrants), North America (more than 19000 immigrants) and Australia and New Zealand (slightly fewer than 2000 immigrants). Perhaps not surprisingly, between 1924 and 1968, the overwhelming majority of immigrant arrivals were from Europe and Canada.

Largely as a result of the Great Depression and the more stringent US immigration policies, the number of immigrants admitted to the US decreased from 4107200 during the 1920s to only 528400 during the 1930s. Even as inflow levels decreased and the composition of arrivals tilted back towards northern and western Europe as the principal source regions, additional steps were taken that affected the demographic composition of the US foreign-born population. For example, the Tydings–McDuffie Act (1934) reduced the annual quota for the Philippines to 50 persons per year and reclassified Filipinos living in the US as 'aliens'. Similarly, in response to rising concerns about immigration from Mexico and Canada, the US Border Patrol was created in 1924. The Mexican Revolution (1910–1920) led many Mexicans to flee to the US. However, between 1929 and 1934, as many as 500000 Mexican citizens and Mexican-Americans were either deported to Mexico or chose to return voluntarily, perhaps fearful of inevitable deportation (Ruiz and Korrol, 2006).

There was, however, some movement towards a more liberal immigration policy. By 1930, due to the restrictions enacted decades earlier, the Chinese population of the US had fallen to 74954 (Taylor, 2002). In that same year, Congress passed legislation to permit admission of Chinese wives who had married American citizens prior to May 1924. In 1935, Congress passed legislation that granted the right to apply for US citizenship to Asian World War I veterans who had fought on the side of the US. Even so, it was not until Congress passed the Chinese Exclusion Repeal Act in 1943 (the Magnuson Act) that immigration from China was again permitted. Due to the quotas set forth by the Immigration Act of 1924, the quota for Chinese immigrants was only 105 arrivals per year; however, Cold War exceptions enabled many more Chinese to migrate and by 1960 there were 237 293 Chinese residents in the US (Purvis, 1997).

The Immigration and Nationality Act of 1952, known as the McCarren–Walter Act, changed the laws governing the naturalization of immigrants; however, it did little to change the laws governing immigrants' entry to the US. In many respects, the Act reaffirmed the restrictionist/ isolationist philosophies of the 1920s. It consolidated the quota system that had been established by the Emergency Quota Act of 1921 and maintained the system which favored immigration from northern and western Europe: Great Britain, Germany and Ireland continued to be allocated the largest number of quota slots each year. The Act limited immigration from the eastern hemisphere but left immigration from the western hemisphere unrestricted; however, other provisions, such as denying entry to those who may become public charges, could still be used to prohibit the entry of unwanted immigrants.

The Act replaced the Asiatic Barred Zone with the Asia-Pacific Triangle. The Triangle consisted of Asian nations that were granted small annual quotas and afforded immigrants from these nations the right of naturalization. Proponents argued that the abolition of the Asiatic Barred Zone was evidence that the law contained no racial bias. Others argued that the low annual quotas and how the quota slots were to be charged were discriminatory. Individuals of Asian descent who were born outside of Asia and who desired to migrate to the US were counted against the quota allocated to their Asian nation rather than to the quota of their country of birth. For example, if the child of Japanese parents who was born in, say, Chile chose to migrate to the US, they would be counted against the quota allotted to Japan. If the same child had been born to, say, Italian parents, then they would enter as a Chilean. Congress also limited immigration from European colonies to 100 individuals each year. This restriction mostly affected black West Indians who previously had emigrated under the large British quota. As a result, emigration to the US from these countries decreased dramatically.

As somewhat of a precursor to the Immigration Act of 1965, the Act of 1952 established a system of preferences for skilled workers and for relatives of US citizens. Additionally, while the Displaced Persons Acts (1948, 1950 and 1951) afforded preferential treatment to refugees from eastern and central Europe following World War II, the 1952 Act permitted the entry of Asian refugees. As a result, more than 3.5 million people were admitted as refugees between 1945 and 1960 (Purvis, 1997). This was due in large part to a provision in the 1952 Act which, in the event that the annual quota for refugees was filled, permitted the US Attorney

General to 'parole' refugees into the US. This procedure was so commonly used that by 1965 nearly two-thirds of the annual immigrant inflow were outside of set quota numbers. For example, Greece had an annual quota of 307 but was sending several times that figure each year. Likewise, Italy had a much larger quota (5800) but was still sending approximately three times their quota each year (Zolberg, 2006).

4.5 WAVE V: 1969–PRESENT

Until about 1890, immigrant inflows were largely comprised of individuals from northern and western European nations. The period from 1890 until World War I was characterized by an increase in the inflows of immigrants from southern and eastern Europe. The restrictive immigration policy embarked upon in the 1880s and expanded in the wake of the First World War severely limited/restricted non-European immigration and led to drastic reductions in the numbers of immigrants arriving in the US. Following World War II, Europe remained the principal source of immigrant arrivals; however, Canada, Mexico and other western hemisphere nations began to contribute significantly to the total inflow. Table 4.1 illustrates.

While it was passage of the Immigration Act of 1965 that marked the beginning of sustained changes in the demographic composition of immigrant inflows, the process that led to passage of the 1965 Act began in 1943 when Congress repealed the Chinese Exclusion Act. The Displaced Persons Acts continued the liberalization of immigration policy. One facet of the Displaced Persons legislation that contributed the most to the eventual abolition of the quota system was the advent of 'quota mortgaging'. Countries were able to mortgage future quota slots, some for more than 100 years, and this led immigrant inflow numbers to frequently exceed stated quota values. While the Displaced Persons Acts did little to change US immigration policy directly, their indirect effects were rather profound in that the restrictive and exclusionary legislation that had been passed during the latter half of the nineteenth century and earlier in the twentieth century could be circumvented.

Although there were piecemeal efforts to alter immigration policy during the 1950s, the US political climate was not conducive to large-scale changes until the 1960s. Beginning with the Kennedy administration and continuing with the Johnson administration, sustained and concerted reform efforts were undertaken. Abba Schwartz, an Assistant Secretary of State in charge of the Bureau of Security and Consular Affairs during the Kennedy–Johnson administrations, was instrumental in crafting the

Table 4.1   Percentage distribution of permanent legal immigration to the US by region of last residence, 1821–30 to 1951–60

Decade	Northwest Europe	Southeast Europe	Asia	Other eastern hemisphere	Canada	Mexico	Other western hemisphere
1821–1830	86.6	2.8	0.0	0.0	2.1	4.4	4.0
1831–1840	92.5	1.1	0.0	0.0	2.6	1.2	2.5
1841–1850	95.9	0.3	0.0	0.0	2.5	0.2	1.1
1851–1860	94.6	0.8	1.6	0.0	2.3	0.1	0.5
1861–1870	88.8	1.1	2.8	0.0	6.7	0.1	0.5
1871–1880	75.9	4.9	4.4	0.4	13.6	0.2	0.5
1881–1890	76.3	13.9	1.3	0.3	7.5	0.0	0.6
1891–1900	55.9	40.8	2.0	0.1	0.1	0.0	0.9
1901–1910	37.4	54.6	3.7	0.2	2.0	0.6	1.5
1911–1920	25.3	50.1	4.3	0.4	12.9	3.8	3.2
1921–1930	32.0	27.9	2.7	0.4	22.5	11.2	3.2
1931–1940	38.1	27.6	3.1	0.8	20.8	4.2	5.5
1941–1950	49.6	10.4	3.6	2.1	16.6	5.9	11.8
1951–1960	39.6	13.4	6.1	1.1	15.1	12.0	12.8

Note: Northwest Europe includes Austria (and Austria-Hungary when Hungary was not specified), Belgium, Denmark, France, Germany, Ireland, the Netherlands, Norway, Sweden, Switzerland, and the United Kingdom. All other European nations are considered part of southeast Europe. Turkey is included in Asia. Prior to 1934, migrants from the Philippines were not recorded as immigrants. From 1820 to 1893, figures for Canada include all of British North America. Complete records on the number of immigrants arriving by land from Canada were not kept until 1908.

Source: Heer (1996).

Immigration and Nationality Act of 1965 Act. Schwartz (1964) commented eloquently on both the inequity of the quota system and its implications for US foreign policy:

> Someplace in American history, Americans, who were immigrants themselves, began to believe that the geographical and national origin of a man determined his suitability as an immigrant.
>
> Subsequently, this was codified into law and became our national immigration policy. At the same time in American history, however, Americans themselves learned to judge their fellow Americans on the basis of ability, industriousness, intelligence, integrity, and all other factors which truly determine a man's value to society. In most laws of our nation we recognize this, except in our immigration laws where we continue to imply judgment of a man on the basis of his national and geographical origin. It is not hard to imagine, therefore, the implication of this policy when it is interpreted to a man from a geographical area or of a national origin, which is not 'favored' by our present

laws. Whether an individual wants to come to the United States or not, he is left with the impression that our standards of judgment are not based on the merits of the individual – but rather on an assumption which can be interpreted as bias and prejudice.

Thus, inasmuch as our immigration laws are interpreted as the basis of how we evaluate others around the world, it is not difficult to understand the impact this has on people abroad and its effect on our foreign relations. Therefore, if for no other reason than to tell people around the world the basis on which we actually judge ourselves and others – not to speak of the contributions all immigrant cultures and traditions have made to our way of life – a revision of our immigration laws is fully justified.

A further indication of how the political landscape had changed, Senator Robert F. Kennedy (1965) made the following statements when addressing the Congressional Subcommittee on Immigration:

It gives me great pleasure to appear today to voice my support of the Administration's immigration bill, S. 500. This bill distills the accumulated experience and wisdom of forty-years – the years since the institution of the discriminatory national origins system. That system was imposed during the postwar crisis in Europe, when many in the United States feared that a continuance of unlimited immigration would lead to the coming here of tens of millions of unlettered, poverty-stricken refugees – and of hundreds of thousands of revolutionaries.

During the corresponding debate on the Senate floor, Senator Ted Kennedy (1965), another proponent of the 1965 Act, described the expected effects of the law as follows:

Under the proposed bill, the present level of immigration remains substantially the same. . . . Secondly, the ethnic mix of this country will not be upset. . . . Contrary to the charges in some quarters, [the bill] will not inundate America with immigrants from any one country or area, or the most populated and deprived nations of Africa and Asia. . . . In the final analysis, the ethnic pattern of immigration under the proposed measure is not expected to change as sharply as the critics seem to think. . . . The bill will not flood our cities with immigrants. It will not upset the ethnic mix of our society.

With its implementation, the 1965 Act replaced the quotas initially established in 1921 by the National Origins Act and modified by the Immigration Act of 1924 with a preference system that focused on: 1) family reunification; 2) filling vacancies in the labor market; and 3) the admittance of refugees and asylum-seekers. The Act eliminated restrictions on Asian emigration and permitted a total of 170 000 immigrants to enter annually from the eastern hemisphere and 120 000 to enter from the western hemisphere. Exclusive of the western hemisphere, the Act placed a

Table 4.2   Immigrant inflows by region, before/after implementation of the Immigration and Nationality Act of 1965

Region	Prior to 1965 Act		Following 1965 Act		ΔShare
	1 July, 1960 –30 June, 1968	Share (per cent)	1 July, 1968 –30 June, 1976	Share (per cent)	
Europe, Canada and Oceania	1 282 644	51.50	858 312	27.96	−23.54
Asia and the Middle East	264 205	10.61	928 108	30.23	+19.63
Latin America and the Caribbean Basin	735 966	29.55	1 054 315	34.35	+4.80
South America	182 374	7.32	174 285	5.68	−1.64
Africa	25 462	1.02	54 664	1.78	+0.76
Total inflows	2 490 651		3 069 684		

limit of 20 000 on the inflow from any particular country; however, immediate family members (that is, children under 21 years of age, spouses and parents) of US citizens were exempt, which resulted in both the 20 000 country-specific caps and the hemisphere-wide maximums regularly being exceeded.

A comparison of immigrant inflow values during the eight years prior to the July 1968 implementation of the Act of 1965 to the eight years immediately following its passage reveals that, contrary to the expectations stated by Senator Ted Kennedy, the number of immigrant arrivals increased substantially and the composition of immigrant inflows in terms of source countries/regions changed considerably.

In Table 4.2 we see that immigrant inflows from Europe, Canada, Oceania (that is, primarily Australia and New Zealand) decreased in absolute numbers by roughly one-third. Conversely, the immigrant inflows from Asia and the Middle East increased by more than 250 per cent during the period, while inflows from Latin America and the Caribbean Basin increased by more than 40 per cent and those from Africa doubled. Changes in the region-specific shares of total immigrant inflows largely mirrored the absolute changes.

During the 1970s, Congress acted to refine and modify US immigration policy. The Immigration and Nationality Act of 1976 limited emigration from all countries to 20 000 per year. Two years later, President Carter signed a bill that replaced the hemisphere-specific caps with a worldwide ceiling of 290000 and a uniform preference system. In general, however, US immigration policy during the past four decades has remained largely as set forth by the 1965 Act. This is evident when one considers the major pieces of recent legislation related to immigration policy that have been passed since 1980. The Refugee Act of 1980 provided the first permanent and systematic procedure for the admission and effective resettlement of refugees of special humanitarian concern to the US. It also set the world-wide ceiling for immigration to the US at 270000, exclusive of refugees. The Immigration Act of 1990 increased total annual immigration to 700000 during fiscal years 1992–4 with a cap of 675000 (480000 family-sponsored, 140000 employment-based and 55000 'diversity immigrants') permitted to enter each year beginning in 1995. The Immigrant Reform and Control Act of 1986 granted legal status to undocumented immigrants who had resided in the US since 1 January, 1982 and established sanctions against employers who knowingly hire persons unauthorized to work in the US. Also, seeking to deter undocumented immigration, the Illegal Immigration Reform and Immigrant Responsibility Act of 1996 established strict measures to control US borders and to deport undocumented immigrants.

NOTES

1. Unless otherwise noted, statistics presented in this part are from Martin and Midgley (1999).
2. The history of US immigration and of US immigration policy is obviously too broad and too rich in detail to be adequately covered in a few pages. For readers who are interested, Briggs (2003), Daniels (2002), Martin and Midgley (1999) and Heer (1996) provide excellent starting points.
3. In 1819, the US acquired Florida from Spain in exchange for dropping its territorial claims to Texas. In 1763, nearly the entire Spanish population of Florida had departed for other Spanish colonies when Great Britain acquired Florida from Spain in exchange for control of Cuba. Spain reacquired Florida in 1783; however, in 1830 there were only 34730 individuals (of which 15501 were slaves) residing in Florida (Mitchell, 1840). Thus, we focus on the settlement of the Massachusetts and Virginia colonies.
4. Although the 1790 census did not count Native Americans, an estimated 150000 Native Americans lived in the US around this time (Lepore, 2002).

5. Primacy, recency and the US immigrant–trade relationship

The notion of primacy effects and recency effects comes from the field of psychology. Simply put, given an ordered sequence of items, individuals are more likely to recall the early and later items in the sequence rather than the middle items. A simple way to think of this is that the remembrance of the early items involves long-term memory while recall of the later items involves short-term (perhaps 'echo') memory. The primacy effect refers to the remembrance of the impressions made by items early in the sequence, while the recency effect refers to the remembrance of impressions made by items at the end of the sequence. If plotted in x–y space with the probability of recall on the y axis and the order in which items are presented along the x axis, a parabolic relationship would be traced out in which recency effects would account for the left arm of the 'U' and primacy effects would account for the right arm. In short, the impressions of items vary according to when each occurs within the sequence. When considered in the context of the US immigrant–trade link, the influence of immigrants from countries generally afforded entry preference prior to 1968 may represent a primacy effect while the influences of immigrants who were largely discouraged or not permitted to immigrate to the US until 1968 may represent a recency effect.

Building on this notion of primacy and recency effects, it is expected that the influence of immigrants from countries that were largely not represented in pre-1968 immigrant inflows will be greater than that of immigrants from home countries that were common source countries prior to 1968. It may also be the case that immigrants who arrived during some period prior to 1968 (the years since the beginning of World War I, for example), being predominantly from European nations, found that the conditions were not conducive for them to exert pro-trade influences. That is, the preference channel may have been inoperable simply because there were relatively fewer immigrant arrivals during this period and, due to earlier immigrant arrivals, the home country goods (or reasonable substitutes) desired by immigrants who arrived between 1914 and 1968 were already available in sufficient quantities. Similarly, the abilities of these immigrants to exert information bridge effects and reduce trade-related transaction costs may have been quite minimal. This could be due to earlier arrivals acting to exploit their abilities to lower transaction costs and enhance/initiate US–home country trade or the result of a large share of the total immigrant inflow during the 1945–68 period being displaced persons who, as refugees, were likely to have had relatively weak ties to their home countries and, hence, may be expected to exert weak or, perhaps, no pro-trade influences.

The primacy effect attributable to pre-1968 home country immigrants is expected to be weaker than the recency effect that is due to immigrants from post-1968 home countries. This is, in part, the result of each home country cohort having achieved different levels of economic development and, as a result, being characterized by differences in terms of their respective trade-facilitating infrastructure. The relative absence or poor quality of such infrastructure would be expected to result in higher trade-related transaction costs. Immigrants from post-1968 home countries would face greater opportunities to increase trade by reducing these costs as compared to immigrants from pre-1968 home countries. Additionally, the influence of immigrants from pre-1968 home countries in terms of shaping the culture and institutions of the US cannot be ignored when considering the relative influences on trade. The basis for this is that greater cultural and institutional dissimilarities are likely to correspond with greater product- and market-related information asymmetries. Immigrants from post-1968 home countries would again face a greater likelihood that they may act to remedy such asymmetries and, by doing so, increase US–home country trade.

5.1   THE DEMOGRAPHIC CONSEQUENCES OF US IMMIGRATION POLICY

To gain an impression of the influence that US immigration policy has had on the composition of immigrant inflows, panel A of Table 5.1 presents US foreign-born population shares by region of immigrants' birth for the period from 1850 to 2000. The combined share of the foreign-born population accounted for by immigrants from Europe, Oceania and North America has generally decreased since 1850. More specifically, between 1850 and 1960, immigrants from these three regions as a share of the foreign-born population decreased from 98.9 per cent of the US foreign-born population to 85.2 per cent. Coincidentally, between 1850 and 1960, the collective share of the US foreign-born population from Asia, the Middle East, Latin America (that is, Mexico and Central America), the Caribbean Basin or South America increased from 1 per cent to 14.5 per cent.

Table 5.1 US foreign-born population: total, composition (by region of birth) and as share of total US population, 1850–2006

Region/Year	1850	1860	1870	1880	1890	1900	1910	1920	1930	1940	1950	1960	1970	1980	1990	2000	2006
Panel A: Immigrant population shares (per cent)																	
Europe	92.2	92.1	88.8	86.2	86.9	86	87.4	85.7	83	---	---	74.5	61.7	39	22.9	15.8	---
Asia and the Middle East	0.1	0.9	1.2	1.6	1.2	1.2	1.4	1.7	1.9	---	---	5.1	8.9	19.3	26.3	26.4	---
Africa	a	a	a	a	a	a	a	0.1	0.1	---	---	0.4	0.9	1.5	1.9	2.8	---
Oceania	a	0.1	0.1	0.1	0.1	0.1	0.1	0.1	0.1	---	---	0.4	0.4	0.6	0.5	0.5	---
Latin America, Caribbean Basin and South America	0.9	0.9	1	1.3	1.2	1.3	2.1	4.2	5.6	---	---	9.4	19.4	33.1	44.3	51.7	---
North America	6.7	6	8.9	10.7	10.6	11.4	9	8.2	9.2	---	---	9.8	8.7	6.5	4	2.7	---
Foreign-born population (mil.)	2.2	4.1	5.6	6.7	9.2	10.3	13.5	13.9	14.2	11.6	10.3	9.7	9.6	14.1	19.8	31.1	37.5
Foreign-born as per cent of total population	9.7	13.2	14.4	13.3	14.8	13.6	14.7	13.2	11.6	8.8	6.9	5.4	4.7	6.2	7.9	11.1	12.5

Panel B: Immigrant stock values (millions)

Europe	2.03	3.78	4.97	5.78	7.99	8.86	11.8	11.91	11.79	---	7.28	5.92	5.5	4.53	4.91	---
Asia and the Middle East	0	0.04	0.07	0.11	0.11	0.12	0.19	0.24	0.27	---	0.49	0.85	2.72	5.21	8.21	---
Africa	---	---	---	---	---	---	---	0.01	0.01	---	0.04	0.09	0.21	0.38	0.87	---
Oceania	---	0.004	0.01	0.01	0.01	0.01	0.01	0.01	0.01	---	0.04	0.04	0.08	0.1	0.16	---
Latin America, Caribbean Basin and South America	0.02	0.04	0.06	0.09	0.11	0.13	0.28	0.58	0.8	---	0.91	1.86	4.67	8.77	16.08	---
North America	0.15	0.25	0.5	0.72	0.98	1.17	1.22	1.14	1.31	---	0.95	0.84	0.92	0.79	0.84	---

Notes

a Less than 0.1 per cent. Totals may not sum to 100 due to rounding.

Source: For all figures other than 1940, 1950 and 2006 total foreign-born population values, foreign-born as a share of total population (all years), and 2000 composition, by region of birth: US Census (2008). Source for 1940 and 1950 total foreign-born population values and foreign-born as a share of total population (except 2006): Briggs (2003). Source for 2006 values: US Census (2009). Source for 2000 composition by region of birth: US Census (2003).

Illustrative of the shifting demographics of the foreign-born population following implementation of the 1965 Act, the collective share from Europe, Oceania and North America has decreased considerably. Between 1960 and 1970, these regions' collective share declined 14.4 percentage points to 70.8 per cent. By 1980, this value had fallen to 46.1 per cent, and by 1990 it had decreased to 27.4 per cent. Finally, in 2000, immigrants from Europe, Oceania and North America collectively accounted for only 19 per cent of the US foreign-born population. The share that was from Asia, the Middle East, Latin America, the Caribbean Basin and South America increased to 28.3 per cent in 1970, to 52.4 per cent in 1980, 70.6 per cent in 1990 and, finally, to 78.1 per cent in 2000. Lastly, it is important to note that the increase in Asian immigration during the 1970s was not primarily the result of the Vietnam War (Sassen, 1992 and 1990). Certainly refugees from Asian nations did enter the US during this period and from Head and Ries (1998) and White and Tadesse (2009c) we know that refugees have, at best, weak effects on trade; however, the Asian nations with consistently the greatest inflows of immigrants to the US were the Philippines, South Korea and Taiwan rather than refugee-sending nations such as Cambodia, Laos and Vietnam.

From 1960 to 2000, the US foreign-born population increased more than threefold from 9.7 million to 31.1 million. Panel B of Table 5.1 indicates that the total number of immigrants from Europe residing in the US in 1960 was approximately 7.25 million. In 2000, this value was roughly 4.9 million persons. This means that the number of immigrants from Europe residing in the US decreased both as a share of the total foreign-born population and in absolute terms. During this same period, the shares of immigrants from Asia and the Middle East and from Latin America, the Caribbean Basin and South America increased by factors of 16.8 and 17.7, respectively. Even more illustrative of the shifting immigrant demographics is that the number of immigrants from Asia and the Middle East increased from less than 0.5 million to nearly 7.75 million. Similarly, the number of immigrants from Latin America, the Caribbean Basin and South America increased from about 900 000 to more than 15 million.

Table 5.2 lists the ten countries with the highest foreign-born population stocks in the US at various times between 1850 and 2000. Up until 1960, with few exceptions, European nations dominate the lists. The notable exceptions are China in 1880 (8th highest value) and Mexico since 1930. Russia and the Soviet Union are each listed in the table. Geographically, both span (or spanned) Europe and Asia; however, the vast majority of Soviet immigrants entering the US following the 1917 Bolshevik revolution were Jewish refugees seeking to escape religious persecution. Given

Table 5.2   *Countries of birth of the US foreign-born population: 1850–2000, ten leading countries*

Rank	1850		1880		1900	
1	Ireland	962000	Germany	1967000	Germany	2663000
2	Germany	584000	Ireland	1855000	Ireland	1615000
3	Great Britain	379000	Great Britain	918000	Canada	1180000
4	Canada	148000	Canada	717000	Great Britain	1168000
5	France	54000	Sweden	194000	Sweden	582000
6	Switzerland	13000	Norway	182000	Italy	484000
7	Mexico	13000	France	107000	Russia	424000
8	Norway	13000	China	104000	Poland	383000
9	Netherlands	10000	Switzerland	89000	Norway	336000
10	Italy	4000	Bohemia	85000	Austria	276000

Rank	1930		1960		1970	
1	Italy	1790000	Italy	1257000	Italy	1009000
2	Germany	1609000	Germany	990000	Germany	833000
3	UK	1403000	Canada	953000	Canada	812000
4	Canada	1310000	UK	833000	Mexico	760000
5	Poland	1269000	Poland	748000	UK	686000
6	Soviet Union	1154000	Soviet Union	691000	Poland	548000
7	Ireland	745000	Mexico	576000	Soviet Union	463000
8	Mexico	641000	Ireland	339000	Cuba	439000
9	Sweden	595000	Austria	305000	Ireland	251000
10	Czechoslovakia	492000	Hungary	245000	Austria	214000

Rank	1980		1990		2000	
1	Mexico	2199000	Mexico	4298000	Mexico	7841000
2	Germany	849000	China	921000	China	1391000
3	Canada	843000	Philippines	913000	Philippines	1222000
4	Italy	832000	Canada	745000	India	1007000
5	UK	669000	Cuba	737000	Cuba	952000
6	Cuba	608000	Germany	712000	Vietnam	863000
7	Philippines	501000	UK	640000	El Salvador	765000
8	Poland	418000	Italy	581000	Korea	701000
9	Soviet Union	406000	Korea	568000	Dominican Rep.	692000
10	Korea	290000	Vietnam	543000	Canada	678000

Note: In general, countries as reported at each census. Data are not totally comparable over time due to changes in boundaries for some countries. Great Britain excludes Ireland. The United Kingdom includes Northern Ireland. China in 1990 includes Hong Kong and Taiwan.

Source: US Census (2001).

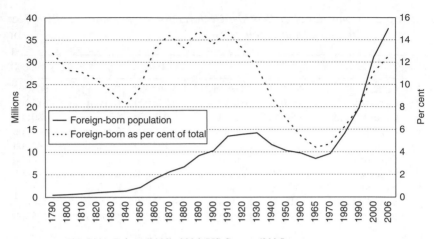

Sources: 1790–2000: Briggs (2003); 2006: US Census (2006).

*Figure 5.1   US foreign-born population in number and as share of total
              population, 1790–2006*

the creation of the Asiatic Barred Zone in 1917, almost all immigration
from Russia and the Soviet Union was from western Russia and eastern
European Soviet satellite nations.

By the mid-1970s, however, immigration from European countries
constituted less than 20 per cent of the total inflow. This shift in the demographic composition of inflows suggests that prior to 1968 residents of
Asian countries were willing but unable to emigrate due to US immigration policy and that many residents in the western hemisphere (exclusive
of Canada) chose not to migrate until after 1968. As a result, we see that,
by 1990, non-European countries top the list of countries of birth for the
US foreign-born population. By 2000, all of the top ten countries of birth
except Canada, which was ranked 10th at that time, are located either in
Asia, Latin America or the Caribbean Basin.

Currently, the share of the US population accounted for by immigrants
is at a level not witnessed since the 1920s. Figure 5.1 details the foreign-
born population in absolute numbers (the solid line) and as a share of the
total population (the dotted line) over the 1790–2006 period. The first
wave of immigration to the US is largely not depicted in this figure due to
the first US census being undertaken in 1790 and as data for earlier years
are largely missing. Focusing first on the line depicting the foreign-born
population in absolute numbers, we see that during the second, third and
even the beginning of the fourth waves (until approximately 1930) this
value increased. It then sharply declines from just under 15 million persons

in 1930 to fewer than 10 million in 1965. This is followed in the years since 1968 by a massive influx of immigrants, with the foreign-born population exceeding 37 million in 2006. This indicates that the foreign-born population has generally increased steadily throughout the nation's history with the sole exception of during the latter portion of the fourth wave of immigration (1918–68). This is not surprising given the quota restrictions that were in place during this era and, to lesser extents, the influences of the Great Depression and World War II on immigrant inflows.

Considering the plot of the foreign-born population as a share of the total population reveals a trough around 1840. While the source for this trough is indeterminable, one potential explanation involves the onset of the industrial revolution in Europe. The industrial revolution began in England in the late 1700s and elsewhere in Europe and in North America in the early 1800s. By the middle of the nineteenth century, industrialization was commonplace in Western Europe and the northeastern US. Given the predominance of England, in particular, and Western Europe in general as sources of US immigrant inflows, the improvements in living standards attributable to industrialization may have acted to diminish the desire to migrate. Certainly, there were negative consequences associated with the industrial revolution as well. Some examples include overcrowded and unsanitary housing arrangements, increased water and air pollution and unsafe working conditions. In considering the potential influence of the industrial revolution on the migration decision, these negative consequences must be considered in conjunction with related benefits that included, among other things, greater product variety and increased purchasing power that resulted from higher average real incomes. The fact that the US pursued, prior to 1882, what may be called an open immigration policy, especially with respect to migration from European nations, since its foreign-born population increased marginally and the share of the population accounted for by immigrants decreased from roughly 13 per cent to about 8 per cent, suggests that migration flows may have been affected by factors other than the policy stance of the US.

Following a sustained increase in the foreign-born population share through to about 1870, a period of relative stability occurred that is reflective of comparable growth rates for the foreign- and native-born populations. This is the period that accounts for much of the third wave of US immigration. Beginning in about 1910, there is a precipitous decline in the foreign-born population share. This decline persists until the mid-1960s and then, as with the absolute number of the foreign-born population, a sharp increase is witnessed. As discussed above, the noted period of decline is largely consistent with the timing of the fourth wave of US immigration, and the subsequent expansion corresponds with the fifth wave.

The basis for a positive direct relationship between immigrants and trade is the assumption that immigrants potentially carry previously unknown information regarding home country markets and products, have connections to specific trade-fostering business and social networks, and/or have somewhat dissimilar preferences from the native-born population and earlier immigrant arrivals. With this in mind, it follows that more recent immigrant arrivals may have found that earlier immigrants exploited information asymmetries between the US and their home countries or had already provided the impetus for increased imports and/or the production of domestic substitutes for home country products. This was alluded to in Chapter 2 as well as earlier in this chapter when it was mentioned that earlier immigrant arrivals had probably forged trading relationships with individuals in their home countries. Both Gould (1994) and Head and Ries (1998) lend support for this notion as they each report decreasing returns to the effect of immigrants on trade. This would suggest that more recent arrivals from European countries, Canada, Australia and New Zealand may have a weaker or, possibly, no effect on US–home country trade, while more recent immigrants – namely, those from the regions that have contributed the largest numbers of immigrants (that is, Asia, the Caribbean Basin and Latin America) – may exert considerable influence on US trade with their home countries. This is not to say that primacy effects are non-existent. In fact, one would expect that earlier waves of immigrant arrivals engaged in behavior similar to that of more recent immigrants. Likewise, what today are viewed as recency effects are expected to diminish with time.

More recent immigrant inflows are likely to differ in many respects from their counterparts who arrived prior to 1968. Most importantly, for the topic at hand, these differences are thought to include their abilities to exploit US–home country information asymmetries to enhance bilateral trade flows. This gives rise to an expected cleavage in the influences of immigrants on US–home country trade, with the typical immigrant from pre-1968 home countries (that is, northern, western and southern Europe along with Canada, Australia and New Zealand) exhibiting weaker, albeit potentially still positive, influences on trade as compared to the influences of more recent arrivals from regions such as Asia and Latin America and the Caribbean Basin. As noted, this cleavage is dichotomized, in an admittedly simple fashion, as primacy effects for the former group and recency effects for the latter.

Figure 5.2 indicates which countries/regions are categorized as part of the pre-1968 home country cohort in the empirical analysis to follow and which countries are categorized as post-1968 home countries. Those without any shading are countries for which data are not available. Section 5.2 lists the countries within each classification.

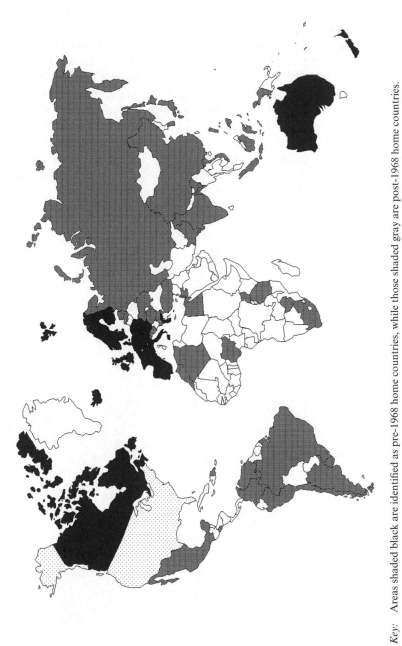

Key: Areas shaded black are identified as pre-1968 home countries, while those shaded gray are post-1968 home countries.

Figure 5.2   World map indicating pre-1968 and post-1968 home countries

5.2   APPENDIX 5.A: COUNTRY LISTING

Pre-1968 home countries: Australia, Austria, Belgium, Canada, Czech Republic, Denmark, Finland, France, Germany, Greece, Hungary, Iceland, Ireland, Italy, Netherlands, New Zealand, Norway, Poland, Portugal, Slovakia, Spain, Sweden, Switzerland, United Kingdom.

Post-1968 home countries: Albania, Algeria, Argentina, Armenia, Azerbaijan, Bangladesh, Brazil, Bulgaria, Chile, China, Colombia, Croatia, Dominican Republic, Egypt, El Salvador, Estonia, India, Indonesia, Israel, Japan, Jordan, Korea (Republic of), Latvia, Macedonia, Mexico, Morocco, Nigeria, Pakistan, Peru, Philippines, Romania, Russia, South Africa, Slovenia, Tanzania, Turkey, Uganda, Ukraine, Uruguay, Venezuela, Vietnam, Zimbabwe.

6. The importance of trade-facilitating infrastructure

In this chapter, we begin our exploration of the possible factors that underlie immigrants' abilities to influence trade between the US and their home countries. Specifically, the topic of trade-facilitating infrastructure (or lack thereof) is explored as is the role that such infrastructure plays with respect to trade-related transaction costs. In Chapters 4 and 5, the history of US immigration is reviewed and a clear distinction is shown in terms of the source countries for immigrant inflows prior to and following the implementation of the Immigration and Nationality Act of 1965. Given the shift in source countries, we also consider whether the pre-1968 and post-1968 home country cohorts vary in terms of the presence and quality of such infrastructure.

The existence and quality of trade-facilitating infrastructure is directly related to trade-related transaction costs. In terms of imports, superior infrastructure aids in the reduction of distribution margins which then results in lower product prices and corresponding increases in consumer welfare. By reducing transaction costs, such infrastructure serves to add value and, in doing so, increases exporters' profits by forming or expanding linkages to global distribution networks (Brooks, 2008). Considering the relationship between infrastructure and exporting, Francois and Manchin (2007) report that infrastructure is a significant determinant of whether exporting occurs and, if it does, the level of exporting that is observed.

Expected variation in the immigrant–trade link, in terms of the proportional influences of immigrants from post-1968 home countries being greater than those of immigrants who are from pre-1968 home countries (that is, that recency effects are proportionally greater than primacy effects), is directly related to the presence and quality of trade-facilitating infrastructure. If a nation's infrastructure is of poor quality or lacking in general then we would expect that transaction costs would be higher than if their infrastructure were of better quality and/or in relative abundance. Thus, poor quality or a lack of infrastructure is expected to inhibit trade. Under such conditions, immigrants potentially face greater opportunities to reduce related transaction costs by acting as intermediaries and would be expected to exert larger positive influences on trade flows. If trade-facilitating infrastructure is abundant and/or of relatively high quality, then trade-related transaction costs will be lower and immigrants' opportunities to offset costs and, hence, to influence trade positively will be diminished.

6.1 WHAT IS TRADE-FACILITATING INFRASTRUCTURE?

Trade-facilitating infrastructure is an important determinant of trade costs; however, it has no formal definition. It is a 'catch-all' term that represents both physical infrastructure and what may be thought of as supporting infrastructure. In a very narrow sense, the term refers to the transportation logistics and customs administration that are associated with international trade. A more expansive definition would also include the environment/business climate in which trade occurs.

Trade costs can be defined as all costs incurred in the delivery of the product to its final user. This would not include, for example, the cost incurred to produce the good but would include costs associated with shipments and transport. These trade costs may be direct or indirect. Direct costs include transportation costs related to ports, air links, highways/roads, and rail lines, warehousing costs, freight insurance, delays experienced at customs, and unofficial payments that may be characterized as bribery and/or corruption. Indirect costs include information search costs associated with the matching of buyers and sellers and with the establishment of production and/or distribution facilities, supply chain management costs, and the regulation of the insurance industry and of currency and capital markets.

Trade-facilitating infrastructure can be categorized as 'hard' or as 'soft'. Traditionally, infrastructure has referred to services that correspond with large and long-lasting capital projects such as highways and railroads, bridges, ports (both air and sea), cool chains, dams and power generation and delivery facilities, and telecommunications systems. These capital-intensive/physical forms of infrastructure can be collectively described as hard infrastructure. Recently, there has been considerable attention devoted to soft (or institutional) infrastructure, which affects the efficiency with which services are delivered via hard infrastructure.

Broadly speaking, soft infrastructure includes the technical assistance that is devoted towards the establishment and maintenance of hard infrastructure. This includes predictable legal rights/procedures, an enforceable and equitable competition policy, a sound regulatory framework, financial services (particularly long-term local currency bond markets to provide financing and currency markets to facilitate payment), and the efficiency of administrative procedures at customs. Soft infrastructure may also include a nation's participation/membership in international agreements that relate to trade and foreign investment. Soft infrastructure is sometimes defined as governance in general, including corporate governance and anti-corruption measures.

Given these descriptions, it is evident that the existence and quality of hard infrastructure aids in the delivery of services that facilitate trade, while the presence and quality of soft infrastructure is necessary to enhance and ensure the efficient operation of existing hard infrastructure. More specifically, Nordas and Piermartini (2004) detail four interactions between trade costs and infrastructure in general. First, the monetary costs associated with delivery of products to their final users are determined by the extent of existing infrastructure and its quality. Second, better quality infrastructure correlates with lower time costs in terms of product delivery. In this regard, the absence of infrastructure or, if present, poor quality infrastructure may translate into higher (monetary) trade costs in the form of higher transportation costs or greater warehousing costs. Third, freight and insurance costs would be likely to be lower if infrastructure is abundant and/or of better quality. Fourth, the existence and quality of infrastructure facilitates greater market access. These four interactions imply that the development of infrastructure (both hard and soft) would probably lead to an increase in trade, assuming that trade was already taking place, and an increase in the likelihood that trading occurs (that is, trade in new products or with new destinations) (Brooks, 2008). Conversely, when trade-facilitating infrastructure is lacking or, if present, of poor quality, it is likely to be the case that less trading occurs both with respect to the intensity of trade and in terms of the breadth of product types being traded.

6.2 DOES THE LEVEL AND QUALITY OF INFRASTRUCTURE VARY ACROSS HOME COUNTRY COHORTS?

Among the examples of infrastructure mentioned, it is likely that transportation infrastructure has the largest influence on trade flows. Brooks (2008) notes that, for developing countries, efficient port operations are particularly important since a large portion of their total trade passes through seaports rather than via rail lines or highways. Haveman et al. (2009) estimate that improvements to port facilities lower port costs with a new harbor, wharf, or terminal decreasing costs by 2 per cent, while a new crane decreases costs by 1 per cent. In addition to port improvements, the quality and extent of complementary transportation infrastructure such as highway and railroad networks can substantially affect trade costs. Limao and Venables (2001) estimated that, for landlocked countries, infrastructure accounts for roughly 60 per cent of transport costs but for only 40 per cent of transport costs for countries that have coastal access. Limao and Venables also estimate land transport to be seven times more costly than transport by water and Brooks (2008) reports that every 1 per cent reduction in transportation costs leads to an estimated 2 per cent rise in a country's exports.

When the high costs of infrastructure development are considered it is not surprising that, relative to their more developed counterparts, developing countries often face considerable structural impediments to hard infrastructure investment and, hence, to trade. This lack of adequate physical and technological infrastructure renders the existence of soft infrastructure moot. Nevertheless, it would be reasonable to assume that the hard infrastructure of developing countries would be less prevalent and/or of reduced quality as compared to the hard infrastructure of the typical developed country. This follows from the former cohort being less able, or less likely, to make sufficient infrastructure investments while the latter cohort would be more likely to undertake such investment.

Similar to the difficulties involved with hard infrastructure, developing countries would be expected to face difficulties in terms of establishing and maintaining well-functioning institutions to support and regulate their financial sectors, insurance industries and credit markets, as well as other trade-supporting services. These countries may also find that integration into the global trading system, either through bilateral dealings or multilaterally via international bodies such as the WTO, is hindered by their inability to adhere to agreements and/or implement necessary reforms effectively. This may compound the difficulties associated with provision of institutional support as the private sector may encounter insufficient financing to fund exporting and may lack access to affordable market intelligence services (Brooks, 2008).

In Chapter 5, the trading partners that are included in the data set for this study are categorized as either pre-1968 home countries or as post-1968 home countries based on preferences afforded historically by US immigration policy. The shift in immigrant source countries/regions that followed the implementation of the Immigration and Nationality Act of 1965 can be characterized as a movement away from the arrival of immigrants from countries that are largely developed to one where the predominant source countries are relatively less developed.

In this section, three questions are addressed. First, are there significant differences across the pre-1968 home country and post-1968 home country groupings in terms of standard economic and social development measures? Second, if a difference is observed, then do the two groupings also differ in terms of their levels of hard infrastructure? Finally, a similar question, do the two groupings differ in terms of their levels of soft infrastructure? If differences are observed, then a basis exists for the notion that because the lack of trade-facilitating infrastructure is likely to lead to higher trade-related transaction costs, such conditions may be conducive for immigrants to exert pro-trade influences. Accordingly, under such circumstances, it would follow that, all else equal, immigrants from the cohort of post-1968 home countries would be expected to exert stronger pro-trade influences than their pre-1968 home country counterparts. This, of course, relates directly to the prior discussion concerning the relative magnitudes of primacy effects and recency effects.

The t-statistics reported in Table 6.1 indicate that the typical member of the cohort of post-1968 home countries is generally, in terms of the standard measures of economic and social development considered, less developed than the typical member of the pre-1968 home country cohort. More specifically, post-1968 home countries are less likely to be members of the Organisation for Economic Co-operation and Development. The OECD is an international organization of 30 representative democracies that adhere to the principles of market-based economics. Generally speaking, OECD members are high-income countries that have achieved high levels of economic and social development. For example, among the countries included in the data here, the correlation coefficient between OECD membership and the United Nations Human Development Index value is 0.66, and the correlation between OECD membership and being categorized as a 'high-income' country according to the World Bank classification system is 0.76.

Given the relationship between OECD membership and HDI values, it is unsurprising that post-1968 home countries have significantly lower average HDI values as compared to the pre-1968 home country cohort. The HDI considers income per capita, life expectancy and two measures of education: adult literacy and school enrolments. As such, it is often considered an aggregate measure of economic development and social development. In terms of simple economic development, the post-1968 cohort has significantly lower average values for gross domestic product per capita and for gross national income per capita. This latter measure is employed by the World Bank to categorize home countries into income classifications. Thus, the post-1968 home countries are, on average, less

Table 6.1   Relative economic and social development, pre-1968 and post-1968 home country cohorts

	All home countries N = 858	Pre-1968 home countries N = 312	Post-1968 home countries N = 546	t-statistic
Non-OECD member dummy	0.5956	0.0449	0.9103	51.01
variable	(0.4911)	(0.2074)	(0.2861)	
Real GDP per capita	11 141.36	23 717.18	3 955.18	28.6
	(12 679.58)	(11 283.36)	(6 155.08)	
Real GNI per capita	11 137.90	23 730.21	3 929.09	26.65
	(13 023.61)	(12 277.06)	(6 141.62)	
UN Human Development	0.7845	0.9131	0.7098	31.52
Index	(0.152)	(0.0344)	(0.1437)	
World Bank income classifications				
High income dummy	0.3485	0.8333	0.0714	31.96
variable	(0.4768)	(0.3733)	(0.2578)	
Upper middle income	0.2273	0.1667	0.2619	3.36
dummy variable	(0.4193)	(0.3733)	(0.4401)	
Lower middle income	0.2576	0	0.4048	19.25
dummy variable	(0.4376)	(0)	(0.4913)	
Middle income dummy	0.4848	0.1667	0.6667	17.11
variable	(0.5001)	(0.3733)	(0.4718)	
Low income dummy	0.1667	0	0.2619	13.91
variable	(0.3729)	(0)	(0.4401)	

Note: Standard deviations in parentheses. t-tests compare mean values for pre-1968 and post-1968 home country cohorts.

likely to be categorized as high-income and more likely to be listed as middle-income (upper or lower) or as low-income.

As the data indicate significant differences across the home country groupings in terms of relative economic and social development, we now turn to the two follow-up questions to address whether the groupings differ with respect to their levels of hard and soft infrastructure. Tables 6.2 and 6.3, respectively, present summary statistics for various types of hard and soft infrastructure. Because individual metrics are insufficient to indicate relative infrastructure development, several measures are considered. Across all measures presented, the corresponding t-statistics indicate significant differences. This applies for both the measures of hard infrastructure and those representing soft infrastructure.

Table 6.2 *Various measures of 'hard' trade-facilitating infrastructure*

	N	All home countries	N	Pre-1968 home countries	N	Post-1968 home countries	t-statistic
Energy							
Electric power consumption (kWh per capita)	845	4623.96 (5116.21)	312	8803.35 (5928.19)	533	2177.48 (2177.59)	19.01
Electric power transmission and distribution losses (per cent of output)	845	12.6966 (8.349)	312	7.1603 (2.3963)	533	15.9374 (8.8731)	21.53
Human Capital							
Researchers in R&D (per million people)	417	2098.97 (1640.73)	211	2877.79 (1524.77)	206	1301.25 (1348.11)	11.19
Technicians in R&D (per million people)	321	621.87 (521.42)	143	927.19 (557.86)	178	376.59 (325.66)	10.46
Telecommunications Services							
Information and communication technology expenditure (per cent of GDP)	215	5.8332 (1.4584)	92	6.2182 (0.7273)	123	5.5452 (1.7722)	3.81
International Internet bandwidth (bits per person)	533	1425.03 (3954.44)	186	3730.74 (5975.89)	347	189.12 (748.3)	8.05
Secure Internet servers (per million people)	323	89.1141 (167.9969)	120	211.2598 (222.6354)	203	16.9097 (41.0684)	9.47
Telephone lines (per hundred people)	857	28.2477 (20.8855)	312	49.1862 (13.0649)	545	16.2609 (13.9069)	34.67

95

Table 6.2 (continued)

	N	All home countries	N	Pre-1968 home countries	N	Post-1968 home countries	t-statistic
Transportation Services							
Air transport, registered carrier departures worldwide	845	167 545 (229 357)	308	262 497 (260 968)	537	113 085 (188 873)	8.81
Non-'passenger car' vehicles (per thousand people)	598	45.2929 (34.1433)	257	61.86 (29.1215)	341	32.8068 (32.3201)	11.52
Rail lines (total route-km)/land area (sq. km)	668	0.0349 (0.0311)	266	0.0575 (0.034)	402	0.02 (0.0169)	16.68
Roads, paved (per cent of total roads)	560	64.0723 (30.8315)	215	80.5841 (22.4764)	345	53.7823 (30.884)	11.85
Roads, total network (km)/land area (sq. km)	626	0.8522 (0.9508)	240	1.3932 (1.1327)	386	0.5158 (0.6126)	11.04
Vehicles (per km of road)	530	35.2746 (31.8015)	231	39.4329 (32.2465)	299	32.062 (31.1283)	2.65
Water and Sanitation							
Improved sanitation facilities (per cent of population with access)	161	80.0497 (22.8273)	48	99.6042 (1.0051)	113	71.7434 (22.5942)	13.08
Improved water source (per cent of population with access)	177	91.4802 (12.0972)	58	99.7414 (0.7389)	119	87.4538 (12.9659)	10.30

Notes: Standard deviations in parentheses. t-tests compare mean values for pre-1968 and post-1968 home country cohorts.

Source: World Bank (2009a).

Table 6.3 *Various measures of 'soft' trade-facilitating infrastructure*

	N	All home countries	N	Pre-1968 home countries	N	Post-1968 home countries	t-statistic
Costs: Financial- and Time-related							
Cost of business start-up procedures (per cent of GNI per capita)	261	28.0448 (47.3708)	94	8.1564 (8.3954)	167	39.2395 (55.9029)	7.05
Time required to build a warehouse (days)	132	220.2652 (115.8795)	48	179.0208 (79.4627)	84	243.8333 (126.7761)	3.61
Time required to register property (days)	197	77.8426 (122.7416)	71	47.5915 (56.3987)	126	94.8889 (145.013)	3.25
Time required to start a business (days)	261	41.5326 (33.7552)	94	25.5426 (22.5802)	167	50.5329 (35.6749)	6.92
Time required to enforce a contract (days)	261	582.8238 (298.3182)	94	523.5532 (252.1968)	167	616.1856 (317.247)	2.59
Time to resolve insolvency (years)	260	2.9154 (1.932)	96	1.9594 (1.7997)	164	3.475 (1.7861)	6.57
Time to prepare and pay taxes (hours)	132	408.5758 (427.1873)	48	227.5 (180.9994)	84	512.0476 (489.5673)	4.79

Table 6.3 (continued)

	N	All home countries	N	Pre-1968 home countries	N	Post-1968 home countries	t-statistic
Governance							
Voice and Accountability	66	0.4104 (0.9033)	24	1.3268 (0.2414)	42	-0.1133 (0.6989)	12.15
Political Stability/No Violence	66	0.0866 (0.9348)	24	0.9891 (0.3106)	42	-0.4292 (0.7628)	10.61
Government Effectiveness	66	0.5113 (1.0034)	24	1.5874 (0.5513)	42	-0.1036 (0.6003)	11.60
Regulatory Quality	66	0.4788 (0.8237)	24	1.3016 (0.3329)	42	0.0086 (0.625)	10.96
Rule of Law	66	0.3583 (1.0284)	24	1.4453 (0.5182)	42	-0.2628 (0.6627)	11.61
Control of Corruption	66	0.3893 (1.13)	24	1.5816 (0.721)	42	-0.2921 (0.6519)	10.51
Miscellaneous							
Informal payments to public officials (per cent of firms)	66	34.9564 (19.8703)	13	27.2023 (13.6144)	53	36.8583 (20.7857)	2.04
Rigidity of employment index (0 = less rigid to 100 = more rigid)	264	35.8447 (15.2301)	96	32.1875 (15.8668)	168	37.9345 (14.4914)	2.92
Strength of legal rights index (0 = weak to 10 = strong)	198	5.9949 (2.0954)	72	6.7361 (1.8764)	126	5.5714 (2.1031)	4.02

Procedures

Procedures to build a warehouse (number)	132	19.3485 (8.2397)	48	16.0417 (7.1962)	84	21.2381 (8.2398)	3.78
Procedures to enforce a contract (number)	261	35.4368 (5.6928)	94	31.7234 (4.8202)	167	37.5269 (5.0537)	9.18
Procedures to register property (number)	197	6.203 (2.9811)	71	4.5775 (2.4358)	126	7.119 (2.875)	6.58
Start-up procedures to register a business (number)	261	9.3295 (3.8248)	94	6.5426 (3.3074)	167	10.8982 (3.1482)	10.39

Notes: Standard deviations in parentheses. t-tests compare mean values for pre-1968 and post-1968 home country cohorts. Governance values are means of country-specific averages over 1996, 1998, 2000, 2002, 2004 and 2006. All other values are averages taken over 2003–06 period.

Source: World Bank (2009a and 2009c).

On a per capita basis, average electricity consumption in pre-1968 home countries is significantly greater than that in post-1968 home countries. As with many infrastructure measures, the difference in electricity consumption may reflect relative levels of development more than the quality or presence of infrastructure. In this instance, to gain a measure of relative quality, electric power transmission and distribution losses as a share of output are also considered. On average, post-1968 home countries lose a significantly greater share of their output relative to pre-1968 home countries.

In terms of human capital, measured on a 'per million residents' basis, post-1968 home countries have fewer researchers and technicians engaged in Research and Development. Across the telecommunications services sub-group, the typical country in the post-1968 grouping is lacking relative to the average pre-1968 home country. A smaller share of GDP is invested in information and communications technology, there are fewer telephone lines and secure Internet servers, and considerably less international Internet bandwith. Likewise, across all measures, transportation services are lacking, as is access to improved water and sanitation.

As with measures of specific types of hard infrastructure, across forms of soft infrastructure the familiar pattern of post-1968 home countries lacking, either in terms of quality or presence, persists. Both financial and time-related costs of doing business are higher, on average, among the post-1968 home country cohort; this is perhaps indicative of poor governmental institutions or a weak overall business climate. The same applies with respect to the number of procedures necessary to complete certain tasks. Bribery is more prevalent in post-1968 home countries, and the strength of legal rights are weaker.

In general, governance is lacking in post-1968 home countries. The World Bank (2009c) defines governance as:

> the traditions and institutions by which authority in a country is exercised. This includes the process by which governments are selected, monitored and replaced; the capacity of the government to formulate and implement sound policies; and the respect of citizens and the state for the institutions that govern economic and social interactions among them.

Across all dimensions of governance, the post-1968 home country cohort is lacking relative to the group of pre-1968 home countries. This is taken as an indication of post-1968 home countries governments' overall ineffectiveness. The implication for soft infrastructure is clear: governments that are less effective in governing, in general, would be likely to be less effective in providing the support necessary for any hard infrastructure that exists and in fostering the development of hard infrastructure.

Since differences are observed across the measures of trade-facilitating infrastructure, a basis exists for the notion that the absence of or relatively poor quality of infrastructure contributes to higher related transaction costs and produces conditions that are conducive for immigrants to exert positive influences on host–home country trade flows. Moreover, this relationship between the timing of immigrant inflows, the presence and quality of infrastructure in the immigrants' home countries, and how such infrastructure (or lack thereof) affects transaction costs suggests that, all else equal, immigrants from post-1968 home countries are likely to face greater opportunities, since they may face higher trade-related transaction costs, to exert pro-trade influences. Again, if immigrants are able to take advantage of these opportunities, then we would expect immigrants from post-1968 home countries to exert stronger influences on trade relative to their counterparts from pre-1968 home countries. In short, the relationships detailed here provide one rationale for the expectation that recency effects will be of greater magnitude than primacy effects.

7. Cultural distance between the US and immigrants' home countries

In an attempt to explain further the underlying basis for the US immigrant–trade link, this chapter introduces a measure of cultural differences (that is, the cultural distance) between the US and each of the home countries in our data set. Hofstede (1981) defines culture as a system of collectively held values which suggests that cultural differences are the degree to which shared norms and values differ from one country to another. Such norms and values reflect societies' behavioral rules, which may be represented through artifacts and symbols, myths and legends, rituals, ceremonies and celebrations, beliefs, and ethical codes (Brown, 1995). Inglehart et al. (2004) also notes that relationship structures, societal obligations, roles and functions are important factors that determine and, hence, reflect a nation's culture. A brief definition of 'culture' may be that it is the totality of behavior, beliefs, arts, institutions and all other avenues by which a population, community or a class collectively expresses its values and attitudes.

If, at the society/country-level, culture is a composite reflection of the population's shared habits and traditions, learned beliefs and customs, attitudes, norms and values, it follows that greater social and/or institutional dissimilarity corresponds with greater cultural dissimilarity (White and Tadesse, 2008a). Greater variation in consumer preferences across immigrants and other host country residents, which may result from cultural (that is, social and institutional) differences between the host and home countries, may increase the likelihood that immigrants will exert positive influences on US imports from their home countries via the preference channel. Similarly, if cultural differences increase the asymmetric nature of information relating to products, markets, and (informal or formal) contracting, immigrants may increase host–home country trade flows by way of their information, cultural or enforcement bridging effects.

Pronounced cultural differences may hinder human interaction as understanding and anticipating behavior becomes more difficult (Elsass and Viega, 1994). Doz and Hamel (1998) note that even if such limitations can be overcome, cultural dissimilarity may still, at times, lead individuals to interpret the same situation or series of events in entirely different ways.

Cross-border transactions can be complicated if cultural differences lead to a lack of uniform legal rights and procedures and/or potential trading partners believe themselves to be vulnerable to opportunistic behavior. This suggests that it is possible (and perhaps quite probable) that cultural dissimilarity between trading partners complicates interactions such that the development of rapport and trust are hindered. This also would potentially result in greater contract enforcement costs or higher transaction costs. For example, search costs may be substantial when seeking to match potential buyers and sellers. As a result, cultural dissimilarity is likely to limit trade (Tadesse and White, 2008b). These increases in transaction costs are important for the immigrant–trade relationship since they would affect trade much in the same manner as would a lack of or poor quality of trade-facilitating infrastructure. Similar to that situation, immigrants may exert pro-trade influences by acting as intermediaries who promote and ensure the trust and degree of commitment that is necessary for the successful completion of international transactions.

7.1   STUDIES INVOLVING CULTURAL DISTANCE, IMMIGRANTS AND TRADE

In Chapter 3, we surveyed the literature relating to the immigrant–trade relationship. As noted, a number of recent studies have used data from the World Values Surveys (WVS) and the European Values Surveys (EVS) (Tadesse and White, 2008a; 2008b; 2007a; White and Tadesse, 2009b; 2008a; 2008b; 2009c). Since we also use the WVS/EVS-based measure of cultural distance here and because the measure is described in section 7.2, we forgo detailed discussion of the variable here and simply note that prior studies that have used this measure of cultural distance have consistently reported that greater cultural differences between the US and its trading partners inhibits both US exports and imports.

A handful of other studies have examined the influences of cultural differences on trade using various other measures. Although a consensus of sorts has emerged from these studies, the findings are not entirely uniform. Linders et al. (2005), for example, used Hofstede's (1980) four-dimensional measure of culture when examining data representing bilateral trade flows between 92 countries during 1999 and reported a positive relationship between cultural distance and bilateral trade. Supporting this notion, Larimo (2003) used both Hofstede's measure of cultural distance and a composite index of cultural distance that was developed by Kogut and Singh (1988). It is thought that cultural differences between countries correspond with greater differences in firms' organizational and management practices and that this makes it more difficult for parent firms to transfer home country business practices to their subsidiaries in culturally-dissimilar locales. As a result, firms may prefer to serve culturally-distant markets at arm's length, choosing to export to them, rather than by establishing local production facilities.

Guiso et al. (2005) used survey data that measures respondents' stereotypes of foreign nationals to construct a proxy variable that represents cultural differences. Examining data for 16 EU member countries over the 1970–96 period, the authors reported that, while cultural differences may increase exports, cultural differences may hinder the development of rapport and the creation of trust required to complete trade deals. If so, then cultural differences would be likely to reduce the probability that trade occurs and, subject to trade taking place, reduce the volume of trade.

A number of recent studies have employed measures of common language usage to represent cultural similarity. In most cases, dummy variables have been used to indicate whether a language is commonly spoken in both trade partners. For example, as a robustness check, Gould (1994) split the sample of trading partners according to whether or not English is commonly spoken in the country. Estimated immigrant links were insignificant with respect to aggregate US imports from English-speaking trading partners; however, the estimated pro-trade immigrant influences were found to be greater when English was commonly used in the home country. Specifically, other than when aggregate imports and consumer imports were employed as dependent variables, estimated elasticities for the immigrant information variable were positive, significant and of greater magnitude for the English-speaking cohort than for the non-English-speaking cohort. Hutchinson (2002) also reported a positive relationship between common language use and bilateral trade. Dunlevy (2006) considered the potential influence of immigrants on US state-level exports and controlled for the possibility of either English or Spanish being commonly spoken in the home country. Supporting the findings of related studies it was found that immigrants from English- and Spanish-speaking countries exerted weaker influences on exports than did immigrants from non-English/non-Spanish-speaking countries. Boisso and Ferrantino (1997) relied on a more complex proxy variable to represent cultural differences. Including an index of linguistic distance and estimating gravity specifications for each year during the 1960–85 period, the authors found that greater linguistic dissimilarity (that is, cultural differences) corresponds with decreased trade flows. In fact, while the trade-inhibiting influence of linguistic dissimilarity remained negative and significant throughout the period, the trade-inhibiting effects of cultural distance are estimated to have increased from 1960 until the early 1970s and then to decrease thereafter.

7.2   MEASURING US–HOME COUNTRY CULTURAL DIFFERENCES

In the review of US immigration history provided in Chapter 4, it was asserted that the US has developed to be more culturally and institutionally akin to Europe, Canada, Australia and New Zealand than it has to other countries/regions. The fact that the source countries and regions of more recent US immigrant inflows have varied from those of earlier immigrant inflows has probably resulted in many recent immigrant arrivals finding a culture that is considerably different from that of their home country. Contrasting this with the observation that earlier waves of immigrant arrivals probably arrived to find a culture somewhat similar to that of their home countries, it would follow that the average cultural distance between the US and the cohort of post-1968 home countries is likely to be greater than the distance between the US and the typical pre-1968 home country. If so, then cultural distance would be expected to hinder US trade with post-1968 home countries more so than it would with pre-1968 home countries. The different effects in terms of reducing trade flows correspond with the notion that greater cultural distance signifies cultural and institutional differences between the US and its trading partners, which results in higher trade-related transaction costs. As with trade-facilitating infrastructure, this may afford immigrants from post-1968 home countries greater opportunities to exert positive effects on US trade with their respective home countries. In this regard, cultural distance is related to primacy and recency effects in the same sense that infrastructure is. The fact that the correlation between the measure of cultural distance we have constructed and the post-1968 home country dummy variable is equal to 0.51 reflects this relationship.

To measure the extent to which trade may be affected by preference-based and institutional differences that would be reflective of product- and market-related information asymmetries, we have constructed a measure of US–home country cultural distance. Data from the WVS and the EVS are used to calculate the cultural distances between the US and each of the 66 home countries identified in Chapter 5 (Inglehart et al., 2004; Hagenaars et al., 2003). The Values Surveys represent a large collection of information regarding individuals' attitudes, values and beliefs. The data are from representative national samples, which allows for the construction of cross-societal standardized measures of cultural differences. These measures are based on answers to a broad set of questions which relate to topics that include economics, politics, religion, sexual behavior, gender roles, family values, communal identities, civic engagement, ethical concerns, environmental protection, and scientific and technological progress (Inglehart et al., 2004).

Inglehart et al. (2004) apply factor analysis to individual survey responses, which permits classification of each respondent in terms of two dimensions of culture: 1) Traditional authority vs. secular-rational authority (*TSR*); and 2) survival values vs. self-expression values (*SSE*). Average *TSR* and *SSE* values have been calculated for each home country. On average, the values surveys provide *TSR* and *SSE* values for 1516 residents of each nation in our sample. These respondents represent a cross-section of each society, with care taken by the survey administrators to sample representative populations in terms of urban and rural locations as well as respondents' age classifications, income levels and gender. For the US, 1200 residents were surveyed. Since the cultural distance measure is calculated using the *TSR* and *SSE* data series, the next section introduces these two underlying dimensions of culture. This is followed by a discussion of the composite measure of US–home country cultural distance.

7.2.1 Traditional Authority vs. Secular-rational Authority

The traditional authority vs. secular-rational authority (*TSR*) dimension of culture reflects the contrast, along a continuum of sorts, between societies in which deference to the authority of the nation, to a god, or to the family is viewed as important or is a general expectation, and those societies that place greater emphasis on the individual. Traditional societies are characterized by an adherence to family and/or communal obligations, national pride, an obedience to religious authority, and on corresponding norms of sharing. In such societies it is not uncommon for large families and large numbers of children to be viewed as positive or desirable achievements. Perhaps not surprisingly, fertility rates in traditional societies tend to be rather high. Divorce, abortion, euthanasia and suicide are generally viewed in a very negative light. Secular-rational societies tend to be characterized by having opposing views on these topics. Members of such societies often adhere to rational-legal norms and emphasize economic accumulation and individual achievement.

Table 7.1 ranks, in ascending order, the home countries included in our data set in terms of their absolute differences from the US along the *TSR* dimension of culture. The countries that have been categorized as pre-1968 home countries are identified in this and in subsequent tables by bold font. Although certain pre-1968 home country sub-groups are clustered together, there is no clear relationship between *TSR* values and categorization as a pre- or post-1968 home country. More specifically, the average *TSR* distance from the US, across all home countries, is 0.69. The US, being one of the most traditional of the western post-industrial societies, is distinct from many pre-1968 home countries in this regard. The

Table 7.1 *Traditional vs. secular-rational authority, US–home country absolute differences in mean values*

Country	$|TSR_i - TSR_j|$	Country	$|TSR_i - TSR_j|$	Country	$|TSR_i - TSR_j|$	Country	$|TSR_i - TSR_j|$
Portugal	**0**	**Australia**	**0.38**	**Hungary**	**0.64**	Russian Fed.	0.99
Poland	**0.03**	Peru	0.41	Armenia	0.64	Bulgaria	1.03
India	0.09	Croatia	0.42	Venezuela	0.66	**Netherlands**	**1.04**
Turkey	0.13	Brazil	0.44	**Iceland**	**0.68**	Slovenia	1.07
Azerbaijan	0.16	**Italy**	**0.47**	**Greece**	**0.69**	**Norway**	**1.12**
Canada	**0.22**	Bangladesh	0.47	**New Zealand**	**0.7**	Estonia	1.12
Argentina	0.23	Uganda	0.48	**France**	**0.7**	Colombia	1.28
Ireland	**0.25**	Mexico	0.49	Jordan	0.72	**Denmark**	**1.29**
Vietnam	0.25	**Spain**	**0.55**	**Belgium**	**0.77**	**Germany**	**1.3**
Romania	0.25	**United Kingdom**	**0.57**	Latvia	0.8	**Czech Rep.**	**1.34**
Chile	0.27	Israel	0.58	Korea, Rep.	0.82	Morocco	1.38
Indonesia	0.29	Zimbabwe	0.58	**Slovakia**	**0.84**	China	1.5
Philippines	0.3	Macedonia	0.58	**Finland**	**0.88**	**Sweden**	**1.56**
S. Africa	0.32	Pakistan	0.6	Tanzania	0.88	Japan	1.58
Uruguay	0.35	**Austria**	**0.61**	Ukraine	0.88	El Salvador	1.86
Albania	0.35	Algeria	0.62	**Switzerland**	**0.9**		
Dominican Rep.	0.36	Egypt	0.64	Nigeria	0.9		

Source: Author's calculations based on data from the WVS/EVS. Available online at www.worldvaluessurvey.org.

correlation between categorization as a pre-1968 home country and what may be referred to as *TSR* distance is 0.01.

7.2.2   Survival Values vs. Self-expression Values

The *SSE* dimension of culture reflects differences in the extent to which societies emphasize hard work and self-denial (that is, survival values) as compared to quality of life issues (that is, self-expression values). Societies in which individuals are more survival-oriented are characterized by a greater emphasis on economic and physical security and by a reduced emphasis on autonomy. Because individuals face uncertainty with respect to their economic stability and their physical security, there is a general perception among members of such societies that foreigners and outsiders are threatening. Likewise, ethnic diversity and cultural change are viewed in a negative light. This corresponds with an intolerance of homosexuals and minorities, an adherence to traditional gender roles and an authoritarian political outlook. Members of societies that emphasize self-expression values frequently hold opposing preferences from individuals in societies that emphasize survival. Societies in which individuals perceive high levels of economic and physical security are often characterized as holding self-expression values. In simple terms, when economic and physical security are commonplace, there is much less uncertainty in one's day-to-day life. Cultural diversity begins to be appreciated and even sought out. This corresponds with an increased tolerance towards deviation from traditional gender roles and sexual norms and greater support for equal rights to be afforded to minorities and other groups.

Average *SSE* values for the countries in our data are presented in Table 7.2. As in the case of *TSR* values, countries are ranked in ascending order by their absolute *SSE* difference from the US. Although categorization as a pre-1968 home country or as a post-1968 home country and *TSR* distance are generally unrelated, the same is not true for *SSE* distance. The correlation between *SSE* distance and categorization as a pre-1968 home country is equal to -0.65. Illustrative of this relationship, 16 of the 17 home countries nearest the US are categorized as pre-1968 home countries. Further, 21 of the 22 home countries farthest from the US are members of the post-1968 home country cohort.

As illustrated in Chapter 6, economic development corresponds with the presence and quality of trade-facilitating infrastructure. Since pre-1968 home countries are, on average, more economically and socially developed, a case has been made for variation in the immigrant–trade relationship across these two home country cohorts. Specifically, immigrants from the post-1968 home country cohort are expected to exert stronger

Table 7.2 Survival vs. self-expression values, US–home country absolute differences in mean values

Country	$|SSE_i - SSE_j|$	Country	$|SSE_i - SSE_j|$	Country	$|SSE_i - SSE_j|$	Country	$|SSE_i - SSE_j|$
Iceland	**0.05**	Japan	0.56	South Africa	1.04	**Hungary**	**1.59**
Norway	**0.05**	Mexico	0.57	**Portugal**	**1.07**	Jordan	1.59
New Zealand	**0.07**	Venezuela	0.62	Tanzania	1.07	Pakistan	1.59
Australia	**0.08**	**Greece**	**0.66**	Vietnam	1.07	Estonia	1.61
Canada	**0.11**	Israel	0.69	Brazil	1.08	China	1.66
United Kingdom	**0.15**	**Germany**	**0.71**	**Slovakia**	**1.1**	Armenia	1.67
Austria	**0.17**	**Spain**	**0.71**	Peru	1.12	Latvia	1.72
Netherlands	**0.19**	Colombia	0.74	Philippines	1.13	Bulgaria	1.74
Switzerland	**0.21**	**Czech Rep.**	**0.76**	Egypt	1.2	Zimbabwe	1.75
Finland	**0.25**	Uruguay	0.78	**Poland**	**1.26**	Azerbaijan	1.78
Denmark	**0.29**	Argentina	0.83	Uganda	1.35	Ukraine	1.94
Ireland	**0.31**	Slovenia	0.83	Indonesia	1.36	Romania	1.96
Belgium	**0.42**	Dominican Rep.	0.89	Korea, Rep.	1.4	Russian Fed.	2
Sweden	**0.49**	Croatia	0.92	Albania	1.5	Macedonia	2.11
El Salvador	0.54	Chile	0.93	Bangladesh	1.51	Morocco	2.16
France	**0.55**	India	0.97	Algeria	1.52		
Italy	**0.56**	Nigeria	0.98	Turkey	1.57		

Source: See Table 7.1.

influences on trade (that is, recency effects) as compared to immigrants from the pre-1968 home country cohort (that is, primacy effects).

Here, through the *SSE* dimension of culture, we see a connection between economic development and institutional development. While there does not appear to be such a relationship in terms of *TSR* distance, the *SSE* dimension of culture may well correspond with variation in consumer preferences across immigrant populations and other host country residents and with product- and market-related information asymmetries. Greater distance along each dimension may correspond with reduced trade flows and afford immigrants the opportunities to increase trade by overcoming asymmetric information. We posit that information is relatively more asymmetric when 1) countries are dissimilar in terms of institutional infrastructure (for example, judicial systems, adherence to the rule of law, and democratic governance); and 2) cultural norms and ideals vary across countries. As institutions are not wholly independent, and often are very much determined by culture, these two factors which contribute to information asymmetry are also not independent. As a result, in our analysis we employ a composite measure of cultural distance between the US and each of the trading partners in the data set and, in a separate set of estimations, the composite measure is replaced by separate component values that represent *TSR* distance and *SSE* distance.

7.3   CALCULATING US–HOME COUNTRY CULTURAL DISTANCES

Figure 7.1 plots the *TSR* and *SSE* values for the US and each country included in our data set. Within this mapping, the US is located near top center in the bottom-right quadrant. The vertical and horizontal differences between the position of the US and each trading partner represent *TSR* distance and *SSE* distance, respectively. These values are presented in Tables 7.1 and 7.2. For instance, the *TSR* distance between the US and Mexico is 0.49, while the corresponding distance between the US and China is 1.5. Similarly, the US–Mexico *SSE* distance is 0.57 and the US–China distance is 1.66. Given the differences in *TSR* and *SSE* values between the US and each home country, application of the Pythagorean Theorem permits calculation of 'cultural distance' rays that run from the US data point to the data point of any home country represented in the cultural map. Specifically, each home country's cultural distance from the US is calculated as $CDIST_{ij} = \sqrt{(TSR_j - TSR_i)^2 + (SSE_j - SSE_i)^2}$. For example, the cultural distance between the US and Mexico is equal to $CDIST_{ij} = \sqrt{0.49^2 + 0.57^2} = 0.7517$.

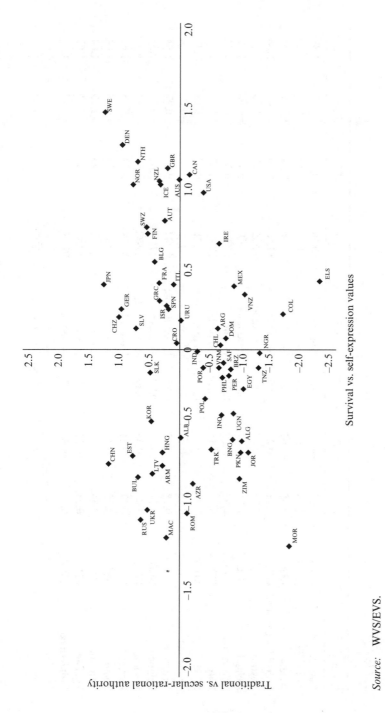

Source: WVS/EVS.

Figure 7.1 Mapping of US–home country cultural distances

111

Table 7.3 Estimated US–home country cultural distances

Country	Abbrev.	SSE_j	TSR_j	$CDIST_j$	Country	Abbrev.	SSE_j	TSR_j	$CDIST_j$
Canada	**CAN**	**1.07**	**−0.15**	**0.25**	Nigeria	NGR	−0.02	−1.27	1.33
Australia	**AUS**	**1.04**	**0.01**	**0.39**	Slovenia	SLV	0.13	0.7	1.35
Ireland	**IRE**	**0.65**	**−0.62**	**0.4**	Egypt	EGY	−0.24	−1.01	1.36
United Kingdom	**GBR**	**1.11**	**0.2**	**0.59**	**Slovakia**	**SLK**	**−0.14**	**0.47**	**1.38**
Austria	**AUT**	**0.79**	**0.24**	**0.63**	Tanzania	TNZ	−0.11	−1.25	1.38
Iceland	**ICE**	**1.01**	**0.31**	**0.69**	Indonesia	INO	−0.4	−0.66	1.39
New Zealand	**NZL**	**1.03**	**0.33**	**0.71**	Uganda	UGN	−0.39	−0.85	1.43
Italy	**ITL**	**0.4**	**0.1**	**0.73**	Colombia	COL	0.22	−1.65	1.48
Mexico	MEX	0.39	−0.86	0.75	**Germany**	**GER**	**0.25**	**0.93**	**1.48**
Argentina	ARG	0.13	−0.6	0.85	Albania	ALB	−0.54	−0.02	1.54
Uruguay	URU	0.18	−0.02	0.85	**Czech Republic**	**CZH**	**0.2**	**0.97**	**1.54**
Belgium	**BLG**	**0.54**	**0.4**	**0.88**	Turkey	TRK	−0.61	−0.5	1.57
France	**FRA**	**0.41**	**0.33**	**0.89**	Bangladesh	BNG	−0.55	−0.84	1.58
Israel	ISR	0.27	0.21	0.9	Korea, Rep.	KOR	−0.44	0.45	1.62
Spain	**SPN**	**0.25**	**0.18**	**0.9**	Algeria	ALG	−0.56	−0.99	1.64
Venezuela	VNZ	0.34	−1.03	0.9	**Sweden**	**SWE**	**1.45**	**1.19**	**1.64**
Finland	**FIN**	**0.71**	**0.51**	**0.91**	Japan	JPN	0.4	1.21	1.67
Switzerland	**SWZ**	**0.75**	**0.53**	**0.93**	Pakistan	PKN	−0.63	−0.97	1.7

Country	Code				Country	Code			
Greece	**GRC**	**0.3**	**0.32**	**0.95**	**Hungary**	**HNG**	**-0.63**	**0.27**	**1.71**
Dominican Rep.	DOM	0.07	-0.73	0.96	Jordan	JOR	-0.63	-1.09	1.74
Chile	CHL	0.03	-0.64	0.97	Armenia	ARM	-0.71	0.27	1.79
India	IND	-0.01	-0.28	0.97	Azerbaijan	AZR	-0.82	-0.21	1.79
Croatia	CRO	0.04	0.05	1.01	Zimbabwe	ZIM	-0.79	-0.95	1.84
Netherlands	**NTH**	**1.15**	**0.67**	**1.06**	Latvia	LTV	-0.76	0.43	1.9
Portugal	**POR**	**-0.11**	**-0.37**	**1.06**	El Salvador	ELS	0.42	-2.23	1.94
South Africa	SAF	-0.08	-0.69	1.09	Estonia	EST	-0.65	0.75	1.96
Vietnam	VNM	-0.11	-0.62	1.09	Romania	ROM	-1	-0.12	1.97
Norway	**NOR**	**1.01**	**0.75**	**1.12**	**Bulgaria**	**BUL**	**-0.78**	**0.66**	**2.01**
Brazil	BRZ	-0.12	-0.81	1.16	Ukraine	UKR	-0.98	0.51	2.13
Philippines	PHL	-0.17	-0.67	1.16	Macedonia	MAC	-1.15	0.21	2.18
Peru	PER	-0.16	-0.78	1.19	China	CHN	-0.7	1.13	2.23
Poland	**POL**	**-0.3**	**-0.4**	**1.26**	Russian Fed.	RUS	-1.04	0.62	2.23
Denmark	**DEN**	**1.25**	**0.92**	**1.32**	Morocco	MOR	-1.2	-1.75	2.56

Note: Corresponding mean *TSR* and *SSE* values for the United States are −0.37 and 0.96, respectively.

Source: See Table 7.1.

Table 7.3 presents average *TSR* and *SSE* values along with corresponding cultural distances from the US. The values reveal that Canada, Australia, Ireland, the UK and Austria are the societies that are most culturally similar to the US, while Morocco, Russia, China, Macedonia and the Ukraine are the most culturally distant. Not surprisingly, many European nations, along with Canada, Australia and Mexico, are estimated as culturally nearest to the US. At the other end of the spectrum, we see that nine of the 13 most distant nations are former Soviet states and Soviet satellites in Eastern Europe. Countries that are included in the pre-1968 home country cohort are identified by a bold font. Similar to the ordering of home countries by *SSE* distance, the order in which countries are ranked according to the composite cultural distance measure reveals that pre-1968 home countries are more commonly found on the left-hand side of the table while post-1968 home countries are more often found on the right-hand side of the table. In fact, the eight home countries that are the most culturally-similar to the US are all in the pre-1968 cohort, while the 14 most culturally-dissimilar countries are in the post-1968 cohort. While the rankings generally conform to expectations, it is important to note that the values are estimates and that strict ordinal interpretation of the rankings may prove problematic.

PART III

Examining the US immigrant–trade link

The results of prior studies provide a set of general expectations regarding the US immigrant–trade link. The review of the associated literature that is provided as part of Chapter 3 led to the generation of a set of hypotheses regarding the relationship. In this section, we present the results of an analysis of these hypotheses. The analysis employs data that span the 1992–2006 period and that represent the US and the 66 home countries/trading partners identified in Chapter 5. Before presenting our results in Chapters 9 and 10, Chapter 8 presents the baseline econometric specification, discusses the variables employed in the analysis and the data sources, and provides a comparison of summary statistics for the pre-1968 and post-1968 home country cohorts.

8. Empirical specification, variable construction and data sources

Following the leads of prior studies, a series of augmented gravity specifications are utilized to address the series of hypotheses that relate to the immigrant–trade link. We begin this chapter by presenting the baseline estimation equation. In later chapters, modified estimation equations are presented, as necessary, to address specific hypotheses. This is followed by a discussion of the data, its sources and the construction of variables that are employed in the analysis. We end this chapter by presenting descriptive statistics for both the dependent variable series and the collection of explanatory variables.

8.1 BASELINE SPECIFICATION: THE AUGMENTED GRAVITY MODEL

Tinbergen (1962) first applies the gravity specification to trade data, and more recent research has established theoretical foundations for the model. See, for example, Anderson (1979), Bergstrand (1985), Helpman and Krugman (1985), Davis (1995), Haveman and Hummels (1997), Deardorff (1998), Feenstra et al. (2001), Eaton and Kortum (2002) and Anderson and van Wincoop (2003). The most basic version of the gravity model posits that trade between two countries i and j during year t ($\widetilde{T}_{ijt}$) increases with the countries' combined economic mass, which is given as the product of their GDP values ($GDP_{it}GDP_{jt}$) and decreases with the geodesic distance ($GDIST_{ij}$) between the trading partners. Higher home country GDP implies greater potential export markets for the host country to serve and an increased probability that the host country will import from the home country. Similarly, higher host country GDP signals an increased capacity for that country to both export and to import. Here, the host country is the US and is denoted with the subscript i, while the subscript j identifies individual home countries. The geodesic distance between Washington, DC and the capital city of each home country is utilized as a proxy variable to represent transport costs. Finally, α is the constant of proportionality. The resulting simple gravity relationship is given by equation (8.1).

The superscripts β and γ are coefficients to be estimated (that is, elasticities once natural logarithms have been taken for both sides of the equation).

$$\tilde{T}_{ijt} = \alpha\left(\frac{GDP_{it}^{\beta_1}GDP_{jt}^{\beta_2}}{GDIST_{ij}^{\gamma_1}}\right) \tag{8.1}$$

Researchers have modified the gravity model to include several additional explanatory variables to represent factors that either facilitate or hinder trade flows. Accordingly, equation (8.1) is augmented with two vectors that contain continuous variables. One of these vectors includes variables representing factors that may facilitate bilateral trade flows (U_{ijt}^{φ}) while the other vector (V_{ijt}^{θ}) contains variables representing factors that may inhibit bilateral trade flows. It may also be that dichotomous explanatory variables represent factors that affect trade flows. Taking this into account, an additional vector of dummy variables that represent potential trade-facilitating influences (X_{ijt}^{λ}) is appended to equation (8.1).

$$\tilde{T}_{ijt} = \alpha\left(\frac{GDP_{it}^{\beta_1}GDP_{jt}^{\beta_2}U_{ijt}^{\varphi}\exp^{X_{ijt}^{\lambda}}}{GDIST_{ij}^{\gamma_1}V_{ijt}^{\theta}}\right) \tag{8.2}$$

At this point, it is worthwhile to define the elements of the three vectors that have been appended to equation (8.1). The vector U contains the (one-year) lagged change in the dependent variable, a measure of the trade openness, population, and economic remoteness of each home country. The vector V contains the change in the US–country j exchange rate, while the vector X contains three dummy variables that indicate if country j is a member of OPEC, whether the US and country j are both parties to at least one regional trade agreement and whether country j has coastal access.

Finally, specific terms are included to represent the primary variables of interest: the stock of immigrants from country j residing in the US (IM_{ijt}^{δ}) and the estimated cultural distance between the US and each home country ($CDIST_{ij}^{\mu}$). These modifications are illustrated in equation (8.3).

$$\tilde{T}_{ijt} = \alpha\left(\frac{GDP_{it}^{\beta_1}GDP_{jt}^{\beta_2}U_{ijt}^{\varphi}\exp^{X_{ijt}^{\lambda}}}{GDIST_{ij}^{\gamma_1}V_{ijt}^{\theta}}\right)\frac{IM_{ijt}^{\delta}}{CDIST_{ij}^{\mu}} \tag{8.3}$$

It can be seen from equation (8.3) that immigrants and cultural distance are assumed to exert positive and negative influences, respectively, on trade flows. The equation also predicts strictly positive realizations of export and import values. Trade data, however, often contain cases wherein values are equal to zero. Following Eaton and Tamura (1994) and Head and Ries (1998), equation (8.3) is modified to allow for the presence of zero trade values. Equation (8.4) results.

$$\widetilde{T}_{ijt} = \alpha\left(\frac{GDP_{it}^{\beta_1}GDP_{jt}^{\beta_2}U_{ijt}^{\varphi}\exp^{X_{ijt}^{\lambda}}}{GDIST_{ij}^{\gamma_1}V_{ijt}^{\theta}}\right)\frac{IM_{ijt}^{\delta}}{CDIST_{ij}^{\mu}}\exp^{(\varepsilon_{ijt}-\eta)} \tag{8.4}$$

In equation (8.4), η is a fixed amount of trade that is subtracted from the predicted level so that when latent trade values are negative, observed imports and/or exports will be zero. Thus, the observed data on country j's imports from or exports to the US can be described as $T_{ijt} = \max\lfloor\widetilde{T}_{ijt}, 0\rfloor$. Substituting this identity, expanding the vectors U_{ijt}^{φ}, V_{ijt}^{θ}, and X_{ijt}^{λ}, appending a vector of time dummies (Ω_t) to absorb time-varying macroeconomic fluctuations and time-specific trade-influencing policy decisions, taking natural logarithms of the continuous variables with minimum values greater than one on both sides of the resulting equation, and assuming that ε_{ijt} is an identically and independently distributed error term results in our baseline estimation equation.[1]

$$\begin{aligned}
\ln(T_{ijt} + \eta) = {} & \alpha_0 + \delta_1 \ln IM_{ijt} - \mu_1 CDIST_{ij} + \beta_1 \ln GDP_{jt} \\
& - \gamma_1 \ln GDIST_{ij} + \varphi_1\Delta \ln(T_{ijt-1} + \eta) + \varphi_2\Delta \ln XRATE_{jt} \\
& + \varphi_3 OPEN_{jt} + \varphi_4 \ln REM_{jt} - \theta_1 \ln POP_{jt} + \lambda_1 OPEC_j \\
& + \lambda_2 RTA_{jt} + \lambda_3 SEAPORT_j + \beta_\Omega\Omega_t + \varepsilon_{ijt}
\end{aligned} \tag{8.5}$$

The vector of dependent variable series includes aggregate exports and imports as well as disaggregated export and import values for manufactured and non-manufactured products, 1-digit SITC industry sectors, Rauch product classifications (that is, organized exchange goods, reference-priced goods, and differentiated goods), non-cultural products and cultural products (at the aggregate level and categorized as core cultural products and related cultural products and corresponding sub-classifications).

Equation (8.5) is modified, as necessary, to address the specific hypotheses presented in Chapter 3. For example, to consider the relative influences of immigrant entry classifications, the immigrant population stock variable is replaced by separate measures of refugees/asylum-seekers and of all other immigrants. Similarly, additional variables are added to the estimation equation when considering whether the average length of time immigrants have been in the US or the skill composition of an immigrant population affect US–home country trade flows. Whenever variations of equation (8.5) are employed, the modified estimation equations are presented and the alterations are explained.

Likelihood ratio tests, Wooldridge tests and Breusch–Godfrey tests, performed using aggregate exports and imports as the dependent variable series, indicate the presence of panel-level heteroskedasticity and first-order autocorrelation in the data. This results in iterative feasible generalized least squares being employed as the principal estimation technique in the analysis; however, the Tobit estimation technique is employed when necessitated by the presence of numerous zero trade values for the dependent variable series. Taking advantage of such instances, when the Tobit technique is applied the resulting coefficients are decomposed, using the procedure developed by McDonald and Moffitt (1980), into trade-intensification and trade-initiation effects.

8.2 VARIABLE CONSTRUCTION AND DATA SOURCES

8.2.1 Dependent Variable Series

Annual bilateral trade values that are used as dependent variable series in the analysis are from the US International Trade Commission (USITC, 2008). These series include aggregate export and import data as well as exports and imports at the 1-digit SITC sector level of detail. These sector-level data have been aggregated to produce export and import series for non-manufactured products (sectors 0–4) and for manufactured products (sectors 5–9). All trade values and values for explanatory variables, when necessary, have been normalized to year 2000 US dollars.

The more disaggregated trade data series require additional explanation. Using Rauch (1999) product classifications, export and import data are categorized at the four-digit SITC industry level as homogeneous goods or as differentiated goods. Homogeneous goods include those products traded on organized exchanges and those for which reference prices are available. Differentiated goods, on the other hand, consist of all other goods. Differentiated goods are characterized by sufficiently imperfect information that prohibits standardized pricing and which discourages the creation of formal or quasi-formal exchanges.

The process undertaken to construct the product classifications is as follows. Beginning with five-digit SITC-level product classifications, Rauch classified industry-level output as organized exchange goods if they were listed in either the *International Commodity Markets Handbook* or *The Knight-Ridder CRB Commodity Yearbook*. Goods were classified as reference-priced goods if price quotations were available in *Commodity Prices.* All other goods were classified as being differentiated goods. Classification at the four-digit SITC level was made based on which of the three product types accounted for the largest share of the value of world trade at the four-digit SITC level.

Definitions of cultural products employed by the United Nations Education, Scientific and Cultural Organization (UN, 2005) are adopted to categorize trade flows, as relevant, into cultural product classifications. Cultural products or services convey ideas, symbols and ways of life. Examples include books, magazines, multimedia products, software, recordings, films, videos, audiovisual programs, crafts and fashion design (Cano et al., 2000). Such goods have both tangible (physical support) and intangible (cultural content) components and are grouped into two broad classifications: core cultural products and related cultural products. More precisely, core cultural products are those goods or services directly associated with cultural content, while related cultural products include the services, equipment and support materials necessary to create, produce or distribute core cultural products. The influences of immigrants on trade in cultural and non-cultural products are considered separately, and variation in the immigrant–trade link is considered across core and related cultural product sub-classifications.

Since the relationship between trade flows and immigrant stock values is the focus of this work, it seems reasonable to examine scatter plots of the immigrant stock variable and the aggregate export and import series. These are illustrated in Figure 8.1. The relationship between the natural logarithm of the immigrant stock data series and the series which represents US exports to the immigrants' home countries is illustrated in the top panel (panel A), while the immigrant stock–US imports relationship appears in the bottom panel (panel B). 'Best fit' lines have been added to each plot, and the simple correlation coefficient for each of the two series is equal to 0.65. Since the correlation coefficient between the export and import series is 0.91, the similarity in the correlation between the immigrant stock and the export and import series is to be expected.

8.2.2 Immigrant Stock Series

Annual estimates of the immigrant stock from home country j residing in the US, IM_{ijt}, is included in the estimation equation to control for the influences of immigrants on US trade with their home countries. The 1990 and 2000 decennial US Censuses provide country-level immigrant stock values (Gibson and Lennon, 1999; US Census, 2006). Annual immigrant inflow data for the years 1991–2006 are from the Immigration and Naturalization Service and the Department of Homeland Security (US INS, 1990–2001; US DHS, 2007b). We accept the census values as benchmarks and incorporate inflow data to estimate immigrant stocks during intra-census years. Estimated immigrant stock values for the years 1991–99 are constructed as follows.

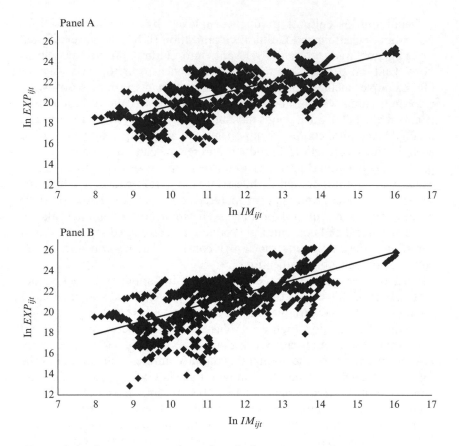

Figure 8.1   Immigrant stocks and trade flows, scatter plots

$$IM_{ijt} = IM_{ij1990} + \sum_{1991}^{t} INFLOW_{ijt} + \tau_j \qquad (8.6)$$

where τ_j is an adjustment factor that accounts for return migration and the death of immigrants during intra-census years. The adjustment factor is constructed as the US immigrant stock from country j given by the 2000 census less the sum of immigrants from country j in the US in 1990 and the cumulative inflow from country j during the years 1991–2000 divided by ten.

$$\tau_j = \frac{IM_{ij2000} - \left[IM_{ij1990} + \sum_{t=1991}^{2000} INFLOW_{ijt}\right]}{10} \qquad (8.7)$$

For the years 2001–06, the immigrant stock variable is constructed similarly. The adjustment made to the post-2000 portion of the sample is based on the adjustment factor derived when estimating 1991–9 immigrant stocks.

$$IM_{ij2001} = (IM_{ij2000} + INFLOW_{ij2001})\left(1 + \frac{\tau_j}{IM_{ij2000}}\right) \qquad (8.8)$$

The final term in equation (8.8), the adjustment percentage, is based on the difference between raw 2000 immigrant values and 2000 benchmark values. Combination of the 1991–9 and 2001–06 estimated immigrant stock values with the 1990 and 2000 benchmark values results in a series of immigrant stock estimates that span the years 1990–2006. Due to an inability to compile complete series for some variables early in the period, the immigrant stock data used in the analysis span only the 1994–2006 period.

To consider the possibility that immigrants' pro-trade influences vary according to their entry classifications, we substitute estimates of the stock of refugees and asylum-seekers (REF_{ijt}) from each trading partner and a measure of all other immigrants (that is, non-refugees/non-asylum-seekers) ($NREF_{ijt}$) in a pair of alternative estimations. The REF_{ijt} and $NREF_{ijt}$ data series, which span the years 1996–2001 and represent 58 of the 66 home countries listed in Chapter 5, are from White and Tadesse (2009c). The refugee/asylee immigrant stock is estimated using inflow data for refugees (REF_INF_{ijt}) and for other immigrants ($NREF\_IM_{ijt}$) that span the years 1946–90 (US DHS, 2004; US INS, 1990–2001). Equation (8.9) indicates how refugee/asylee stock values for 1990 were generated. The non-refugee immigrant stock was estimated as $NREF\_IM_{ij1990} = IM_{ij1990} - REF\_IM_{ij1990}$.

$$REF\_IM_{ij1990} = IM_{ij1990} \times \frac{\sum_{t=1946}^{1990} REF\_INF_{ijt}}{\sum_{t=1946}^{1990} (REF\_INF_{ijt} + NREF\_INF_{ijt})} \qquad (8.9)$$

For the non-census years, 1991–9 and 2001, refugee/asylee and non-refugee immigrant stocks were estimated as $REF\_IM_{ijt} = (REF\_IM_{ijt-1} + REF\_INF_{ijt}) \times (1 + \tau_j)/(IM_{ij2000})$ and $NREF\_IM_{ijt} = IM_{ijt} - REF\_IM_{ijt}$, where τ is as described above. Combining the 1990 and 2000 census values with the estimates that were generated for the years 1991–9 and 2001 produces estimates of the refugee and non-refugee immigrant stocks that span the years 1990–2001; however, due to incomplete data for a number of other control variables, White and Tadesse (2009c) were restricted to study only the years 1996–2001.

8.2.3 Additional Explanatory Variables

Given that the measure of US–home country cultural distance is discussed in Chapter 7, the focus of this section is on the remaining explanatory variables. The variables representing home country GDP and the geodesic distances between the US and each home country are as described in section 8.1. The source for the GDP data is the World Bank (2009a), while geodesic distance values have been calculated using the Great Circle method. As noted earlier, higher home country GDP implies greater export markets for the US and an increased probability of US imports. Since geodesic distance is included as a measure of transport costs, all else equal, greater distance between Washington, DC and the capital city of country j is expected to correspond with lower trade flows.

Following Eichengreen and Irwin (1996), the one-year lagged change of the dependent variable ($\Delta \ln (T_{ijt-1} + \eta)$) is included in the estimation equation in order to control for the effects of inertia on annual trade flows. The *a priori* expectation is that the sign for the corresponding coefficient estimate is positive. Annual changes in the US–country j exchange rate ($\Delta \ln XRATE_{jt}$), given as home country currency units per US dollar, represents terms of trade effects. While the coefficient on the variable is listed as being positive in equation (8.5), an increase in the variable signals a depreciation of the home country's currency vis-à-vis the US dollar, which would be expected to increase US imports and decrease US exports. The sources for the exchange rate series data are the International Financial Statistics (IFS) (IMF, 2008) and, when IFS data are unavailable, the FXHistory database (OANDA, 2008). A measure of each home country's general propensity to trade is given by the trade openness variable ($OPEN_{jt}$) which is calculated as the sum of a country's total imports and exports divided by its GDP (Head and Ries, 1998). This is the 'volume of trade' variable first discussed in Chapter 1. Following Wagner et al. (2002), a measure of economic remoteness is included in the estimation equation to control for each home country's relative lack of outside trading opportunities. The variable, which is a measure of quasi-distance, is calculated as $REM_{jt} = 1/\Sigma_{k=1}^{K}[(GDP_{kt}/GGP_{wt})/GDIST_{jk}]$, where GGP_{wt} is gross global product and k identifies potential trading partners for country j other than the US. Internal distance (when $k = j$) is calculated as per Head and Mayer (2000) as $0.4 \times \sqrt{LandMass_j}$. Coefficient estimates for both the trade openness and economic remoteness variables are expected to be positive. The population of country j (POP_{jt}) serves as a proxy variable for the size of the home country's domestic market. Accordingly, the corresponding coefficient estimates are expected to be positive.

A set of dummy variables is included in the estimation equation to capture various factors that may determine trade flows. $OPEC_{jt}$, for example, is included to control for imports of petroleum and related goods. The variable is equal to 1 if country j was an OPEC member for six or more months in year t, and is equal to 0 otherwise. Capturing the effects of common regional trade agreement membership, RTA_{ijt} is equal to 1 if country j was a signatory to an agreement that the US was also party to for six or more months during year t (Ghosh and Yamarik, 2004).[2] To capture related geographic effects on trade flows, a variable that is equal to 1 if the home country is not landlocked ($SEAPORT_j$) is included. Finally, as previously noted, the vector of time dummies, Ω_t, is included to absorb macroeconomic fluctuations and trade-influencing policy decisions.

In a separate set of estimations, we consider whether the skill composition of prior immigrant inflows, a proxy variable for the skill composition of the immigrant stock, is significantly related to the level of US–home country trade. The variable that is used is the ratio of skilled-to-unskilled immigrants ($SKUK_{jt}$). The skilled/unskilled categorization is based on immigrants' stated occupations at the time of entry. Skilled immigrants include those classified as 'professional, technical and kindred workers', while those classified as 'general machine operators', 'laborers', 'farm workers' or 'service workers' are classified as unskilled. All other occupational categories are considered insufficiently skilled or unskilled, in general, to be used when constructing the variable. We also include a variable ($STAY_{ijt}$) which represents the average length of time, in years, since each immigrant's arrival in the US and, since the influence of an immigrant's stay with respect to trade flows may be non-linear, we also include the squared value of this variable in the corresponding econometric specifications.

8.3   DESCRIPTIVE STATISTICS

Table 8.1 presents descriptive statistics for the explanatory variable series. Values are provided for the full sample and for both the pre-1968 and post-1968 home country cohorts. T-tests of differences in mean values have been employed to compare the summary values for each cohort to the corresponding 'full sample' values.

Although highly variable, during the 1994–2006 period, the immigrant stock from the typical home country was estimated to equal 371 858 persons. While data is lacking for all years, what is available indicates that immigrant stocks have largely been comprised of non-refugee and non-asylee immigrants. The ratio of skilled-to-unskilled immigrants indicates an inflow of nearly three skilled immigrants having arrived for every one

Table 8.1 *Descriptive statistics, non-trade flow variables*

Variable	Description	N	All home countries	Pre-1968 home countries	Post-1968 home countries
IM_{jt}	Immigrant stock	858	371 858 (1 090 521)	203 040*** (257 106)	468 325 (1 344 130)
$NREF_{jt}$	Non-refugee/non-asylee immigrant stock	348	363 364 (1 105 354)	177 805*** (223 009)	476 761 (1 381 152)
REF_{jt}	Refugee/asylee immigrant stock	348	26 201 (84 563)	23 353 (45 794)	27 942 (101 270)
$SKUK_{jt}$	Skilled-unskilled ratio, cumulative inflows since 1970	854	2.7392 (1.9607)	2.6791 (1.4587)	2.7738 (2.1989)
$STAY_{jt}$	Stay in US (average duration, in years)	858	15.8872 (6.9583)	22.579*** (4.6697)	12.0633*** (4.8382)
$CDIST_j$	Cultural distance, US-to-home country	66	1.3136 (0.5007)	0.9757*** (0.3926)	1.5067** (0.4512)
$|SSE_i - SSE_j|$	Survival vs. self-expression values, absolute difference: US-to-home country	66	0.9979 (0.5844)	0.4921*** (0.4148)	1.2869*** (0.4569)
$|TSR_i - TSR_j|$	Traditional vs. secular-rational authority, absolute difference: US-to-home country	66	0.6864 (0.41)	0.7304 (0.3987)	0.6612 (0.4146)
$OPEC_j$	OPEC membership	66	0.0606 (0.2387)	0** (0)	0.0952 (0.2938)

126

		N			
RTA_{jt}	Common regional trade agreement membership	858	0.1841 (0.3878)	0.125*** (0.3313)	0.2179* (0.4132)
$SEAPORT_j$	Seaport (that is, not landlocked)	66	0.8636 (0.3434)	0.7917 (0.4068)	0.9048 (0.2938)
$\Delta lnXRATE_{jt}$	Logged (1-year) change in annual US-home country exchange rate	858	−0.0607 (0.2909)	0.0057*** (0.1106)	−0.0986** (0.3495)
$GDIST_j$	Geodesic distance between Washington, DC and capital of country j	66	8267.69 (3230.99)	7453.42 (3224.21)	8732.99 (3144.35)
GDP_{jt}	Real gross domestic product (in 2000 US dollars)	858	338581887558 (687963086914)	488096856411*** (607111388031)	253144762499** (716800203067)
$OPEN_{jt}$	Trade openness	858	0.7256 (0.3401)	0.8217*** (0.3513)	0.6707*** (0.3211)
POP_{jt}	Population	858	71545386 (195260992)	21144990*** (22298675)	100345612*** (239551003)
REM_{jt}	Economic remoteness	858	4139.02 (2747.66)	2687.04*** (2627.65)	4968.71*** (2456.63)

Notes

See text for explanations of variables.

Standard deviations in parentheses.

***, **, and * denote statistical significance from the 'full sample' cohort values at the 1 per cent, 5 per cent and 10 per cent levels, respectively.

unskilled immigrant, and the timing of inflows has been such that the average duration since arrival in the US is nearly 16 years. Only four of the 66 home countries in the data are members of OPEC, the US is party to at least one regional trade agreement with about one in five home countries, the overwhelming majority of home countries have coastal access, and the typical home country saw its currency appreciate relative to the US dollar during the period.

In a typical year, there were significantly fewer immigrants from the average pre-1968 home country (203 040 persons) residing in the US as compared to the average post-1968 home country (468 325 persons, which was not significantly different from the overall average value). Likewise, relative to the overall average of 363 364 persons and the post-1968 home country average of 476 761 persons, there were fewer non-refugee/non-asylee immigrants from the typical pre-1968 home country (177 805 persons). Immigrants from pre-1968 home countries had an average duration of stay in the US (22.6 years) that was greater than the overall average, while the average stay of immigrants from post-1968 home countries (12.1 years) was significantly shorter in duration.

As discussed in Chapter 7, the post-1968 home country cohort is, on average, more culturally-distant from the US ($CDIST_{ij}$ = 1.51) than is the typical home country in the pre-1968 home country grouping (0.98). As there are no significant differences across mean values for each cohort in terms of the traditional vs. secular-rational authority (TSR) dimension of cultural distance, the significant difference in overall cultural distance is largely the result of differences across cohorts in terms of the survival vs. self-expression values (SSE) dimension. Specifically, the pre-1968 home country grouping has an average SSE distance value of 0.49 while the post-1968 grouping has an average value of 1.29. In both instances, the mean values are significantly different from the overall average.

Table 8.1 also indicates that no pre-1968 home countries were members of OPEC; however, four of the 42 post-1968 home countries (9.5 per cent of the grouping) were. The US is significantly more likely to be party to a regional trade agreement with a post-1968 home country than with a pre-1968 home country. In a typical year, the average member of the pre-1968 home country cohort saw its currency depreciate significantly relative to the dollar while the average member of the post-1968 home country realized a currency appreciation. Similarly, the typical pre-1968 home country realized higher GDP values, was more open to trade, less remote, and had smaller populations. In terms of the remaining explanatory variables – namely, refugee/asylee immigrant stocks, skilled–unskilled compositions of immigrant inflows, TSR distance, coastal access, and geodesic distance from the US – average values for the pre-1968 and post-1968 home countries are not significantly different from the overall mean values.

To gain a measure of the relationships between the variables – explanatory variables, in particular – a correlation matrix is provided as Table 8.2. The values presented in columns (a) and (b) indicate simple correlations between aggregate trade values and the full complement of explanatory variables used in the analysis. As noted in Figure 8.1, when the scatter plots depicting the relationships between immigrant stocks and exports and imports (in natural logarithms) were presented, a positive relationship was illustrated between aggregate trade flows and the immigrant stock series. This relationship persists for the correlations between non-refugee/non-asylee immigrants and trade series; however, the correlations for refugee and asylee immigrants and trade flows, while near zero, are negative. Likewise, the correlations between the skilled-to-unskilled immigrant inflow series and exports and imports are negative, while the values for the duration of stay are positive. As expected, cultural distance is negatively related to trade flows; however, the magnitude of the correlation coefficient is much larger with respect to the *SSE* dimension of culture as compared to the *TSR* dimension. The US trades less, in general, with OPEC members, members of the post-1968 home country cohort, countries that are geographically more distant and those that generally trade more intensively. Conversely, the US trades more with those countries that it is party to the same regional trade agreement with and those that have coastal access, higher GDP values, and larger populations.

A review of the correlation coefficients presented in columns (c) to (s) reveals four correlation values that, in absolute magnitude, are in excess of 0.50. Specifically, the correlation between the variable that measures the average duration of immigrants' stays in the US and the dummy variable that identifies members of the post-1968 home country cohort is equal to −0.73. The correlation between the duration of stay variable and *SSE* distance is equal to −0.59. A third excessively high correlation is found for the overall measure of cultural distance and the measure of *SSE* distance (0.83). To avoid the influence of collinearity, none of the econometric specifications that we estimate include any of these pairs of variables. The fourth correlation in excess of 0.5 is that between the dummy variable, which identifies post-1968 home countries, and the overall measure of cultural distance (0.51). In Chapter 6, it was explained that the recency effects on trade that are attributable to immigrants from post-1968 home countries are expected to be larger than the primacy effects on trade that are exerted by immigrants from pre-1968 home countries. The dummy variable that identifies members of the post-1968 home country cohort is used (see Chapter 10), exclusive of the cultural distance variable, to explore this

Table 8.2 Correlation matrix

Variable	(a)	(b)	(c)	(d)	(e)	(f)	(g)	(h)
(a) EXP_{jt}	1							
(b) IMP_{jt}	0.905	1						
(c) IM_{jt}	0.4745	0.4706	1					
(d) $NREF_{jt}$	0.4926	0.4552	0.9985	1				
(e) REF_{jt}	−0.066	−0.0373	0.0592	0.0141	1			
(f) $SKUK_{jt}$	−0.0392	−0.0499	−0.2121	−0.235	−0.1967	1		
(g) $STAY_{jt}$	0.2312	0.2131	−0.0091	−0.0549	−0.0371	−0.1208	1	
(h) $CDIST_j$	−0.3178	−0.1743	−0.1471	−0.1418	0.0892	−0.0398	−0.486	1
(i) $|SSE_i − SSE_j|$	−0.3092	−0.2263	−0.0989	−0.095	0.1484	−0.0402	−0.5919	0.8262
(j) $|TSR_i − TSR_j|$	−0.0233	0.1106	−0.0582	−0.0523	−0.095	0.0014	0.0564	0.4427
(k) $OPEC_j$	−0.0707	−0.0334	−0.0676	−0.0732	−0.0682	0.0987	−0.0972	0.001
(l) $Post-1965_j$	−0.1518	−0.0748	0.1184	0.1314	0.0264	0.0233	−0.7271	0.5137
(m) RTA_{jt}	0.4519	0.4977	0.3768	0.3538	0.1417	0.0702	0.0423	−0.1211
(n) $SEAPORT_j$	0.1326	0.1397	0.1198	0.0935	0.0357	−0.0647	−0.0541	−0.1426
(o) $\Delta lnXRATE_{jt}$	0.0518	0.0622	0.0125	0.0775	−0.0217	−0.1186	0.1833	−0.1321
(p) $GDIST_j$	−0.3155	−0.2192	−0.1772	−0.2015	0.2262	0.4001	−0.2045	0.1024
(q) GDP_{jt}	0.4524	0.6061	0.1295	0.095	0.0333	0.0315	0.3186	−0.0719
(r) $OPEN_{jt}$	−0.0913	−0.1324	−0.077	−0.0362	0.1099	−0.0346	0.0554	0.0836
(s) POP_{jt}	0.0806	0.3118	0.1774	0.1394	0.041	0.0122	−0.0769	0.1453
(t) REM_{jt}	0.0227	−0.0346	0.1092	0.102	−0.1198	0.256	−0.2937	−0.1796

Note: Sample sizes are equal to 348 for correlations relating to $NREF_{jt}$ and REF_{jt} and are equal to 854 for all other variables.

possibility. However, in equation (8.5), which is the baseline estimation equation, and nearly all other variants, the cultural distance variable is utilized and the post-1968 home country dummy variable is excluded. Again, this is done to minimize the influence of collinearity. The cultural distance variable was chosen for inclusion over the post-1968 dummy variable since the latter is dichotomous and the former is more descriptive in terms of its cross-societal variation. Further, due to the high correlation between the two series, the cultural distance variable is, to a degree, representative of the categorization of home countries into the pre-1968 or post-1968 home country groupings.

Tables 8.3 and 8.4 present mean values, for the full sample and for the pre-1968 and post-1968 home country cohorts, for each of the dependent variable series. Generally speaking, the US imports more than it exports. This is found for aggregate trade flows, across all Rauch product classifications and for trade in both manufactured products and non-manufactured products. It is only for a handful of more disaggregated trade classifications that the US is a net exporter: crude materials, inedible, except fuels (SITC-2); animal and vegetable oils, fats and waxes (SITC-4); printed matter and music and the performing arts (core cultural

(i)	(j)	(k)	(l)	(m)	(n)	(o)	(p)	(q)	(r)	(s)
1										
−0.1012	1									
0.053	−0.0435	1								
0.656	−0.0791	0.1932	1							
−0.0884	−0.0498	0.0426	0.1173	1						
−0.1305	−0.0455	0.1015	0.1574	0.1898	1					
−0.1878	0.0791	−0.0695	−0.1738	0.0454	0.057	1				
0.2505	−0.2632	0.045	0.192	0.2437	−0.0348	−0.0701	1			
−0.2436	0.273	−0.0865	−0.163	0.2701	0.1503	0.0745	0.0108	1		
0.0298	0.14	−0.0747	−0.2162	−0.1421	−0.2368	0.0487	−0.2014	−0.287	1	
0.1444	0.0588	0.0322	0.1968	0.237	0.1275	0.0057	0.2481	0.2377	−0.2538	1
−0.0201	−0.2653	0.1626	0.4037	0.3226	0.1091	−0.1266	0.2137	−0.2674	−0.4121	0.0084

products); and New media (a related cultural product). For all related cultural product classifications and for both printed matter and for music and the performing arts, the US has a trade surplus, collectively, with respect to the pre-1968 home country cohort. In terms of the data categorized at the 1-digit SITC sector level of detail, the US tends to have trade surpluses in beverages and tobacco (SITC-1), crude materials, inedible, except fuels (SITC-2), Animal and vegetable oils, fats and waxes (SITC-4), and chemicals and related products (SITC-5). At the aggregate level, the US trades significantly more with the pre-1968 home country cohort than it does with those in the post-1968 home country grouping. This pattern is largely mirrored when other dependent variable series are examined; however, the US does export more to members of the post-1968 cohort in terms of products classified as animal and vegetable oils, fats and waxes (SITC-4) and imports more miscellaneous manufactured articles (SITC-8), audio and audiovisual media products and goods categorized as television and radio. In absolute terms, with some exceptions, the US tends to trade more with countries in the pre-1968 home country cohort as compared to its trade with those countries categorized as post-1968 home countries.

Table 8.3 Descriptive statistics, aggregate trade flows

Description	Exports All	Exports Pre-1968 home countries	Exports Post-1968 home countries	Imports All	Imports Pre-1968 home countries	Imports Post-1968 home countries
Aggregate trade	7 974 547 099 (20 630 565 438)	12 143 448 376*** (28 248 685 737)	5 592 317 798*** (14 081 099 032)	14 348 894 340 (35 747 006 214)	17 943 900 507* (41 325 698 069)	12 294 605 102 (31 987 660 897)
Rauch product classifications						
Differentiated goods	4 922 392 496 (14 263 741 488)	7 960 702 082*** (20 331 338 489)	3 186 215 589*** (8 702 880 726)	9 723 787 530 (25 996 636 908)	11 216 548 316 (24 932 002 760)	8 870 781 366 (26 570 678 994)
Reference-priced goods	1 089 307 115 (2 855 299 225)	1 531 791 831*** (3 761 253 636)	836 458 705** (2 137 980 005)	1 566 982 405 (3 825 634 972)	2 704 861 950*** (5 666 774 577)	916 765 523*** (1 877 371 677)
Organized-exchange goods	475 151 088 (1 122 512 437)	603 081 233** (1 092 063 551)	402 048 148 (1 134 064 493)	1 550 419 827 (4 332 427 992)	1 742 851 321 (5 668 383 491)	1 440 458 973 (3 338 699 702)
Cultural product classifications						
Core cultural products	132 286 754 (364 603 785)	259 640 416*** (530 546 599)	44 731 111*** (111 592 699)	189 081 525 (484 671 235)	262 095 375** (472 443 257)	138 884 503 (487 246 142)
Cultural heritage products	6 047 431 (21 915 216)	12 522 051*** (31 711 301)	1 596 131** (8 495 601)	21 822 587 (73 450 275)	43 657 485*** (108 667 553)	6 811 095*** (21 258 256)
Printed matter	59 724 582 (244 539 996)	120 807 773** (371 944 276)	17 729 889* (41 242 208)	37 755 604 (109 588 319)	63 790 217** (143 868 969)	19 856 808*** (72 728 861)
Music and the performing arts	16 019 358 (39 338 549)	21 487 675* (42 666 514)	12 259 890 (36 465 838)	6 612 129 (20 575 587)	11 469 937** (29 576 621)	3 272 386*** (9 335 666)

132

Visual arts	41 978 967 (128 410 907)	88 518 588*** (187 040 373)	9 982 978*** (36 299 976)	75 602 537 (218 558 021)	134 769 393*** (295 623 740)	34 925 324*** (128 931 378)
Audio and audiovisual media	8 544 550 (40 695 272)	16 373 879* (62 373 974)	3 161 886 (7 439 036)	47 291 799 (264 517 878)	8 429 782*** (29 385 245)	7 409 436 (340 383 494)
Related cultural products	171 525 542 (444 426 172)	247 518 923* (591 446 466)	119 280 091 (294 604 171)	396 392 071 (1 313 283 965)	136 807 416*** (205 373 776)	574 856 521* (1 675 253 817)
Music	36 181 398 (77 692 475)	42 617 826 (73 369 217)	31 756 353 (80 333 856)	89 573 626 (346 476 508)	21 422 081*** (40 352 116)	136 427 813* (443 047 237)
Cinema and photography	55 250 288 (119 046 525)	80 554 010** (140 191 663)	37 853 979* (98 507 734)	77 592 633 (247 765 888)	73 366 705 (130 361 986)	80 497 958 (303 353 240)
Television and radio	46 670 907 (171 687 261)	68 836 017 (241 369 422)	31 432 395 (96 054 290)	212 758 959 (902 075 446)	23 622 859*** (60 944 899)	342 790 027* (1 153 520 764)
New media	33 450 726 (120 041 609)	55 527 262* (176 858 375)	18 273 108 (47 975 552)	16 529 191 (80 591 322)	18 372 572 (37 614 732)	15 261 867 (99 987 764)

Notes

***, **, and * denote statistical significance from the corresponding 'full sample' value at the 1 per cent, 5 per cent and 10 per cent levels, respectively.

For aggregate trade values and Rauch product classifications, sample sizes are 858, 312 and 546, while sample sizes corresponding to cultural product classifications are 594, 242 and 352 for the full sample, pre-1968 home countries and post-1968 home countries, respectively.

Table 8.4 *Descriptive statistics – trade values: manufactures, non-manufactures and 1-digit SITC sectors*

Description	All home countries N = 858	Pre-1968 home countries N = 312	Post-1968 home countries N = 546
Non-manufactured goods, exports	930 512 600 (2 362 697 648)	931 445 450 (2 119 282 200)	929 979 543 (2 493 018 899)
0: Food and live animals, exports	8 103 631 (26 548 725)	12 667 091*** (33 071 463)	5 495 940** (21 574 947)
1: Beverages and tobacco, exports	158 588 859 (557 059 988)	142 118 359 (305 973 265)	168 000 573 (659 012 265)
2: Crude materials, inedible, except fuels, exports	414 900 100 (1 075 630 534)	444 534 320 (905 169 752)	397 966 260 (1 162 321 194)
3: Mineral fuels, lubricants and related materials, exports	180 239 607 (560 354 579)	243 785 604** (714 435 141)	143 927 609 (445 931 584)
4: Animal and vegetable oils, fats and waxes, exports	168 743 637 (436 993 871)	88 381 212*** (269 088 930)	214 665 023** (503 146 732)
Manufactured goods, exports	7 043 811 471 (18 681 527 873)	11 212 532 080*** (26 195 214 693)	4 661 685 408*** (11 899 224 783)
5: Chemicals and related products, n.e.s., exports	1 087 164 535 (2 540 234 171)	1 738 688 504*** (3 494 749 308)	714 865 123*** (1 672 000 790)
6: Manufactured goods classified chiefly by material, exports	779 437 209 (2 873 143 666)	1 244 061 259*** (4 112 469 099)	513 937 752** (1 770 760 632)
7: Machinery and transport equipment, exports	3 889 542 418 (10 484 789 191)	6 188 479 727*** (14 982 240 727)	2 575 863 956*** (6 326 017 342)
8: Miscellaneous manufactured articles, exports	963 715 450 (2 426 220 584)	1 501 126 354*** (3 108 275 959)	656 623 505*** (1 866 400 913)
9: Commodities and transactions, n.e.c., exports	324 396 785 (772 511 112)	541 349 189*** (994 165 397)	200 423 983*** (576 252 395)

Table 8.4   (*continued*)

Description	All home countries N = 858	Pre-1968 home countries N = 312	Post-1968 home countries N = 546
Non-manufactured goods, imports	2017956947 (6805124040)	2979514809** (10081958611)	1468495311** (3739753611)
0: Food and live animals, imports	26335500 (154206506)	56306947*** (240357728)	9208958*** (60148102)
1: Beverages and tobacco, imports	187451729 (440408432)	403176370*** (617290858)	64180506*** (213751769)
2: Crude materials, inedible, except fuels, imports	332155912 (1422528060)	636887716*** (2299366123)	158023453*** (285430043)
3: Mineral fuels, lubricants and related materials, imports	1409996952 (5017269183)	1755416006 (6956319210)	1212614635 (3444273838)
4: Animal and vegetable oils, fats and waxes, imports	61977572 (253734617)	127338587*** (406801889)	24628421*** (54411054)
Manufactured goods, imports	12333261045 (31190064055)	14968490211* (31977833703)	10827415808 (30658794361)
5: Chemicals and related products, n.e.s., imports	1192634466 (2653175819)	2280037469*** (3810351288)	571261321*** (1311655841)
6: Manufactured goods classified chiefly by material, imports	1799911890 (4523875845)	2453412965** (6314810247)	1426482703** (3006969296)
7: Machinery and transport equipment, imports	6388577607 (18796814086)	7281141945 (17426940331)	5878540843 (19533771103)
8: Miscellaneous manufactured articles, imports	2327925751 (7261037453)	1823727020* (3057235647)	2616039312 (8794479569)
9: Commodities and transactions, n.e.c., imports	624013591 (1934230734)	1128483010*** (2877505886)	335745351*** (963922602)

Notes
Standard deviations in parentheses.
***, ** and * denote statistical significance from corresponding full sample values at the 1 per cent, 5 per cent and 10 per cent levels, respectively.

NOTES

1. Natural logarithms are not taken for the cultural distance ($CDIST_j$) and trade openness variables ($OPEN_{jt}$), as the logarithm of values between 0 and 1 would be negative and interpretation of corresponding estimated elasticities would be affected.
2. The Regional Trade Agreements considered are the European Union/European Economic Community, European Free Trade Arrangement, European Economic Area, Canada–US Free Trade Arrangement/North American Free Trade Agreement, Asia Pacific Economic Community, Central American Common Market, Latin America Free Trade Association/Latin America Integration Agreement, Andean Community, Caribbean Community/Carifta, Organization of Eastern Caribbean States, Southern Cone Common Market (Mercado Comùn del Sur), Group of Three, Association of Southeast Asian Nations, The Papua New Guinea–Australia Trade and Commercial Relations Agreement, Bangkok Agreement, South Pacific Regional Trade and Economic Agreement, Australia–New Zealand Closer Economic Relations Trade Agreement, East Asian Economic Caucus, South Asian Association for Regional Cooperation/SAARC Preferential Trading Arrangement, Central European Free Trade Area, Arab Common Market, Economic Cooperation Council, Gulf Cooperation Council, Economic and Monetary Community of Central Africa, East African Community/East African Cooperation, South African Customs Union Agreement, Economic Community of West African States, South Africa Development Community/Southern African Development Coordination Conference, and the Common Market for Eastern and Southern Africa.

9. Verification of the immigrant–trade link

In this and the following chapter, results obtained when estimating equation (8.5) and variants of the baseline estimation equation are presented and discussed. We begin by verifying an immigrant–trade link between the US and the full set of home countries examined in this study. This also involves examination of the robustness, in terms of sample composition and econometric specification, of this primary result. We then turn our attention to variation in the influences of immigrants across entry classifications and in terms of the average length of stay in the US and the skill composition of immigrant populations, before finally considering in greater detail the effects of cultural distance and its component dimensions on US–home country trade flows and the corresponding connection to immigrants' pro-trade influences.

9.1 THE INFLUENCE OF IMMIGRANTS ON US–HOME COUNTRY TRADE

To determine whether an immigrant–trade links exists for the US and the 66 home countries for which complete data are available, three econometric specifications have been estimated using both aggregate exports and imports, in turn, as the dependent variable. The estimation results are presented in Table 9.1. Results obtained when estimating our baseline specification are provided in columns (c) and (f). Since natural logarithms have been taken for each of the dependent variable series, estimated coefficients on explanatory variables that also have been transformed into logarithms can be interpreted as elasticities. This is to say that the coefficients represent the expected proportional change in the respective dependent variable that would result from a marginal increase in the explanatory variable, all else held constant. In the cases of the coefficients for the immigrant stock variables that are presented in columns (c) and (f), it can be said that a 1 per cent increase in the immigrant stock from a given home country is estimated to increase US exports to that country by 0.24 per cent and increase US imports by 0.28 per cent. Extrapolating to

Table 9.1 Verifying the US immigrant–trade link

Expl. Var.:	Dep. Var.: ln EXP_{jt} (a)	ln EXP_{jt} (b)	ln EXP_{jt} (c)	ln IMP_{jt} (d)	ln IMP_{jt} (e)	ln IMP_{jt} (f)
ln IM_{jt}	0.2835***	0.2616***	0.2449***	0.2715***	0.3076***	0.2762***
	(0.0131)	(0.0155)	(0.018)	(0.0116)	(0.0192)	(0.0155)
$CDIST_j$		−0.4824***	−0.4951***		−0.2164***	−0.1303***
		(0.0363)	(0.0305)		(0.0422)	(0.0311)
ln $GDIST_j$	−0.8868***	−0.6546***	−0.6196***	−0.8112***	−0.7363***	−0.5668***
	(0.0295)	(0.0293)	(0.0403)	(0.0203)	(0.0346)	(0.0386)
ln GDP_{jt}	0.8915***	1.3362***	1.089***	0.9827***	1.3006***	1.2088***
	(0.0087)	(0.042)	(0.0353)	(0.0101)	(0.0481)	(0.0378)
Lagged Δ dep. var.		−0.0298	−0.0067		−0.0219	−0.0147
		(0.0214)	(0.0141)		(0.023)	(0.0171)
Δln$XRATE_{jt}$		−0.0634	−0.0776		0.0099	−0.0392
		(0.0483)	(0.0518)		(0.0725)	(0.0559)
$OPEN_{jt}$		0.005***	0.0037***		0.0092***	0.0096***
		(0.0004)	(0.0005)		(0.0006)	(0.0005)
ln POP_{jt}		0.0061	0.0731***		0.0264	0.0334*
		(0.0153)	(0.0208)		(0.0245)	(0.0173)
ln REM_{jt}		0.4749***	0.2471***		0.3907***	0.2317***
		(0.0365)	(0.0318)		(0.0414)	(0.0344)
$OPEC_j$			0.3402			1.7541***
			(0.2527)			(0.0588)

	(1)	(2)	(3)	(4)	(5)	(6)
RTA_{jt}			0.6983***			0.7242***
			(0.0392)			(0.0353)
$SEAPORT_j$			0.436***			0.2058***
			(0.0493)			(0.0523)
Constant	3.3222***	−13.7063***	−4.7247***	0.5258	−12.7514***	−9.6791***
	(0.2997)	(1.41)	(1.2196)	(0.3267)	(1.5362)	(1.3042)
N	858	858	858	858	858	858
Adjusted R^2	0.852	0.87	0.8926	0.8379	0.8483	0.8897
Wald chi^2 statistic	23 170***	21 888***	39 272***	19 825***	13 130***	28 197***
Log-likelihood statistic	−763.2	−673	−581.9	−837.82	−783.17	−600.87

Notes

Robust standard errors in parentheses.

Estimated coefficients on year dummy variables not reported.

***, ** and * denote statistical significance at the 1 per cent, 5 per cent and 10 per cent levels, respectively.

consider a 10 per cent increase in the immigrant stock from any particular home country, the estimation results predict respective increases of 2.45 per cent and 2.76 per cent in US exports to and imports from the home country. It is important to note at this point that, given the specifications for which results are presented in Table 9.1, the elasticity estimates apply to all home countries. Beginning in section 9.3, where we introduce the measure of US–home country cultural distance, and throughout chapter 10, we allow for variation in elasticity estimates across the pre-1968 and post-1968 home country classifications.

Both of the estimated coefficients on the immigrant stock variable are significant from zero at the 1 per cent level. Comparing across columns, we see persistence in terms of the pattern of significance for the immigrant stock coefficients. Further still, we see that the relative magnitudes of coefficients are comparable across specifications. Columns (a) and (d) present results obtained from the estimation of specifications in which the only modifications from equation (8.1) are the inclusion of the immigrant stock variable and the vector of year dummy variables. Results obtained after augmenting the initial estimation equation to include the series of continuous explanatory variables, but not the dummy variables, are presented in columns (b) and (e). The coefficient estimates for the immigrant stock variables presented here, while larger with respect to exports, are comparable to the averages of the values that are reported in panel A of Table 3.1: 0.16 for exports and 0.26 for imports. Taken collectively, the coefficient estimates for the immigrant stock variable indicate that, dependent upon the specification being estimated, a 10 per cent increase in the immigrant stock variable yields expected increases in US exports to the immigrants' home countries ranging from 2.45 per cent to 2.84 per cent. Similarly, like immigrant stock increases are estimated to increase US imports from the immigrants' home countries by 2.72 per cent to 3.08 per cent.

The estimation results also indicate that, as expected, greater US–home country cultural distance acts to hinder trade flows. As mentioned earlier, the relationship between immigrants, cultural distance and trade is discussed in greater detail in section 9.3. The remaining coefficient estimates presented in Table 9.1 indicate that greater geodesic distance between the US and its trading partners, implying higher transport costs, acts to reduce trade. Higher home country GDP values, on the other hand, correspond with increases in both US exports and imports. While the coefficients for the lagged change in the dependent variable series are negative, none are significant from zero. Likewise, all coefficients on the annual change in the US–host country exchange rate are insignificant. This may be the result of annual exchange rate changes masking variation that occurs within each year and which may have been more influential in determining trade flows. The coefficients on the variable representing trade openness are positive and significant in all estimations, indicating that the US is more likely to engage in trade with nations that trade more intensively relative to the sizes of their economies. Indicative of the expected correspondence between larger markets and trade flows, positive coefficients are reported for the home country population variables; however, only the coefficients from estimation of the full specification (that is, equation (8.5)) that are presented in columns (c) and (f) are statistically significant. The results also indicate that home country economic remoteness corresponds with increased trade flows while, reflective of the extent to which the US imports petroleum, the coefficient on the variable that indicates OPEC membership is positive and significant in column (f). Similarly, the US trades more with countries if they are both parties to at least one regional trade agreement and those that have coastal access.

The similarities across specifications in the signs and the magnitudes of the coefficients and in terms of the incidence/levels of statistical significance are taken to indicate the robustness of the immigrant–trade relationship to specification choice/inclusion of additional explanatory variables. Just as it is important to determine whether the choice of econometric specification influences the signs, magnitudes and statistical significance of coefficient estimates, whether inclusion of any particular home country significantly affects coefficient estimates also needs to be considered. For example, the relative magnitude of US trade with countries such as Canada, China and Mexico, coupled with the high numbers of immigrants in the US from these countries may influence the overall findings. As an additional robustness check, equation (8.5) was estimated while removing one home country at a time from the sample. For example, in the first round Albania was excluded, while in the second round Albania was included but Algeria was excluded. This process was repeated 66 times with a different home country excluded each time. If the removal of any particular home country leads to considerable variation in the estimated coefficients for the immigrant stock variables, then the excluded country can be said to significantly impact the results obtained when using data representing the full complement of home countries. Table 9.2 reports the immigrant stock coefficients that were obtained from this series of ancillary estimations.

Of the 132 coefficients listed, only nine lay outside of the 95 per cent confidence intervals constructed around the immigrant stock coefficients that are reported in columns (c) and (f) of Table 9.1. These instances include three post-1968 home countries (Armenia, Israel and El Salvador) and four pre-1968 home countries (Canada, Greece, Italy and New Zealand). Removal of either Canada or New Zealand from the sample

Table 9.2 Sample composition robustness check

Dep. Var: Excluded:	ln EXP_{jt} (a)	ln IMP_{jt} (b)	Excluded:	ln EXP_{jt} (c)	ln IMP_{jt} (d)	Excluded:	ln EXP_{jt} (e)	ln IMP_{jt} (f)
Albania	0.2626 (0.0171)	0.2992 (0.0151)	Finland	0.2367 (0.0182)	0.2821 (0.0155)	Pakistan	0.2432 (0.0181)	0.2709 (0.0151)
Algeria	0.2597 (0.018)	0.28 (0.0159)	France	0.2312 (0.0189)	0.2694 (0.0161)	Peru	0.2379 (0.0182)	0.2712 (0.0157)
Argentina	0.2446 (0.0181)	0.2781 (0.0157)	Germany	0.2488 (0.0182)	0.2829 (0.0162)	Philippines	0.2249 (0.0192)	0.2595 (0.0155)
Armenia	0.2023 (0.0191)	0.2946 (0.0154)	Greece	0.2627 (0.0173)	0.3224 (0.0165)	Poland	0.2688 (0.0177)	0.2997 (0.0157)
Australia	0.2508 (0.0184)	0.278 (0.0157)	Hungary	0.2516 (0.0183)	0.2698 (0.0157)	Portugal	0.2542 (0.0179)	0.2973 (0.0163)
Austria	0.2442 (0.0183)	0.2771 (0.0158)	Iceland	0.2428 (0.018)	0.2743 (0.0156)	Romania	0.256 (0.0178)	0.2854 (0.0156)
Azerbaijan	0.2491 (0.0182)	0.2627 (0.0138)	India	0.2391 (0.0182)	0.2798 (0.0153)	Russia	0.2315 (0.0184)	0.2635 (0.0158)
Bangladesh	0.2397 (0.0179)	0.2865 (0.0154)	Indonesia	0.2419 (0.0177)	0.2739 (0.0151)	Slovakia	0.248 (0.0185)	0.277 (0.0158)
Belgium	0.2801 (0.0167)	0.2906 (0.0171)	Ireland	0.2431 (0.0181)	0.2594 (0.0152)	Slovenia	0.2207 (0.0186)	0.2906 (0.0153)
Brazil	0.2594 (0.0179)	0.2812 (0.0153)	Israel	0.2212 (0.0185)	0.2385 (0.0139)	South Africa	0.2472 (0.0184)	0.2732 (0.0161)
Bulgaria	0.2455 (0.018)	0.2805 (0.0158)	Italy	0.2618 (0.0173)	0.3126 (0.0173)	Spain	0.2217 (0.0188)	0.2627 (0.0151)
Canada	0.1713 (0.0216)	0.2329 (0.015)	Japan	0.2456 (0.0181)	0.3016 (0.0159)	Sweden	0.2454 (0.018)	0.2761 (0.0153)

Country			Country			Country		
Chile	0.2547	0.2809	Jordan	0.2228	0.2758	Switzerland	0.2523	0.2792
	(0.0183)	(0.0157)		(0.0188)	(0.0152)		(0.0173)	(0.0148)
China	0.2527	0.3032	Korea, Rep. of	0.2424	0.2746	Tanzania	0.2493	0.2558
	(0.0181)	(0.0151)		(0.018)	(0.0161)		(0.0187)	(0.015)
Colombia	0.2455	0.2707	Latvia	0.2397	0.2712	Turkey	0.2541	0.2708
	(0.0177)	(0.0147)		(0.0182)	(0.0158)		(0.018)	(0.0159)
Croatia	0.2347	0.2776	Macedonia	0.2518	0.2776	Uganda	0.2424	0.261
	(0.0183)	(0.0152)		(0.018)	(0.016)		(0.0182)	(0.0155)
Czech Rep.	0.2476	0.2677	Mexico	0.2589	0.285	Ukraine	0.2533	0.2849
	(0.0184)	(0.0155)		(0.021)	(0.0169)		(0.018)	(0.0155)
Denmark	0.2403	0.2772	Morocco	0.2563	0.2631	United Kingdom	0.242	0.2855
	(0.0181)	(0.0155)		(0.0179)	(0.0155)		(0.0181)	(0.0162)
Dominican Rep.	0.246	0.2695	Netherlands	0.2602	0.278	Uruguay	0.238	0.2689
	(0.0175)	(0.0141)		(0.0174)	(0.0156)		(0.0186)	(0.0154)
Egypt	0.2548	0.2763	New Zealand	0.2874	0.3349	Venezuela	0.2515	0.275
	(0.0177)	(0.0156)		(0.0169)	(0.016)		(0.0177)	(0.0156)
El Salvador	0.209	0.2492	Nigeria	0.2555	0.2627	Vietnam	0.2693	0.2991
	(0.019)	(0.0148)		(0.0182)	(0.0157)		(0.0175)	(0.0156)
Estonia	0.2427	0.2771	Norway	0.241	0.2742	Zimbabwe	0.2483	0.2898
	(0.0179)	(0.0159)		(0.018)	(0.0154)		(0.0179)	(0.0164)

Notes

Lower bound and upper bound values for 95 per cent confidence intervals calculated for the estimated coefficients on the immigrant stock variable (presented in columns (c) and (f) of Table 8.1) are equal to 0.2097 and 0.2802 when US exports to country *j* are used as the dependent variable and are equal to 0.2458 and 0.3066 when US imports from country *j* are used as the dependent variable.

Values noted here by being 'boxed' indicate that immigrants' stock coefficients estimated when the indicated country is removed from the data sample lay outside the corresponding confidence interval.

All coefficients reported above are significant from zero at the 1 per cent level.

leads to higher estimated immigrant influences on both US exports and imports. Exclusion of Armenia or El Salvador increases only the estimated immigrant-export effect, while exclusion of Greece, Israel or Italy increases only the estimated immigrant-import effect. It is important to note that all coefficient estimates are positive and are significantly different from zero at the 1 per cent level. This indicates that, while the magnitude of the estimated influence of immigrants on US–home country trade is, at times, sensitive to the composition of the home country data sample, the observed immigrant–trade link is not driven by the inclusion of any individual home country. Thus, the general result of a pro-trade immigrant effect can be considered robust to sample composition.

9.2   IMMIGRANTS' CHARACTERISTICS AND THE IMMIGRANT–TRADE LINK

To explore the immigrant–trade relationship further, we follow Gould (1994), Bardhan and Guhathakurta (2004) and Mundra (2005) and modify the baseline estimation equation to produce equation (9.1). The skill composition of prior immigrant inflows ($SKUK_{ijt}$) is included in this modified specification as a proxy for the skill composition of the immigrant population. Since assimilation to the culture of the host country and/ or the amount of time spent in the host country may weaken immigrants' ties to their home countries, a variable which represents the average duration of immigrants' stays in the US ($STAY_{ijt}$) is also included in the modified estimation equation. To capture any non-linearity in the relationship, the squared value of the $STAY_{ijt}$ variable is also included. The coefficients on the variables representing skill composition and length of stay are expected to be positive, while a negative coefficient is expected for the squared value of the length of stay variable. The vector X contains all explanatory variables other than the measures of the immigrant stock that are listed in the baseline estimation equation (that is, equation (8.5)).

$$\ln(T_{ijt} + \eta) = \alpha_0 + \delta_1 \ln IM_{ijt} + \beta_1 SKUK_{ijt} + \beta_2 STAY_{ijt}$$
$$+ \beta_3 STAY_{ijt}^2 + +\psi_X X + \varepsilon_{ijt} \qquad (9.1)$$

Estimation results are provided in columns (a) and (c) of Table 9.3. As was the case with the initial series of estimations, the coefficients on the immigrant stock variable are positive and significant from zero. As is the case with the cultural distance and trade openness variables, the $SKUK_{ijt}$ and $STAY_{ijt}$ variables are in levels rather than logarithms.

Table 9.3 *Variation across immigrant attributes and entry classifications*

Dep. Var.: Expl. Var.:	ln EXP_{jt} (a)	ln EXP_{jt} (b)	ln IMP_{jt} (c)	ln IMP_{jt} (d)
ln IM_{jt}	0.3322*** (0.0178)		0.3607*** (0.019)	
ln REF_{jt}		0.0595*** (0.0074)		0.0891*** (0.0044)
ln $NREF*_{jt}$		0.2692*** (0.0217)		0.3038*** (0.0205)
$CDIST_j$	−0.3733*** (0.0277)	−0.1898*** (0.0437)	−0.174*** (0.0369)	−0.2876*** (0.035)
$SKUK_{jt}$	0.1085*** (0.008)		0.0558*** (0.0111)	
$STAY_{jt}$	0.1406*** (0.0108)		0.0463*** (0.0146)	
$STAY_{jt} \times STAY_{jt}$	−0.0041*** (0.0003)		−0.0022*** (0.0004)	
ln $GDIST_j$	−0.7093*** (0.0354)	−0.573*** (0.0533)	−0.552*** (0.0324)	−0.6302*** (0.0494)
ln GDP_{jt}	1.0081*** (0.036)	1.0491*** (0.0398)	1.3682*** (0.0447)	1.1733*** (0.043)
Lagged Δ dep. var.	−0.0147 (0.0178)	0.2339*** (0.0865)	−0.017 (0.0168)	0.3509*** (0.0969)
Δln$XRATE_{jt}$	−0.0849* (0.0507)	0.0069 (0.0728)	−0.0399 (0.0621)	−0.1446*** (0.0564)

Table 9.3 (continued)

Expl. Var.:	ln EXP_{jt} (a)	ln EXP_{jt} (b)	ln IMP_{jt} (c)	ln IMP_{jt} (d)
Dep. Var.:				
$OPEN_{jt}$	0.0036***	0.0081***	0.0092***	0.0118***
	(0.0005)	(0.0008)	(0.0004)	(0.0005)
ln POP_{jt}	0.066***	0.1657***	0.1831***	0.0631***
	(0.0197)	(0.0237)	(0.0208)	(0.0222)
ln REM_{jt}	0.2398***	0.1162***	0.2878***	0.1759***
	(0.031)	(0.036)	(0.0407)	(0.0372)
$OPEC_j$	0.2611	0.4342	1.6765***	1.581***
	(0.2467)	(0.2656)	(0.0633)	(0.0779)
RTA_{jt}	0.4737***	0.7724***	0.4043***	0.6937***
	(0.0384)	(0.0451)	(0.044)	(0.0485)
$SEAPORT_j$	0.4033***	0.2458***	0.352***	0.3436***
	(0.0544)	(0.072)	(0.0597)	(0.0377)
Constant	-4.2669***	-1.7015	-12.7196***	-6.8208***
	(1.1615)	(1.448)	(1.483)	(1.5141)
N	854	348	854	348
Adjusted R^2	0.9112	0.9177	0.9014	0.9153
Wald chi^2 statistic	41616***	18960***	24513***	17168***
Log-likelihood statistic	-480.9	-159.82	-606.92	-116.12
Hausman test statistic:				
$\beta_{\ln REF} = \beta_{\ln NREF}$	----	191.18***	----	366.64***

Notes: See Table 9.1.

146

The results indicate that an increase in the skill composition of the immigrant population is positively related to US–home country trade. Skilled immigrants are those who self-identified at their time of entry as 'professional, technical and kindred workers'. The unskilled are those immigrants who reported their occupations as classified as 'general machine operators', 'laborers', 'farm workers' or 'service workers'. While immigrants in either category have the potential to exert pro-trade influences, it seems reasonable that skilled immigrants would be more likely to do so as they may be more likely to be connected to social and business networks in their home countries and, being more skilled, may consume at a higher level than would lower-skilled immigrants and, hence, likely lower-income individuals; thus, they potentially increase US imports from their home countries as they satisfy their demand for home country products.

The lengthier the average stay in the US of immigrants from a given country, the more the US trades with that country. Considered in relation to the immigrant–trade relationship, this would suggest that the longer immigrants have resided in the US, the stronger their effects on US–home country trade flows. This influence increases at a decreasing rate, however, and eventually would begin to wane. However, it is important to note that, for both the $SKUK_{ijt}$ and $STAY_{ijt}$ variables, the measures employed here are 'summary' values of sorts and may reflect the trade-related influences of something other than immigrants.

To explore potential variation in the pro-trade influences of immigrants across entry classifications, equation (8.5) was modified such that the immigrant stock variable was replaced by estimates of the refugee/asylee population and the stock of all other immigrants. The vector **X** remains as described with respect to equation (9.1). Equation (9.2) illustrates.

$$\ln (T_{ijt} + \eta) = \alpha_0 + \delta_1 \ln REF_{ijt} + \delta_2 \ln NREF_{ijt} + \psi_X \mathbf{X} + \varepsilon_{ijt} \quad (9.2)$$

Estimation results are provided in columns (b) and (d) of Table 9.3. Substitution of the REF_{ijt} and $NREF_{ijt}$ variables for the IM_{ijt} variable allows examination, broadly, of the immigrant–trade effect across entry classifications and, hence, immigrant types.[1] The estimated coefficients on the $NREF_{ijt}$ variable are considerably greater in magnitude as compared to the coefficients on the REF_{ijt} variable. Hausman tests confirm that the REF_{ijt} and $NREF_{ijt}$ coefficients are significantly different from one another regardless of whether exports or imports are utilized as the dependent variable series. The difference makes sense intuitively since it would be more likely that refugees and asylum-seekers would have difficulty maintaining close connections to business and social networks in their home countries. Also, as many refugees and asylum-seekers spend considerable time in countries other than their home countries prior to their arrival in the US it is possible that their preferences are not as strongly oriented toward home country goods, generally speaking, as are the preferences of other immigrants. The overall message is that entry classification matters in terms of the magnitude of the immigrant–trade link; however, we do see that even refugees and asylum-seekers exert positive influences on US trade with their home countries.

9.3   IMMIGRANTS AND THE EFFECTS OF CULTURAL DISTANCE

Using a number of measures to represent cultural dissimilarity, several studies have reported a negative relationship between cultural distance and bilateral trade flows. The negative and significant coefficients on the cultural distance variables presented in Table 9.1 and in Table 9.3 buttress the findings of these studies. In this section, we consider the pro-trade influences of immigrants in terms of offsetting the trade-inhibiting effects of cultural distance. To accomplish this, we modify estimation equation (8.5) as follows.

$$\ln(T_{ijt} + \eta) = \alpha_0 + \delta_1 \ln IM_{ijt} - \mu_1 CDIST_{ij} + \beta_1 (\ln IM_{ijt} \times CDIST_{ij})$$
$$+ \psi_X \mathbf{X} + \varepsilon_{ijt} \qquad (9.3)$$

Again, the vector $\mathbf{X}$ contains all explanatory variables other than the immigrant stock and cultural distance variables that are listed in equation (8.5). In equation (9.3), a positive and significant coefficient on the term which interacts the immigrant stock and cultural distance variables would signal that immigrants from home countries that are more culturally-distant from the US exert relatively stronger pro-trade influences. This would suggest that, if the estimated coefficient on the variable which represents cultural distance is negative, immigrants act to offset, at least in part, the corresponding trade-inhibiting influences.

Following estimation of equation (9.3), we decompose the cultural distance variable to examine the respective influences of the traditional authority vs. secular-rational authority (*TSR*) and the survival values vs. self-expression values (*SSE*) dimensions of culture on trade flows, and again consider the interaction of each term with the variable that represents immigrant stocks. Equation (9.4) illustrates.

$$\ln(T_{ijt} + \eta) = \alpha_0 + \delta_1 \ln IM_{ijt} - \mu_1|SSE_i - SSE_j| - \mu_2|TSR_i - TSR_j|$$
$$+ \beta_1(\ln IM_{ijt} \times |SSE_i - SSE_j|)$$
$$+ \beta_2(\ln IM_{ijt} \times |TSR_i - TSR_j|) + \psi_X\mathbf{X} + \varepsilon_{ijt} \qquad (9.4)$$

Results generated when estimating equations (9.3) and (9.4) are presented in Table 9.4. The first set of results (reported in columns (a) and (c)) correspond to the specification where the composite cultural distance variable and an interaction term between the immigrant stock variable and the measure of cultural distance are included. The estimated coefficients on the immigrant stock variables and the interaction terms are both positive and significant. Since, for a number of home countries, the value of the cultural distance variable is less than 1, and taking the logarithm of a value less than 1 results in a negative number, the cultural distance variable is in levels rather than in logarithms. Otherwise, coefficient interpretation becomes problematic. For example, a negative coefficient would be interpreted as indicative of a positive effect of cultural distance on trade between the US and less culturally-distant countries and a negative effect on US trade with more distant partners.

The proportional influence of immigrants from a typical home country, holding constant the trade-inhibiting effects of cultural distance, is given by summation of the coefficients on the immigrant stock variable and the interaction variable.[2] From the results provided in columns (a) and (c), we estimate that an assumed 10 per cent increase in the immigrant stock increases US exports to and imports from a typical home country by 2.51 per cent and 2.55 per cent, respectively. Similarly, if we hold the effects of immigrants on trade constant, the estimated effect of cultural distance on trade is given by the sums of the coefficients on the cultural distance and interaction variables. As anticipated, cultural distance inhibits trade flows while immigrants enhance trade flows. The positive and significant coefficients on the interaction terms indicate that immigrants from more culturally-distant home countries exert stronger influences on US trade with their respective home countries. That is, immigrants can be said to offset, at least in part, the trade-inhibiting influence of cultural distance.

To examine the separate influences of *TSR* distance and *SSE* distance on US–home country trade flows, we decompose the composite measure of cultural distance into variables that represent the *TSR* and *SSE* dimensions of cultural distance and include each as explanatory variables. As before, we interact each of these variables with the immigrant stock variable. Results are presented in columns (b) and (d) of Table 9.4. In both estimations, the coefficients on the immigrant stock variables are

Table 9.4 Cultural distance and the US immigrant–trade link

Expl. Var.:	Dep. Var.: $\ln EXP_{jt}$ (a)	$\ln EXP_{jt}$ (b)	$\ln IMP_{jt}$ (c)	$\ln IMP_{jt}$ (d)
$\ln IM_{jt}$	0.2092*** (0.0281)	0.1837*** (0.0272)	0.0973*** (0.0218)	0.2009*** (0.0206)
$CDIST_j$	−0.9878*** (0.228)		−1.9712*** (0.2028)	
$\ln IM_{jt} \times CDIST_j$	0.0416** (0.0188)		0.1576*** (0.0169)	
$|SSE_i - SSE_j|$		0.4576** (0.191)		−2.0012*** (0.1833)
$|TSR_i - TSR_j|$		−2.6526*** (0.268)		0.7559*** (0.2463)
$\ln IM_{jt} \times |SSE_i - SSE_j|$		−0.0972*** (0.0164)		0.1351*** (0.0161)
$\ln IM_{jt} \times |TSR_i - TSR_j|$		0.2098*** (0.0216)		−0.0363* (0.0193)
$\ln GDIST_j$	−0.6472*** (0.0408)	−0.5886*** (0.0382)	−0.7035*** (0.0294)	−0.6256*** (0.0224)
$\ln GDP_{jt}$	1.083*** (0.0354)	0.9589*** (0.0321)	1.21*** (0.0351)	1.0712*** (0.0325)
Lagged Δ dep. var.	−0.0076 (0.0144)	−0.0126 (0.0144)	−0.0121 (0.018)	−0.0105 (0.0237)
$\Delta \ln XRATE_{jt}$	−0.1079** (0.0546)	−0.0761 (0.0554)	−0.0504 (0.0543)	−0.0566 (0.0564)

	(1)	(2)	(3)	(4)
$OPEN_{jt}$	0.0035***	0.0055***	0.0095***	0.0094***
	(0.0005)	(0.0005)	(0.0004)	(0.0004)
ln POP_{jt}	0.0853***	0.0006	-0.0224	0.095***
	(0.0207)	(0.0227)	(0.0147)	(0.0136)
ln REM_{jt}	0.2486***	0.1938***	0.267***	0.2358***
	(0.0314)	(0.0256)	(0.0319)	(0.0286)
$OPEC_j$	0.3668	0.2923	1.6851***	1.6212***
	(0.2529)	(0.2619)	(0.0572)	(0.0534)
RTA_{jt}	0.7043***	0.7475***	0.6692***	0.6616***
	(0.0399)	(0.0387)	(0.0332)	(0.0291)
$SEAPORT_j$	0.41***	0.4256***	0.1714***	0.1143*
	(0.0509)	(0.0456)	(0.054)	(0.0611)
Constant	-3.6409***	-1.7239	-6.8135***	-6.8587***
	(1.2912)	(1.1245)	(1.1041)	(0.9829)
N	858	858	858	858
Adjusted R²	0.893	0.9004	0.8915	0.8977
Wald chi² statistic	30 841***	25 969***	29 842***	39 568***
Log-likelihood statistic	-588.81	-564.7	-563.8	-493.04
Joint significance z-statistic	13.6***	----	20.09***	----
Hausman test statistic: $\beta_{\ln IM \times dSSE} = \beta_{\ln IM \times dTSR}$	----	124.37***	----	42.19***
Hausman test statistic: $\beta_{dSSE} = \beta_{dTSR}$	----	89.72***	----	76.75***

Notes: See Table 9.1.

significant and positive. Summation of the coefficients on the immigrant stock variables with those on the interaction terms reveals positive immigrant influences on trade. However, with respect to US exports, the influence of immigrants in terms of offsetting TSR distance (0.394) is greater than the corresponding influence relating to SSE distance (0.087). For US imports, the influence of immigrants is greater for SSE distance (0.336) than it is for TSR distance (0.165).

For the variables which measure SSE distance and TSR distance, coefficient signs and magnitudes vary according to whether US exports or imports are used as the dependent variable series. Specifically, the US exports less to and imports more from home countries that are of greater SSE distance, while it exports more to and imports less from home countries that are of greater TSR distance. While the results presented in columns (a) and (c) indicate that the composite measure of cultural distance is negatively related to trade and that immigrants act to counter this negative relationship, the results presented in columns (b) and (d) indicate that even though the signs on the coefficients for the SSE distance and TSR distance variables vary across exports and imports, immigrants exert positive influence on trade for each. In the cases where the coefficients on the decomposed distance variables are negative, the corresponding influence of immigrants is larger than when the coefficient on the distance variable is positive. This suggests that when coefficients on the distance variables are negative there may be greater opportunities for immigrants to exert pro-trade influences and, hence, larger corresponding coefficients on the immigrant stock variables.

In summary, these results indicate that immigrants exert positive influences on US exports to and imports from their home countries. Further, this effect appears to be robust to sample composition and econometric specification. There is, however, variation across immigrants' entry classifications, with refugees and asylum-seeking immigrants estimated to exert positive yet weaker effects on US–home country trade relative to the effects estimated for other immigrants. The US tends to trade more with home countries that send proportionally more skilled immigrants to the US. In terms of the time-path of immigrants' influences on trade, it appears that the positive influences of immigrants grow stronger initially; however, these influences grow at a decreasing rate and, eventually, dissipate. Cultural distance is found to inhibit US–home country trade, with the positive influences of immigrants on trade offsetting the trade-inhibiting influences of cultural distance at least partially.

NOTES

1. REF_{ijt} and $NREF_{ijt}$ data series, spanning the years 1996–2001, are available for all countries listed in Appendix 5.A (Section 5.2) with the exceptions of Canada, Dominican Republic, Finland, New Zealand, Norway, Philippines, Romania and the Ukraine.
2. Since immigrant effects are estimated by the summation of coefficients on the immigrant stock and interaction variables, determination of statistical significance for immigrant effects reported in columns (a) and (c) is based on a modified z-statistic that accounts for the value of each coefficient, its variance and the covariance of the variable pairs:

$$z = \frac{\hat{\beta}_{IM} + \hat{\beta}_{IM \times CDIST}}{\sqrt{\text{var}(\hat{\beta}_{IM}) + \text{var}(\hat{\beta}_{IM \times CDIST}) + 2\text{cov}(\hat{\beta}_{IM}, \hat{\beta}_{IM \times CDIST})}}.$$

10. Variation in the immigrant–trade link

Having established a positive influence of immigrants on US–home country trade in Chapter 9, we continue our examination of the hypotheses listed in Chapter 3. First, we consider whether or not variation exists in the pro-trade influences of immigrants across the pre-1968 and post-1968 home country cohorts. As discussed earlier, it is expected that the recency effects of immigrants from post-1968 home countries are greater than the primacy effects of immigrants from pre-1968 home countries. We then examine variation in immigrant–trade effects across a number of disaggregated trade measures. The use of such dependent variable series provides for a more detailed understanding of how immigrants affect trade and affords the opportunity to consider whether immigrants only affect trade when it is already taking place (that is, a trade-intensification effect) or if they also exert trade-initiation effects when US–home country trade is not occurring.

10.1 PRE-1968 AND POST-1968 HOME COUNTRY COHORTS

The history of US immigration policy was reviewed in Chapter 4 and immigrants' home countries were categorized in Chapter 5, based on whether or not entry preference was afforded historically, as either pre-1968 home countries or post-1968 home countries. It was then shown in Chapter 6 that pre-1968 home countries are, on average, significantly different from the average home country in the post-1968 cohort in terms of both hard and soft trade-facilitating infrastructure. The existence and quality of such infrastructure are directly related to trade-related transaction costs. When infrastructure is lacking or of lower quality, transaction costs are likely to be higher. The presence of higher transaction costs is anticipated to afford immigrants greater opportunities to exert pro-trade influences. To determine whether the pro-trade influences of immigrants from post-1968 home countries (that is, recency effects) are in fact greater than those exerted by immigrants from pre-1968 home countries (that is, primacy effects), we estimate a battery of specifications in which the immigrant stock variable is interacted separately with dummy variables that identify home countries as belonging to either the pre-1968 cohort or the post-1968 cohort. Equation (10.1) illustrates. As before, the vector **X** contains all explanatory variables other than the immigrant stock variable that are listed in equation (8.5).

$$\ln(T_{ijt} + \eta) = \alpha_0 + \delta_1(\ln IM_{ijt} \times PRE1968_j) + \delta_2(\ln IM_{ijt}$$
$$\times POST1968_j) - \nu_1 POST1968_j + \psi_X\mathbf{X} + \varepsilon_{ijt} \quad (10.1)$$

The a priori expectation is that $\delta_2 > \delta_1 \geq 0$. That is, while the recency effect is expected to exceed the primacy effect, both are expected to be positive and potentially significantly different from zero. Estimation results are presented in Table 10.1. Columns (a) and (b) report results obtained from estimations in which home countries have been categorized as indicated at the end of Chapter 5. The remaining columns, which will be discussed in turn, include results obtained from the estimation of an alternative econometric specification and when different criteria are employed to categorize home countries into the pre-1968 and post-1968 groupings.

Beginning with columns (a) and (b), we see that the estimated coefficients on the terms which interact the immigrant stock variable with dummy variables that identify trading partners according to classification as pre-1968 or post-1968 home countries reveal a proportional influence of immigrants from the latter group that is greater than the influence estimated for the former group. Specifically, a 10 per cent increase in the immigrant stock from a post-1968 home country is estimated to increase US exports to and imports from that country by 1.9 per cent and 3.58 per cent, respectively. An identical increase in the number of immigrants from a pre-1968 home country is estimated to increase US exports to that country by 0.76 per cent and to increase imports from that country by 1.08 per cent. Hausman test statistics, noted among the summary statistics, indicate that the differences in immigrants' proportional influences on trade across the pre-1968 and post-1968 home country cohorts are significant.

To gain an indication of the robustness of the results presented in columns (a) and (b), a series of alternative estimations has been undertaken. Due to the high correlation between the home country dummy variables and the measure of US–home country cultural distance (that is, that the correlation between the post-1968 home country dummy variable and the cultural distance measure is equal to 0.51), we remove the cultural distance variable and re-estimate equation (10.1). Results are presented in columns (c) and (d). For both home country groupings and both dependent

Table 10.1 Variation across pre-1968 and post-1968 home country cohorts

Dep. Var.: Expl. Var.:	ln EXP_{jt} (a)	ln IMP_{jt} (b)	ln EXP_{jt} (c)	ln IMP_{jt} (d)	ln EXP_{jt} (e)	ln IMP_{jt} (f)	ln EXP_{jt} (g)	ln IMP_{jt} (h)
ln IM_{jt} × $Post\text{-}968_j$	0.1901***	0.3575***	0.2632***	0.3919***	0.2795***	0.4404***	0.2697***	0.4403***
	(0.0184)	(0.0181)	(0.0158)	(0.0179)	(0.0228)	(0.0193)	(0.0203)	(0.0174)
ln IM_{jt} × $Pre\text{-}1968_j$	0.0755***	0.1079***	0.184***	0.1227***	0.2389***	0.2566***	0.1941***	0.2262***
	(0.0236)	(0.0218)	(0.0241)	(0.0216)	(0.0201)	(0.0149)	(0.0213)	(0.0177)
$CDIST_j$	−0.7401***	−0.3889***			−0.5388***	−0.1474***	−0.7343***	−0.315***
	(0.0425)	(0.0358)			(0.0391)	(0.0358)	(0.0405)	(0.0324)
$Post\text{-}1968_j$	−0.3886	−2.1403***	−0.3795	−2.7004***	−0.3875*	−1.9122***	−0.0826	−1.8081***
	(0.2404)	(0.2223)	(0.252)	(0.2233)	(0.228)	(0.1984)	(0.2276)	(0.1979)
ln $GDIST_j$	−0.7636***	−0.7562***	−0.8101***	−0.7189***	−0.6923***	−0.766***	−0.7436***	−0.6929***
	(0.0288)	(0.0333)	(0.0384)	(0.0389)	(0.0451)	(0.0328)	(0.0361)	(0.0261)
ln GDP_{jt}	1.0094***	1.2033***	1.1734***	1.279***	1.0648***	1.2413***	1.0317***	1.2391***
	(0.0282)	(0.0325)	(0.0317)	(0.0333)	(0.0346)	(0.0324)	(0.0315)	(0.0351)
Lagged Δ dep. var.	−0.0105	−0.0103	−0.0102	−0.0088	−0.0076	−0.0166	−0.0076	−0.0166
	(0.0134)	(0.0193)	(0.0157)	(0.0199)	(0.0141)	(0.0187)	(0.013)	(0.0181)
Δln$XRATE_{jt}$	−0.0363	0.0314	−0.0898*	0.0286	−0.1102**	−0.0606	−0.0505	−0.0118
	(0.0482)	(0.0697)	(0.0518)	(0.0685)	(0.0543)	(0.0583)	(0.0486)	(0.0648)
$OPEN_{jt}$	0.0078***	0.0096***	0.2982***	0.8705***	0.3488***	0.8941***	0.6514***	0.9914***
	(0.0006)	(0.0005)	(0.069)	(0.0416)	(0.0505)	(0.0394)	(0.0516)	(0.0413)
ln POP_{jt}	0.094***	0.1659***	0.2275***	0.1399***	0.0762***	0.1158***	0.1176***	0.1986***
	(0.0195)	(0.0222)	(0.0204)	(0.0217)	(0.0226)	(0.0181)	(0.02)	(0.02)
ln REM_{jt}	−0.0012	0.0721**	0.1538***	0.1797***	0.2299***	0.2462***	0.0643**	0.1394***
	(0.0259)	(0.0285)	(0.0269)	(0.0287)	(0.031)	(0.0301)	(0.0277)	(0.0313)

$OPEC_j$	0.1171	1.6681***	0.4892	1.7163***	0.3164	1.783***	0.1661	1.7431***
	(0.1445)	(0.0681)	(0.3441)	(0.0645)	(0.2547)	(0.0597)	(0.1462)	(0.0714)
RTA_{jt}	0.5417***	0.4028***	0.5631***	0.3856***	0.6797***	0.5772***	0.5952***	0.4433***
	(0.0355)	(0.0409)	(0.0453)	(0.0433)	(0.0411)	(0.0343)	(0.0371)	(0.0384)
$SEAPORT_j$	0.1549***	0.1458**	0.2606***	0.0043	0.4102***	0.1108**	0.1443***	0.104*
	(0.0494)	(0.0579)	(0.0544)	(0.0557)	(0.0507)	(0.0566)	(0.0484)	(0.0581)
Constant	2.905***	−2.0464*	−1.7638	−6.0758***	−3.1132**	−7.1397***	0.786	−4.9801***
	(1.0301)	(1.183)	(1.1765)	(1.1795)	(1.281)	(1.0667)	(1.1115)	(1.1968)
N	858	858	858	858	858	858	858	858
Adjusted R^2	0.9025	0.9042	0.8856	0.9013	0.8931	0.8935	0.9015	0.9018
Wald chi² statistic	24798***	21049***	24163***	19970***	38479***	31672***	25781***	25710***
Log-likelihood statistic	−540.42	−585.47	−594.17	−596.28	−585.56	−561.13	−544.94	−562.4
Hausman test statistic	32.49***	173.46***	14.01***	202.01***	4.41**	137.52***	15.59***	165***

Notes:

Robust standard errors in parentheses

Estimated coefficients on year dummy variables not reported

***, ** and * denote statistical significance at the 1 per cent, 5 per cent and 10 per cent levels, respectively.

variable series, the estimated coefficients on the immigrant stock variables increased; however, the ordering of coefficients by magnitude remains the same. Immigrants from post-1968 home countries are again estimated to exert, for both exports and imports, significantly larger proportional effects than do their counterparts from pre-1968 home countries.

Since the results presented in columns (a) to (d) could result from the composition of the pre-1968 and post-1968 home country cohorts, two final pairs of estimation results – generated when employing alternative home country categorizations – are provided in columns (e) to (h). The first pair of results (columns (e) and (f)) is obtained after re-categorizing Mexico, which initially was included in the post-1968 home country grouping, as a pre-1968 home country. The reasons for this modification are twofold. First, Mexico is the source country for the largest number of immigrants in the US and is one of the largest trading partners of the US. Second, a large number of immigrants from Mexico did arrive in the US prior to the implementation of the Immigration and Nationality Act of 1965. The decennial census values indicate that in 1930 there were only seven countries with larger US immigrant stocks than that of Mexico (641 000 persons). By 1960, this number had decreased to 576 000; however, by 1970, the immigrant stock from Mexico was equal to 760 000, and only Italy, Germany and Canada were source countries for larger immigrant stocks. The differences between estimated coefficients on the immigrant stock variable that are presented in columns (e) and (f) decreased relative to those presented in columns (a) to (d). However, we see that immigrants from the modified post-1968 cohort were still estimated to exert significantly larger proportional effects on US trade as compared to immigrants from this modified pre-1968 home country cohort.

The second pair of results (columns (g) and (h)) is obtained after further modification of the pre-1968 and post-1968 home country cohorts. In this iteration, all nations in the western hemisphere have been added to the original 24-nation pre-1968 home country cohort. The justification for this change is that, although western hemisphere nations (with the exceptions of Canada and, to a lesser extent, Mexico) were not principal sources for US immigration prior to implementation of the Immigration and Nationality Act of 1965, there were few, if any, explicit restrictions that hindered or banned migration from these countries (as did the Asiatic Barred Zone and, later, the Asia-Pacific Triangle). Even with this modification, the estimated coefficients follow the same ordering in terms of their magnitudes and, as before, the Hausman test statistics indicate that immigrants from post-1968 home countries generally exert proportional effects on trade that are significantly larger as compared to the influences of immigrants from pre-1968 home countries. It is important to note that modifying the cohorts of pre-1968 and post-1968 home countries results in larger immigrant stock coefficients than the values reported in columns (a) and (b).

Application of the estimated coefficients on the interaction terms, even though they are only reflective of significant differences in immigrant effects across broad cohorts, allows for better estimation of country-level per-immigrant effects than would, say, the estimated coefficients from columns (c) and (f) of Table 8.1. The results presented in columns (a) and (b) are employed to estimate the country-specific per-immigrant trade effects that are reported in Table 10.2.

We see that while the proportional effects of immigrants from the typical post-1968 home country are larger than those of immigrants from the typical pre-1968 home country in absolute terms (that is, in terms of the estimated per-immigrant effects) immigrants from pre-1968 home countries generally exert larger effects on US trade with their home countries than do immigrants from post-1968 home countries. The average annual effects of an immigrant from a pre-1968 home country are increases of $657 in US exports and $939 in US imports. By comparison, the average effects of an immigrant from a post-1968 home country are $365 for exports and $442 for imports. While there is considerable overlap in the distributions for the two cohorts, t-tests of differences in mean values indicate that for both exports and imports the listed differences are significant. It is also important to note the relative magnitudes of per-immigrant export and import effects across the two cohorts. For the pre-1968 home country classification, in all 24 instances the estimated influence of immigrants on US imports is greater than the estimated per-immigrant export effect. This cannot be said for the post-1968 home country classification. Here, the estimated per-immigrant export effects are greater than the corresponding import effects in 24 out of 42 cases.

The pattern of the relative magnitudes of immigrant effects is the result of variation in coefficient magnitudes across specifications where exports and imports are employed as the dependent variable series and the amounts that the US exports to and imports from each home country. As noted in Chapter 2, the welfare effects of an increase in imports that is attributable to the preference channel are unclear; however, increases in exports or imports that result from immigrants' information bridging effects are clearly welfare-enhancing. The preference channel would only affect US imports from immigrants' home countries, while the information bridge channel could affect both US exports to and imports from the home country. This implies that the average per-immigrant trade effects that are calculated for the post-1968 home country classification may be more likely to be associated, as compared to those estimated for the pre-1968 home country classification, with overall improvements in the social welfare of the US.

Table 10.2   Estimated annual per-immigrant trade effects

Pre-1968 home countries			Post-1968 home countries		
Country	EXP_{jt}	IMP_{jt}	Country	EXP_{jt}	IMP_{jt}
Australia	645.95	923.15	Albania	9.49	3.22
Austria	356.42	509.37	Algeria	1 570.63	3 248.11
Belgium	1 957.05	2 796.89	Argentina	579.59	225.05
Canada	1 755.37	2 508.67	Armenia	22.62	4.24
Czech Rep.	202.65	289.61	Azerbaijan	116.87	22.97
Denmark	652.15	932.02	Bangladesh	55.30	227.52
Finland	951.53	1 359.88	Brazil	1 116.71	737.68
France	1 232.12	1 760.87	Bulgaria	75.84	88.31
Germany	568.82	812.93	Chile	770.24	464.89
Greece	24.70	35.30	China	293.27	927.05
Hungary	128.98	184.33	Colombia	157.78	119.54
Iceland	336.21	480.49	Croatia	73.19	51.63
Ireland	607.33	867.96	Dominican Rep.	93.27	63.53
Italy	330.79	472.74	Egypt	495.96	91.63
Netherlands	684.78	978.65	El Salvador	31.29	19.81
New Zealand	627.63	896.97	Estonia	144.41	204.60
Norway	905.06	1 293.46	India	64.77	104.74
Poland	15.53	22.20	Indonesia	690.87	1 351.61
Portugal	56.39	80.60	Israel	838.24	960.66
Slovakia	62.49	89.31	Japan	2 782.10	3 846.72
Spain	477.54	682.47	Jordan	126.99	49.23
Sweden	1 198.63	1 713.00	Korea, Rep.	494.21	398.58
Switzerland	1 604.22	2 292.66	Latvia	94.99	71.63
United			Macedonia	30.77	73.66
Kingdom	388.76	555.59	Mexico	158.45	139.48
			Morocco	261.23	108.93
			Nigeria	120.75	697.62
			Pakistan	72.95	92.86
			Peru	111.23	82.93
			Philippines	84.89	75.76
			Romania	40.75	38.58
			Russia	147.98	210.85
			Slovenia	525.24	809.77
			South Africa	844.13	676.26
			Tanzania	110.94	24.94
			Turkey	721.96	380.05
			Uganda	49.90	21.78
			Ukraine	22.68	27.39
			Uruguay	265.57	116.97
			Venezuela	907.38	1 585.36

Table 10.2   (continued)

	Pre-1968 home countries		Post-1968 home countries		
Country	EXP_{jt}	IMP_{jt}	Country	EXP_{jt}	IMP_{jt}
			Vietnam	8.84	20.36
			Zimbabwe	126.21	115.07
Average	657.13	939.13	Average	364.54	442.42
Maximum	1 957.05	2 796.89	Maximum	2 782.10	3 846.72
Minimum	15.53	22.20	Minimum	8.84	3.22
t test of dif. in mean values	2.11**	2.45**			

Notes
Estimates are in 2000 US dollars.
Calculations are based on estimated immigrant stock coefficients presented in columns
(a) and (b) of Table 9.1 and average bilateral trade values observed during the 1994–2006
period.
** denotes statistical significance at the 5 per cent level.

*Table 10.3   Correlations between estimated per-immigrant effects and
various country classifications*

	EXP effects	IMP effects
Post-1968 home country cohort	−0.2585**	−0.2917**
US–home country SSE distance	−0.4591***	−0.437***
US–home country TSR distance	0.1867	0.243**
US–home country Cultural distance	−0.2965**	−0.2491**
OECD member	0.5021***	0.4894***

Note: ** and *** denote statistical significance at the 5 per cent and 10 per cent levels,
respectively.

That pre-1968 home countries have, on average, larger estimated
per-immigrant effects is also indicated in Table 10.3. The correlation coefficients between being classified as a post-1968 home country and the
average per-immigrant export and import effects are −0.259 and −0.292,
respectively. Similarly, home countries that are members of the OECD
also have, again on average, larger estimated per-immigrant effects. Here,
the correlation coefficients with respect to the export and import effects
are 0.502 and 0.489. T-tests of the correlation coefficients indicate that,
even with small sample sizes, the values are significant from zero.[1] Across

all home countries, those that are more culturally distant from the US tend to have smaller per-immigrant effects. The negative relationships between per-immigrant effects and *SSE* distance and the positive effects for *TSR* distance (although significant only with respect to the import effect) confirm that *SSE* distance acts to inhibit trade more than *TSR* distance. Given the relationship between *SSE* distance and relative economic and social development (as discussed in Chapter 6), such distance would correlate with the absence of or poor quality of trade-facilitating infrastructure, leading to higher trade-related transaction costs and greater opportunities for immigrants to influence trade. In other words, because of the high correlation coefficient between the cultural distance variable and the dummy variable which identifies trading partners as being categorized as post-1968 home countries, and because the pre-1968 and post-1968 home country cohorts differ significantly with respect to the presence and quality of infrastructure, the measure of cultural distance captures, albeit imperfectly, the influences of inferior/lacking hard and soft infrastructure as well as product- and market-related information asymmetries.

10.2   DISAGGREGATED TRADE DATA: TRADE-INTENSIFICATION AND TRADE-INITIATION

The results presented thus far indicate that immigrants exert positive influences on aggregate levels of trade and that these influences vary across home country cohorts and according to immigrant characteristics. This leads to additional questions that include whether the positive influence of immigrants also varies across product types, and whether the pro-trade influences exerted by immigrants are limited to the enhancement of trade when it is already taking place, or whether it extends to the creation of trade when, initially, trade flows are zero or at a sufficiently low level as to not be reflected in the data.

Given the channels through which immigrants are thought to influence trade flows, it seems reasonable to expect that variation in immigrants' influences will exist across product classifications. For example, there may be greater opportunities for immigrants to affect trade in differentiated products – through their preferences or their abilities to reduce associated transaction costs – relative to homogeneous goods. The same is likely to be the case for trade in cultural products relative to non-cultural products and across manufactured products and non-manufactured products or industrial sector sub-classifications. As trade data becomes more disaggregated, it is also more likely that the data which represent particular product groups or industry classifications will contain 'zero' values that reflect that either no trade is taking place between the US and a particular home country or that, if trade is occurring, it is at a sufficiently low level as to appear as a zero value in the trade data. Comparison of estimated immigrant–trade effects across product classifications provides information relating to the channels through which immigrants influence the intensity of trade. Examining the influence of immigrants using data that contain zero trade values offers an indication of the influence of immigrants on the initiation of trade flows.

Beginning with the first question of whether, and to what extent, variation is found across product classifications, we estimate equation (8.5) separately using data for US trade in manufactured products (that is, 1-digit SITC sectors 5 to 9 taken collectively) and non-manufactured products (SITC sectors 0 to 4) as the dependent variables. Table 10.4 presents the corresponding estimation results. In all instances, the estimated influences of immigrants are positive and significant; however, the proportional influences of immigrants on trade in manufactured products are greater in magnitude than the corresponding influences of immigrants on trade in non-manufactured products. Specifically, in response to an assumed 10 per cent increase in the immigrant stock variable, US exports and imports of manufactured products are estimated to increase by 2.68 per cent and 2.91 per cent, respectively. The same increase in the immigrant stock would be expected to increase exports of non-manufactured products by 0.73 per cent and imports of such products by 1.4 per cent. Revisiting the descriptive statistics presented in Table 8.4 reveals that US trade in manufactures is considerably greater than trade in non-manufactures. Thus, in addition to having larger proportional effects, immigrants' absolute effects (evaluated at the overall sample mean) are greater for manufactured products than for non-manufactured products.

Given the breadth of products across the manufactured or non-manufactured product groupings, the finding of proportional and absolute variation in immigrants' pro-trade influences is not particularly informative. It does suggest, however, that at higher levels of disaggregation the trade data may reveal greater variation in terms of immigrants' influences. To explore this possibility, we again estimate equation (8.5) while using the export and import series for each of the 1-digit SITC sectors in turn. Columns (a) and (b) of Table 10.5 summarize the resulting estimates of immigrants' trade-intensification effects. Focusing first on the sectors identified as SITC-0 to SITC-4 (that is, the non-manufactured product sectors) and comparing the magnitudes of the immigrant stock coefficients, we see striking variation.

It is important to note that because of the parameter η, the resulting coefficients are not true elasticities. However, because values of η relative

Table 10.4   *Variation across manufactures/non-manufactures product classifications*

Dep. Var.:	ln *MANU* EXP_{jt}	ln *Non-MANU* EXP_{jt}	ln *MANU* IMP_{jt}	ln *Non-MANU* IMP_{jt}
Expl. Var.:	(a)	(b)	(c)	(d)
ln IM_{jt}	−0.2677***	0.0726***	0.2909***	0.14***
	(0.019)	(0.0211)	(0.0162)	(0.0208)
$CDIST_j$	−0.6395***	−0.2595***	−0.108***	−0.6493***
	(0.0326)	(0.0459)	(0.0284)	(0.0456)
ln $GDIST_j$	−0.5779***	−0.8233***	−0.5472***	−0.9042***
	(0.0435)	(0.0401)	(0.0363)	(0.0387)
ln GDP_{jt}	1.1358***	0.8132***	1.1872***	1.0293***
	(0.0385)	(0.0293)	(0.031)	(0.04)
Lagged Δ	−0.0037	−0.0227	−0.0138	−0.0116
dep. var.	(0.0119)	(0.0237)	(0.0189)	(0.0284)
$\Delta\ln XRATE_{jt}$	−0.0389	−0.1538**	−0.0939	−0.1149
	(0.0616)	(0.0754)	(0.0579)	(0.0877)
$OPEN_{jt}$	0.0046***	0.0015**	0.0103***	0.0002
	(0.0005)	(0.0007)	(0.0005)	(0.0007)
ln POP_{jt}	−0.099***	0.1872***	0.0386**	0.0305
	(0.0226)	(0.0259)	(0.0172)	(0.0217)
ln REM_{jt}	0.2632***	0.1324***	0.1521***	0.3069***
	(0.0346)	(0.0216)	(0.0283)	(0.0335)
$OPEC_j$	0.3446***	0.4259	−0.0155	3.0295***
	(0.0643)	(0.2984)	(0.1263)	(0.071)
RTA_{jt}	0.6734***	0.8265***	0.8239***	1.019***
	(0.0447)	(0.0425)	(0.0323)	(0.0555)
$SEAPORT_j$	0.285***	1.2557***	0.1386***	1.6049***
	(0.046)	(0.0726)	(0.0527)	(0.0727)
Constant	−6.1924***	−0.8287	−10.0569***	−2.9832**
	(1.3162)	(0.9149)	(1.105)	(1.308)
N	858	858	858	858
Adjusted R²	0.893	0.7327	0.8703	0.7755
Wald chi² statistic	31 858***	8 164***	38 444***	10 553***
Log-likelihood statistic	−639.34	−831.03	−663.13	−944.96

Notes: See Table 10.1.

Table 10.5 Summary of immigrants' trade-intensification and trade-initiation effects, 1-digit SITC sectors

1-digit SITC sector	Intensification ln EXP_{jt} (a)	Intensification ln IMP_{jt} (b)	Initiation ln EXP_{jt} (c)	Initiation ln IMP_{jt} (d)
0: Food and live animals	1.5392*** (0.1848)	0.378** (0.1566)	0.03*** (0.0036)	0.042** (0.0174)
1: Beverages and tobacco	0.7824*** (0.0893)	0.7396*** (0.113)	8.2E-13*** (9.4E-14)	1.7E-08*** (2.5E-09)
2: Crude materials, inedible, except fuels	0.0954 (0.0633)	−0.0478 (0.0731)	--- (0.58%)	--- (0.93%)
3: Mineral fuels, lubricants and related materials	0.2109** (0.1005)	0.2867* (0.1567)	1.1E-10** (5.1E-11)	3.6E-06* (1.9E-06)
4: Animal and vegetable oils, fats and waxes	0.2696*** (0.0929)	1.0049*** (0.1429)	5.3E-13*** (1.8E-13)	0.0001*** (1.1E-05)
5: Chemicals and related products, n.e.s.	0.1159*** (0.0444)	0.2202*** (0.058)	--- (0.12%)	--- (0.58%)
6: Manufactured goods classified chiefly by material	0.2848*** (0.0337)	0.2133*** (0.0655)	--- (0%)	--- (0.12%)
7: Machinery and transport equipment	0.1648*** (0.0287)	0.4663*** (0.0675)	--- (0%)	--- (0.47%)
8: Miscellaneous manufactured articles	0.3518*** (0.0305)	0.6538*** (0.0563)	--- (0%)	--- (0%)
9: Commodities and transactions, n.e.c.	0.4292*** (0.0503)	0.2919*** (0.0383)	--- (0.23%)	--- (0%)

Notes: See Table 10.1.

to the mean values of corresponding dependent variable measures are small, we heuristically interpret the coefficients as elasticities. Overall, coefficient estimates range from 0 for both exports and imports of 'crude materials, inedible, except fuels' (SITC-2) to 1.539 for exports of 'food and live animals' (SITC-0) and 1.005 for imports of 'animal and vegetable oils, fats and waxes' (SITC-4). This is a considerably broader range than is estimated for the 1-digit sectors that comprise the broader manufacturing sector (SITC-5 to SITC-9). The estimated proportional immigrant effects on exports range from 0.116 for 'chemicals and related products, n.e.s.' (SITC-5) to 0.429 for 'commodities and transactions, n.e.c.' (SITC-9) while for imports the range is from 0.263 for 'manufactured goods, classified chiefly by material' (SITC-6) to 0.654 for 'miscellaneous manufactured articles' (SITC-8).

It may be the case that the sectors for which the estimated proportional immigrant effects are of greater magnitude consist of a higher proportion of differentiated products. If so, then information would be likely to be more asymmetric, resulting in more abundant opportunities for immigrants to exert pro-trade influences. Employing trade data that have been produced using the Rauch product classifications allows for the estimation of immigrant–trade effects for differentiated products and two categories of homogeneous products: those for which reference-prices are available (that is, reference-priced products) and those which are traded on organized exchanges (that is, organized-exchange products). Estimation of equation (8.5) for each of these product classifications, using US exports and imports separately, produces the coefficients reported in Table 10.6.

Comparison of the coefficients on the immigrant stock variables across the trade measures reveals a stronger influence of immigrants on trade in differentiated products than is reported for either of the two homogeneous product classifications. Assuming a 10 per cent increase in the immigrant stock variable, as before, the estimated increase in US exports of differentiated products is 2.84 per cent and the expected increase in imports is equal to 3.66 per cent. The proportional influence of immigrants on trade in products that are traded on organized exchanges is greater than that which is estimated for products that have reference prices. This ordering is to be expected since product differentiation would correspond with greater information asymmetries which, in turn, provide immigrants with greater opportunities to exert pro-trade influences.

To address the relationship between product differentiation and immigrants' influences more specifically, we employ data for a set of product classifications that are likely to be generally representative of differentiated products. Columns (a) and (b) of Table 10.7 summarize the trade-intensification effects of immigrants on trade in cultural products.[2] Due

Table 10.6 Variation across homogeneous/differentiated product classifications

Dep. Var.:	ln ORG. EXCH. EXP$_{jt}$ (a)	ln REF. PRICED EXP$_{jt}$ (b)	ln DIFF. EXP$_{jt}$ (c)	ln ORG. EXCH. IMP$_{jt}$ (d)	ln REF. PRICED IMP$_{jt}$ (e)	ln DIFF. IMP$_{jt}$ (f)
Expl. Var.:						
ln IM$_{jt}$	0.2978***	0.1014***	0.2838***	0.176***	0.0798***	0.3659***
	(0.034)	(0.0253)	(0.0168)	(0.0363)	(0.0242)	(0.0153)
CDIST$_j$	−0.1197*	−0.6849***	−0.6587***	−0.6329***	−0.0839*	−0.0441
	(0.0667)	(0.0435)	(0.0275)	(0.1019)	(0.048)	(0.0291)
ln GDIST$_j$	−0.6123***	−0.8446***	−0.6205***	−0.8523***	−0.8497***	−0.5214***
	(0.06)	(0.0545)	(0.0369)	(0.0532)	(0.0477)	(0.031)
ln GDP$_{jt}$	1.2396***	1.1751***	1.0741***	1.4158***	1.3162***	1.1269***
	(0.0531)	(0.0453)	(0.0328)	(0.0992)	(0.053)	(0.0369)
Lagged Δ dep. var.	0.0746**	0.0041	0.0036	0.038	−0.0007	−0.0137
	(0.0318)	(0.021)	(0.0123)	(0.0435)	(0.0179)	(0.016)
ΔlnXRATE$_{jt}$	−0.0057	−0.0038	−0.0337	−0.692***	−0.3598***	−0.1219*
	(0.1398)	(0.0853)	(0.0489)	(0.1581)	(0.0955)	(0.0711)
OPEN$_{jt}$	0.0016	0.0074***	0.0031***	0.0029**	0.0109***	0.0083***
	(0.0012)	(0.0006)	(0.0005)	(0.0015)	(0.0009)	(0.0005)
ln POP$_{jt}$	0.0509	0.1337***	0.1271***	0.1424**	0.2048***	−0.023
	(0.0444)	(0.0298)	(0.0223)	(0.0575)	(0.0328)	(0.018)
ln REM$_{jt}$	0.2451***	0.3034***	0.2098***	0.528***	−0.0404	0.0695**
	(0.0422)	(0.04)	(0.0293)	(0.0829)	(0.0445)	(0.0312)

167

Table 10.6 (continued)

Dep. Var.:	ln ORG. EXCH. EXP_jt (a)	ln REF. PRICED EXP_jt (b)	ln DIFF. EXP_jt (c)	ln ORG. EXCH. IMP_jt (d)	ln REF. PRICED IMP_jt (e)	ln DIFF. IMP_jt (f)
Expl. Var.:						
$OPEC_j$	0.929***	−0.0358	0.2613***	3.5354***	1.9603***	−0.1301
	(0.1515)	(0.08)	(0.0584)	(0.1212)	(0.1155)	(0.1491)
RTA_{jt}	0.5704***	1.0217***	0.7792***	0.5277***	0.6079***	0.8732***
	(0.0652)	(0.0581)	(0.0411)	(0.1074)	(0.0633)	(0.0394)
$SEAPORT_j$	1.2881***	0.9631***	0.123***	1.5356***	0.1845***	0.1565***
	(0.1597)	(0.0562)	(0.0351)	(0.1578)	(0.0701)	(0.0463)
Constant	−15.6316***	−9.9127***	−3.7063***	−20.0912***	−4.9829***	−8.3679***
	(1.7133)	(1.5955)	(1.1414)	(3.1401)	(1.747)	(1.1851)
N	858	858	858	858	858	858
Adjusted R^2	0.6266	0.8008	0.8947	0.5581	0.7733	0.8509
Wald chi^2 statistic	5476***	14459***	47646***	6715***	9332***	34024***
Log-likelihood statistic	−1,282.99	−915	−582.73	−1,502.06	−984.49	−748.93

Notes: See Table 10.1.

Table 10.7 Summary of immigrants' trade-intensification and trade-initiation effects, cultural products classifications

	Intensification ln EXP_{jt} (a)	Intensification ln IMP_{jt} (b)	Initiation ln EXP_{jt} (c)	Initiation ln IMP_{jt} (d)
Core cultural products	0.1128** (0.0474)	0.0893 (0.0752)	--- (0%)	--- (0.67%)
Cultural heritage products	0.6262*** (0.2013)	0.4366*** (0.1444)	0.0065*** (0.0021)	2.0E-06*** (6.5E-07)
Printed matter	−0.0358 (0.0509)	0.4224*** (0.1149)	--- (0%)	2.4E-09*** (6.5E-10)
Music and the performing arts	0.2657*** (0.0974)	0.4252** (0.1841)	1.5E-12*** (5.4E-13)	0.0019** (0.0008)
Visual arts	0.7871*** (0.1257)	0.1472 (0.1011)	1.4E-07*** (2.2E-08)	8.1E-14 (5.5E-14)
Audio and audiovisual media	1.1799*** (0.1586)	0.162 (0.2125)	0.0002*** (2.4E-05)	0.004 (0.0053)
Related cultural products	0.1943*** (0.0473)	0.3196*** (0.1048)	--- (0%)	1.9E-12*** (6.2E-13)
Music	0.3355*** (0.0688)	0.2516* (0.1405)	--- (0.51%)	2.7E-06* (1.5E-06)

Table 10.7 (continued)

	Intensification ln EXP_{jt} (a)	Intensification ln IMP_{jt} (b)	Initiation ln EXP_{jt} (c)	Initiation ln IMP_{jt} (d)
Cinema and photography	0.086	0.4502**	---- (0.84%)	0.0011**
	(0.0761)	(0.198)	----	(0.0005)
Television and radio	0.1911***	0.7607***	---- (0.34%)	0.0003***
	(0.0615)	(0.1812)	----	(0.0001)
New media	0.1852***	0.5827***	7.6E-12***	0.0025***
	(0.0691)	(0.2046)	(1.4E-12)	(0.0009)
Cultural products, total	0.1783***	0.1417*	---- (0%)	---- (0.67%)
	(0.0445)	(0.0731)	----	----
Non-cultural products, total	0.0843**	0.1789***	---- (0%)	---- (0%)
	(0.0362)	(0.0453)	----	----

Notes: See Table 10.1.

170

to a lack of data, only 54 of the 66 trading partners listed in Chapter 5 are included in our analysis of trade in cultural products and the data span only the period from 1994 to 2004.[3]

A positive link is reported between immigration and trade in both cultural products and non-cultural products; however, for imports, the estimated proportional influence is greater for non-cultural products. Trade in cultural products is quite limited, equal to roughly 4 per cent of all trade. This means that the absolute influences of immigrants on trade in cultural products are quite small relative to their influences on non-cultural products. What is of importance and can be gleaned from the estimated coefficients is that variation exists across product sub-classifications and that often the corresponding coefficient estimates are quite large relative to those commonly reported in studies that consider the influence of immigrants on aggregate trade flows. (Tables 3.1 and 3.2 summarize these estimated effects.) Here, we see that the estimated effects of a 1 per cent increase in the immigrant stock on non-cultural exports and imports are equal to 0.84 per cent and 1.79 per cent, respectively. In all instances where the estimated immigrant effects on trade in a cultural product category are significantly different from zero, the magnitude of the effect exceeds the effect reported on trade in non-cultural products. This suggests that, predicated on the notion that cultural products are more highly differentiated than non-cultural products, immigrants exert stronger proportional influences on trade in differentiation goods. This is again consistent with the assertion that immigrants exert pro-trade influences through their preferences for home country products, which may be quite dissimilar to host country variants, and/or by reducing trade-related transaction costs which would be expected to be higher if goods are differentiated than if they are homogeneous.

As is the case for manufactured and non-manufactured products, there are no zero values for the dependent variables when the Rauch product classifications are employed. Accordingly, in both instances, the feasible generalized least squares technique has been used to estimate the reported coefficients. Thus, the resulting coefficients cannot be decomposed into trade-initiation and intensification effects. Dependent variable series that contain a high frequency of zero values can also be thought of as being censored at a lower bound value of zero. Under such conditions, the Tobit estimation procedure is appropriate. We follow Ranjan and Tobias (2005), Eaton and Tamura (1994) and Head and Ries (1998) and employ the Tobit estimation procedure to estimate equation (8.5), when possible, using the 1-digit SITC-level trade data. As mentioned at the outset of this chapter, a unique feature of the Tobit estimation procedure is that it generates coefficient estimates that can be decomposed using the procedure developed by

McDonald and Moffitt (1980) into trade-intensification effects and trade-initiation effects. Simply stated, trade-intensification effects are estimates of the change in the dependent variable series given a small change in the immigrant stock variable if trade is already taking place. Trade-initiation effects represent the change, in response to a change in the immigrant stock variable, in the likelihood that the dependent variable will take a value greater than its lower bound value of zero.

Returning to columns (c) and (d) in Tables 10.6 and 10.7, trade-initiation effects are reported for all dependent variable series for which there are sufficient zero trade values as to permit estimation of such effects. For all other dependent variable series, the proportions of dependent variables that were equal to zero are noted parenthetically. The trade-initiation effects of immigrants on 1-digit SITC-level trade values (SITC-0, 1, 3 and 4) are positive and significantly different from zero for both US exports and imports. The marginal effects represent the estimated changes in the probabilities that the dependent variable series takes values greater than zero given small increases in the immigrant stock values. As these are marginal effects, we focus on the signs of the effects more than on the magnitudes. The estimated trade-initiation effects reported for cultural products indicate that immigrants' effects are positive and significant in nearly all instances where an effect can be estimated. This indicates that immigrants not only enhance trade when it is already taking place (that is, trade-intensification) but also act to create trade when, initially, no trade is occurring or, if trade is taking place, is at a level so low as to not be reflected in the trade data (that is, trade-initiation).

10.3   APPENDIX 10.A: CORE AND RELATED CULTURAL GOODS CLASSIFICATIONS[4]

I.   Core Cultural Goods

- Cultural heritage – Collections and collectors pieces (9705); antiques of an age exceeding 100 years (9706).
- Printed matter – Printed reading books, brochures, leaflets, etc. (4901); children's picture, drawing and coloring books (4903); newspapers, journals and periodicals, whether or not illustrated or containing advertising material (4902); music, printed or in manuscript, whether or not bound or illustrated (4904); maps and hydrographic or similar charts, including atlases, wall maps (4905); postcards, printed or illustrated, and printed greeting cards (4909); calendars of any kind, printed, including calendar blocks (4910); pictures,

designs and photographs (491191); used postage/revenue stamps and the like/unused not of current/new issue (9704).

- Music and the performing arts – Gramophone records (852410); discs for laser reading systems for reproducing sound only (852432); magnetic tape recorded (excluding 852440) of a width not greater than 4 millimeters (852451); magnetic tape recorded (excluding 852440) of widths of 4 millimeters to 6.5 millimeters (852452); magnetic tape recorded (excluding 852440) of a width greater than 6.5 millimeters (852453); other recorded media for sound (852499).
- Visual arts – Paintings, drawings, pastels, collages, etc (hand-made) (9701); original engravings, prints and lithographs (9702); original sculptures and statuary, in any material (9703); statuettes and other ornamental articles (392640); statuettes and other ornaments, of wood (442010); statuettes and other ornamental ceramic articles (6913); statuettes and other ornaments, of base metal plated with precious metal (830621); other statuettes and other ornaments, of base metal (830629); worked ivory, bone, tortoiseshell, horn, antlers, coral, mother-of-pearl and other animal carving material, and articles of these materials (including articles obtained by moulding) (9601).
- Audio and audiovisual media – Photographic plates and film, exposed and developed, other than cinematographic film, other than for offset reproduction and microfilms (370590); cinematograph film, exposed and developed without incorporated sound track (3706); videogames used with a television receiver (940510).

II. Related Cultural Goods

- Music – Musical instruments, parts and access of such articles (92); electronic sound reproducing equipment, non-recording (8519); electronic sound recording equipment (8520); video recording and reproducing apparatus (8521); prepared unrecorded sound recording media (8523).
- Cinema and photography – Photographic cameras (except cine), accessories (9006); cinematographic cameras and projectors (9007); image projectors, photographic enlargers and reducers (9008); equipment for photographic laboratories, not elsewhere specified (9010); photographic plate, film, not rolls, exposed, paper (3701); photographic film, rolls, unexposed, not paper (3702); photographic paper, board, etc., sensitized, unexposed (3703); photographic plate, film, paper, exposed, undeveloped (3704); photographic plates and

film, exposed and developed, other than cinematographic film for offset reproduction (370510); microfilms (370520).

● Television and radio – Television receivers, video monitors, projectors (8528); radio, radio-telephony receivers (8527).

● New media – Magnetic tapes for reproducing phenomena other than sound or image (852440); recorded discs for laser reading systems for reproducing phenomena other than sound or image (852431); other recorded disks for laser reading systems (852439); other recorded media for reproducing phenomena other than sound or image, not elsewhere specified (852491).

10.4   APPENDIX 10.B: COUNTRY LISTING

Pre-1968 home countries: Australia, Austria, Belgium, Canada, Czech Republic, Denmark, Finland, France, Germany, Hungary, Iceland, Ireland, Italy, Netherlands, New Zealand, Norway, Poland, Portugal, Spain, Sweden, Switzerland, United Kingdom.

Post-1968 home countries: Albania, Argentina, Bangladesh, Brazil, Bulgaria, Chile, China, Colombia, Dominican Republic, Egypt, El Salvador, India, Indonesia, Israel, Japan, Jordan, Korea (Republic of), Mexico, Morocco, Nigeria, Pakistan, Peru, Philippines, Romania, South Africa, Tanzania, Turkey, Uganda, Uruguay, Venezuela, Vietnam, Zimbabwe.

NOTES

1. The t-statistic to determine the statistical significance of the correlation coefficient, ρ, is given as

$$t_\rho = \frac{\rho\sqrt{\eta - 2}}{\sqrt{1 - \rho^2}}.$$

2. Descriptions of core and related cultural products classifications are provided in Appendix 10.A.
3. A listing of the nations for which trade in cultural products is available is provided in Appendix 10.B.
4. Source: UN (2005). HS96 product codes in parentheses.

PART IV

Implications and opportunities

The construction and implementation of public policies that secure socially-optimal outcomes, and thus which maximize social welfare, may be impeded by political expediency, the lobbying efforts of special interest groups, or if public opinion is at odds with proposed policy changes. It would be difficult, if not impossible, to offer a detailed prescription for US immigration policy that circumvents these limitations; however, while these limitations are real and cannot be ignored when policy is formulated, they are also, quite often, issue- and time-specific. Rather than assume away the difficulties which are intrinsic to the policymaking process, we follow an alternative tack by acknowledging these difficulties and offering broad suggestions for potential changes in US immigration policy. We begin this part by discussing risk-averse preferences for immigration and the related implications for the optimal level of the annual immigrant inflow to the US. This is followed by a summary of the econometric results that are presented in Chapters 9 and 10 and, finally, by general recommendations that relate to the composition of immigrant inflows.

11. Lessons for US immigration policy

In Chapter 1 we stressed that immigrants' pro-trade influences are welfare-enhancing. The benefits of immigration include increased domestic output that results when immigrants fill labor market vacancies, increased overall employment as immigrants are more likely to start businesses, and enhanced competitiveness of domestic firms that results from the immigration of highly-skilled individuals. Aside from labor market-related benefits, immigrants add cultural diversity and, through connections to their home countries, act as an arm of US foreign policy. While viewed in a positive light by many, added cultural diversity is seen by some as a cost of immigration. Similarly, while immigrants offer benefits to the labor market they may also generate adverse earnings and employment effects for competing domestic workers. Other criticisms include the argument that immigrants constitute a net tax burden to the native-born and may even represent a national security threat; however, as mentioned earlier, the review of opinion poll data conducted by Scheve and Slaughter (2001) found that worries over the labor market effects of immigrants were the primary concern underlying opposition to immigration.

Focusing on the related labor market consequences of immigration, the winners include the owners of factors of production other than domestic labor that is in competition with immigrant labor. These individuals gain to the extent that the arrival of immigrants makes other factors more productive. Also, if immigrants are unskilled or semi-skilled, the middle and upper classes of the host country gain if they consume the services of unskilled labor. The list of those who lose from immigration includes the host country's resident wage-earning population. Within this population, the distribution of losses depends on the skill composition of immigrant inflows. While a high number of skilled immigrants arrive in the US each year, the change in immigrant source countries/regions that resulted from passage of the Immigration Act of 1965 represents a general decline in the skill sets possessed by immigrant arrivals. Due to fewer immigrants having arrived from relatively more prosperous northern and western Europe and an increase in the inflow from Asia and Latin America and the Caribbean Basin, more recent immigrants differ considerably from the native-born population in terms of basic skills. In 2003, for example, a third of all immigrants in the US had completed fewer than 12 years of education. The corresponding value for the native population was 13 per cent (Hanson, 2005).

Perhaps coming as a surprise when one considers opposition to immigration on the basis of adverse labor market effects, the estimated wage, earnings and unemployment effects of immigration are, generally speaking, rather minor. For example, illustrating the increased competition faced by low- or semi-skilled native-born workers, Borjas (2003) estimated that between 1980 and 2000 immigration reduced wages for native-born high school dropouts by as much as 9 per cent. This constitutes an average annual decrease of less than one-half of 1 per cent. Altonji and Card (1991) examine the effects of immigration on wages in US cities between 1970 and 1980. The authors report that a 1 per cent increase in the labor force due to immigration decreases the earnings of low-skilled domestic labor by 1.2 per cent. Card (2001), examining earnings of workers in US cities during the 1985–90 period, reports a smaller effect – a 1 per cent increase in the labor force corresponds with a 0.15 per cent decline in earnings. Borjas et al. (1997) estimate that 1 per cent increases in the labor force increased wages, annually, during the 1960s and 1970s by 0.59 per cent and 0.07 per cent, respectively. During the 1980s, a like increase was estimated to lower wages by 0.01 per cent.

Smith and Edmonston (1997) note that the large size of the US economy and its population relative to the annual inflow of immigrants makes it very unlikely that immigration has pronounced effects on either relative earnings or GDP per capita. More specifically, the US labor supply increased during the 1980s by about 2 to 4 per cent as a result of immigration. Based on results in the literature relating to labor demand, the corresponding wage effect of immigrants was a decline in wages of competing native-born workers of about 1 to 2 per cent. The wages of non-competing native-born workers would rise, and all workers (those who compete with immigrants and those who do not alike) were likely to gain as consumers. Often, immigration is reported to correspond with decreased unemployment while other studies report that immigration is positively related to unemployment. Thus, it appears that labor demand often keeps pace with increases in labor supply that are caused by immigration. As a result, the typical native-born worker is not very likely to experience an immigration-induced adverse labor market outcome and when they do realize such an outcome, it may be less harmful than many would anticipate.

Scheve and Slaughter (2001) found that opposition to immigration is inversely related to respondents' levels of education and that this corresponds with a general skepticism regarding globalization. The authors also make light of the fact that the observed labor market effects of immigrants are simply too weak to explain the sustained opposition to immigration. This is important, of course, if public policy is formulated with the maximization of social welfare in mind. The results of public opinion polls, however, consistently indicate that a large share of the population is skeptical of the net benefits of trade and that only a small minority of poll respondents favor increasing immigrant inflows, with respondents often expressing concern regarding the associated labor market effects. This places policymakers in a difficult position as they may be held accountable by the public if they pursue policy reforms that, while aimed to increase social welfare, are perceived by voters as welfare-reducing. Scheve and Slaughter also concluded that American public opinion is characterized in part by incomplete and inaccurate information and suggested that the public exhibits risk-averse preferences with respect to both immigration and trade. A review of more recent polls shows that American public opinion on these two issues has not changed fundamentally. Thus, the public appears to overstate the costs of immigration while understating its benefits. As risk aversion is rooted in loss aversion, how the public views associated benefits and costs is important and needs to be considered when formulating public policy.

11.1 PERCEIVED VS. REAL BENEFITS/COSTS AND THE INFLUENCE OF RISK-AVERSE PREFERENCES

Public opinion poll results indicate a general preference for either holding the number of immigrant arrivals constant or reducing the number of arrivals. Likewise, the public is skeptical regarding the net effects of trade. For example, a dozen Gallup polls conducted between March 2001 and June 2008 asked the question 'In your view, should immigration be kept at its present level, increased or decreased?' On average, only 14 per cent of respondents favored allowing more immigrants to enter each year, while more than 46 per cent favored decreasing the number of arrivals, and over 36 per cent favored holding the number of arrivals constant. Similarly, eight Gallup Poll surveys conducted between 2001 and 2009 asked 'What do you think foreign trade means for America? Do you see foreign trade more as an opportunity for economic growth through increased US exports or a threat to the economy from foreign imports?' Less than 45 per cent, on average, considered trade to be a threat, while barely more than 46 per cent of respondents, again on average, considered trade to be an opportunity for economic growth.

As mentioned, we see little evidence of systemic or sufficiently widespread job loss and/or wage and income decline/stagnation that would justify the extent of opposition to current levels of immigration or to increased trade that opinion polls reflect. This becomes even more evident when one considers that between 1980, the beginning of the most recent period of globalization, and 2006 there was a fourfold increase in the value of US exports (measured in 2000 dollars) from $324 billion to $1.3 trillion, and a sixfold increase in US imports (from $311 billion to $1.9 trillion). This represents a rise in trade intensity of the US – measured as the sum of US imports and exports as a share of GDP – from 12 per cent to 28 per cent (World Bank, 2009a). Coincidentally, the US foreign-born population increased from 14.1 million individuals in 1980 (6.2 per cent of the total population) to 37.5 million in 2006 (12.5 per cent) (Briggs, 2003; US Census, 2006). As these increases in the foreign-born population and trade occurred, total US employment increased from 105 million workers to 148 million workers. The labor force participation rate increased from 64 per cent of the population (aged 15 years and older) to 66 per cent, and the unemployment rate, which was 7 per cent in 1980, peaked at 10 per cent in 1982 and 1983, and was only 5 per cent in 2006. Finally, average income (measured by GDP per capita in 2000 dollars) increased from $22 568 in 1980 to $37 707 in 2006 (World Bank, 2009a).

While studies of the wage and earning effects of immigration for competing domestic workers report adverse effects that are of modest magnitudes, when viewed from a macroeconomic perspective we see that the US economy's increased exposure to international trade and increases in its foreign-born population have not coincided with large changes in aggregate employment, the unemployment rate, labor force participation or average earnings that would justify fears of detrimental labor market outcomes. This leads to two related issues. First, as mentioned, the public's perception of the benefits and costs attributable to immigration and trade do not appear to reflect the real benefits and costs. Second, the apparent divergence between perceived and real benefits and costs suggests that the public lacks correct information regarding immigrants' labor market effects and/or exhibits risk-averse preferences for immigration. Figure 11.1 illustrates expected changes in individual levels of utility (that is, their life satisfaction) given varying levels of benefits and costs. Although risk-seeking, risk-neutral and risk-averse preferences are represented, given public opinion, we largely focus the following discussion on expected changes in utility for risk-averse individuals.

The horizontal axis represents the gains and losses (that is, benefits and costs) an individual would expect to realize given an event's occurrence. The vertical axis depicts the expected change in the individual's utility conditional on a gain or a loss being realized. Here, the event is immigration to

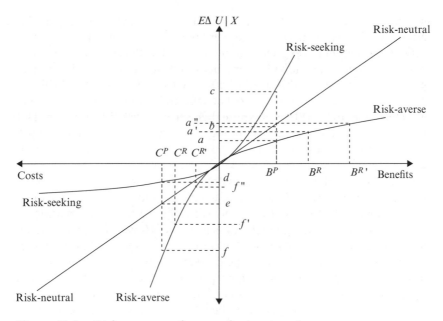

Figure 11.1 Risk-averse preferences for immigration

the US, and the individuals who are facing possible changes in their levels of utility are US residents, whether native-born or immigrants themselves. Assume, for simplicity, that the typical individual expects the benefits and costs associated with immigration to be equivalent and believes there to be an equal likelihood of either a positive or a negative outcome being experienced. In other words, the perceived costs of immigration, C^P, are equal to the perceived benefits, B^P, and it is just as likely that the individual will incur costs as it is that benefits will be received. From this description, it would seem that the individual would be neither better off nor worse off due to immigration; that is, $0.5 \times -C^P + 0.5 \times B^P = 0$. Although the expected payoff (in terms of the value of net benefits) is equal to zero, the expected payoff does not account for individuals' preferences for accepting or avoiding risk.

Under the conditions described in the preceding paragraph, if a gain of B^P were to be realized, the expected increase in utility for an individual with risk-averse preferences for immigration would be represented by the vertical distance from the origin of the cross plot to point a. If, however, a loss of C^P were to be incurred, the individual would incur an expected utility loss equal to the vertical distance from the origin to point f. Since $|-f| > a$, the expected net change in the utility of a risk-averse individual who faces an equal probability of experiencing equivalent benefits and losses is equal to $0.5 \times -f + 0.5 \times a < 0$. That is, since the individual is averse to being exposed to risk, the event would be expected to lower their utility even though the expected payoff is such that the event would not be expected to make the individual any better off or any worse off. Another way of thinking about this would be to say that, because of a dislike of risk, the individual requires expected benefits to be sufficiently greater than expected losses to be willing to expose themselves to risk. From Figure 11.1 we can also see that the corresponding expected changes for risk-neutral and risk-seeking individuals in utility are zero ($0.5 \times -e + 0.5 \times b = 0$) and positive ($0.5 \times -d + 0.5 \times c > 0$), respectively.

If an individual is risk-averse with respect to immigration then, as shown above, with $C^P = B^P$ and an equal probability of the two outcomes being realized, the expected corresponding change in utility conditional on an event (X) occurring ($E\Delta U|X$) is negative. However, because we do not see evidence on any large scale of immigration-induced labor market consequences that would justify the preference for fewer immigrant arrivals which is expressed by such high proportions of poll respondents, it seems likely that the perceived costs of immigration are greater than the real costs and/or that the perceived benefits of immigration are less than the real benefits. If we assume equal likelihoods of receiving benefits and of incurring costs but allow for the real benefits of immigration to exceed real costs (that is, $B^R > C^R$), then whether the expected change in utility conditional on immigration occurring ($E\Delta U|X'$) is positive, negative or equal to zero depends on the relative levels of benefits and costs and on how risk-averse the individual is. In Figure 11.1, this is depicted as an expected decrease in utility since $|-f'| > a'$.

If, on the other hand, benefits and costs are as noted by B^R and C^R, and the probability of receiving benefits is greater than the probability of incurring costs, then the corresponding expected change in utility ($E\Delta U|X''$) will be a smaller decrease than if the likelihoods of receiving benefits or incurring costs were equal. In other words, $E\Delta U|X < E\Delta U|X' < E\Delta U|X''$. In fact, if B^R or the probability of receiving B^R is sufficiently large relative to C^R or the probability of incurring C^R, respectively, the resulting expected change in utility would be positive. This would indicate that, even with risk-averse preferences, the expected increase in utility from the event's occurrence would be large enough to fully offset the individual's expected decrease in utility from the event. For example, Figure 11.1 indicates that if the probability of receiving benefits is at least 0.5 and benefits and costs indicated as $B^{R'} > C^{R'}$, the expected change in utility would be positive since $a'' > |-f''|$.

In the event that the public is properly informed of the real benefits and costs of immigration, preferences for reduced immigrant inflows that are largely based on worries or fears regarding associated labor market outcomes would be consistent with risk-averse preferences for immigration. However, Scheve and Slaughter (2001) conclude that the public is not well-informed on these issues. Incomplete information or information that is of poor quality may lead perceived benefits and costs of immigration to be inconsistent with real benefits and costs and/or to differences between perceived and real likelihoods of benefits being received or of costs being incurred. If the public overstates and understates the costs and benefits of immigration, respectively, then the level of immigration collectively preferred by the public falls short of the level that would maximize social welfare. The corresponding policy change would seem to be an increase in immigrant inflows; however, since policymakers may either look to public opinion for guidance or consider that voters may hold them accountable during the next election cycle, the extent to which the public is risk-averse and the degree to which information is lacking become quite important for the creation/implementation of public policy.

Before discussing policy changes in greater detail, the next section revisits the hypotheses relating to the immigrant–trade link that were presented in Chapter 3 and summarizes the findings of our analysis.

11.2 REVISITING THE IMMIGRANT–TRADE LINK HYPOTHESES

Results obtained from the estimation of equation (8.5), our baseline equation, and its variants confirm the principal hypothesis. Specifically, the values presented in columns (c) and (f) of Table 9.1 reveal a pro-trade influence of immigrants when either aggregate US exports to or imports from the immigrants' respective home countries are considered as the dependent variable. Results presented, from alternative estimation equations, in the remaining columns of Table 9.1 suggest that the immigrant–trade link is robust to changes in the econometric specification. Additionally, trade elasticities that were estimated after removing individual home countries, in turn, from the data sample are all positive and significantly different from zero. These values are reported in Table 9.2. From this, it can also be said that the estimated relationship appears robust to sample composition, at least in the sense that no single home country is influencing the overall results. Finally, while the default estimation technique employed is feasible generalized least squares (FGLS), the Tobit technique is employed when there is a large enough proportion of dependent variable values that are equal to zero (that is, that are censored at the lower bound value). The persistent finding of pro-trade influences, across FGLS and Tobit estimations, suggests that the immigrant–trade link is also robust to the estimation technique.

Trade elasticities estimated when aggregate export or import values are used as dependent variables are summarized in Table 11.1. In 16 of 17 instances, export-elasticity values are within the range of 0.05 to 0.3 that was posited by our second hypothesis. Specifically, export-elasticities range from 0.06 when the influences of refugees and asylum-seekers are estimated to 0.33 in the modified estimation equation that includes the composite immigrant stock variable and variables representing the skill composition of immigrant populations and their average lengths of stay in the US. A somewhat similar pattern is found for estimated import-elasticities. The lowest estimated value (0.09) again applies to the influences of refugees and asylum-seekers; however, import-elasticity estimates exceed the hypothesized upper bound value of 0.3 in eight of the 17 instances. In fact, in two instances the import-elasticity estimates exceed 0.4.

A summary of trade-elasticities that were generated using disaggregated measures of trade as the dependent variable series is provided in Table 11.2. Here we see much broader variation in the magnitudes of immigrant–trade links. Specifically, estimated elasticities are equal to zero for several cultural product sub-classifications and, among the 1-digit SITC industry sectors, for the 'crude material, inedible, except fuels' industry sector (SITC-2). The export-elasticity is estimated to be as high as 1.54 for 'food and live animals' (SITC-0) while the estimated import-elasticity is equal to 1.0 for 'animal and vegetable oils, fats and waxes' (SITC-4). It should also be noted that these more disperse elasticity estimates were obtained when using the Tobit technique. Restricting the comparison to only those elasticities generated when using the FGLS technique results in a more narrow range of elasticity estimates.

Table 11.2 also reports the influences of immigrants on trade for a variety of product types and industry classifications. As anticipated, and noted in our third hypothesis, a stronger proportional immigrant–trade relationship is found for differentiated products as compared to the two classes of homogeneous products considered. This is taken as confirmation of differentiated products being more likely to be characterized by asymmetric information and, thus, more amenable to being positively influenced via the channels through which immigrants are thought to affect trade flows.

The fourth, fifth and sixth hypotheses relate to immigrant-specific characteristics, namely, whether the influence of immigrants on trade diminishes as the length of time in the US increases, whether the proportional pro-trade influences of skilled immigrants are greater than those of unskilled immigrants, and if pro-trade influences vary across immigrants'

Table 11.1   Summary of estimated export- and import elasticities: Aggregate trade values used as dependent variables

Table	Immigrant Stock Measure	Notes	Export-elasticity	Import-elasticity
9.1	Immigrant stock: $\ln IM_{ijt}$	Minimum estimated value	0.2449*** (0.018)	0.2715*** (0.0116)
		Maximum estimated value	0.2835*** (0.0131)	0.3076*** (0.0192)
9.2	Immigrant stock: $\ln IM_{ijt}$ with individual home countries excluded in turn	Minimum estimated value	0.1713*** (0.0216)	0.2329*** (0.015)
		Maximum estimated value	0.2874*** (0.0169)	0.3349*** (0.016)
9.3	Immigrant stock: $\ln IM_{ijt}$ with 'skilled-to-unskilled ratio' and 'average duration of immigrants' stay' variables included in the specifications	—	0.3322*** (0.0178)	0.3607*** (0.019)
9.3	Refugees/asylees: $\ln REF_{ijt}$	—	0.0595*** (0.0074)	0.0891*** (0.0044)
	Non-refugees/asylees: $\ln NREF_{ijt}$	—	0.2692*** (0.0217)	0.3038*** (0.0205)
9.4	Immigrant stock: $\ln IM_{ijt}$ and the $\ln IM_{ijt}$ variable interacted with the $CDIST_{ij}$ variable	—	0.2508*** (0.0184)	0.2549*** (0.0127)
9.4	Immigrant stock: $\ln IM_{ijt}$ and the $\ln IM_{ijt}$ variable interacted with the SSE_{ij} and TSR_{ij} variables	—	0.2963	0.2997
10.1	Immigrant stock: $\ln IM_{ijt}$ interacted separately with the $PRE\text{-}1968_j$ and $POST\text{-}1968_j$ dummy variables: original home country *with* the $CDIST_{ij}$ variable included	Pre-1968 home country cohort	0.0755*** (0.0236)	0.1079*** (0.0218)
		Post-1968 home country cohort	0.1901*** (0.0184)	0.3575*** (0.0181)

Migration and International Trade

Table 11.1 (*continued*)

Table	Immigrant Stock Measure	Notes	Export-elasticity	Import-elasticity
10.1	Immigrant stock: ln IM_{ijt} interacted separately with the *PRE-1968$_j$* and *POST-1968$_j$* dummy variables: original home country *without* the $CDIST_{ij}$ variable Included	Pre-1968 home country cohort	0.184*** (0.0241)	0.1227*** (0.0216)
		Post-1968 home country cohort	0.2632*** (0.0158)	0.3919*** (0.0179)
10.1	Immigrant stock: ln IM_{ijt} interacted separately with the *PRE-1968$_j$* and *POST-1968$_j$* dummy variables – alternative categorization of home countries: Mexico moved to the Pre-1968 cohort	Pre-1968 home country cohort	0.2389*** (0.0201)	0.2566*** (0.0149)
		Post-1968 home country cohort	0.2795*** (0.0228)	0.4404*** (0.0193)
10.1	Immigrant stock: ln IM_{ijt} interacted separately with the *PRE-1968$_j$* and *POST-1968$_j$* dummy variables – alternative categorization of home countries: all western hemisphere countries moved to the Pre-1968 cohort	Pre-1968 home country cohort	0.1941*** (0.0213)	0.2262*** (0.0177)
		Post-1968 home country cohort	0.2697*** (0.0203)	0.4403*** (0.0174)

Notes
*** denotes statistical significance at the 1 per cent level.

entry classifications. Returning to the estimation results presented in Table 9.3, we see that for both exports and imports there is a positive and significant coefficient on the variable that estimates the skill composition of the immigrant population. That is, trade flows are positively related to the share of the home country's immigrant stock who are considered 'skilled' (as defined by the occupations listed at the time of entry to the US). The coefficients on the variables that estimate the average duration of

Table 11.2 *Summary of estimated export- and import-elasticities:*
Disaggregated trade values used as dependent variables

Table	Dependent variable	Notes	Export-elasticity	Import-elasticity
10.4	Manufactured and non-manufactured products	Manufactured products	0.2677*** (0.019)	0.2909*** (0.0162)
		Non-manufactured products	0.0726*** (0.0211)	0.14*** (0.0208)
10.5	Homogeneous (organized exchange and reference-priced) products and differentiated products	Organized exchange products	0.1978*** (0.034)	0.176*** (0.0363)
		Reference-priced products	0.1014*** (0.0253)	0.0798*** (0.0242)
		Differentiated products	0.2838*** (0.0168)	0.3659*** (0.0153)
10.6	1-digit SITC sectors (estimated trade-intensification effects listed)	0: Food and live animals	1.5392*** (0.1848)	0.378** (0.1566)
		1: Beverages and tobacco	0.7824*** (0.0893)	0.7396*** (0.113)
		2: Crude materials, inedible, except fuels	0.0954 (0.0633)	−0.0478 (0.0731)
		3: Mineral fuels, lubricants and related materials	0.2109** (0.1005)	0.2867* (0.1567)
		4: Animal and vegetable oils, fats and waxes	0.2696*** (0.0929)	1.0049*** (0.1429)
		5: Chemicals and related products, n.e.s.	0.1159*** (0.0444)	0.2202*** (0.058)
		6: Manufactured goods classified chiefly by material	0.2848*** (0.0337)	0.2133*** (0.0655)
		7: Machinery and transport equipment	0.1648*** (0.0287)	0.4663*** (0.0675)
		8: Miscellaneous manufactured articles	0.3518*** (0.0305)	0.6538*** (0.0563)
		9: Commodities and transactions, n.e.c.	0.4292*** (0.0503)	0.2919*** (0.0383)

Table 11.2   (continued)

Table	Dependent variable	Notes	Export-elasticity	Import-elasticity
10.7	Cultural products (aggregate and sub-classifications and non-cultural products (estimated trade-intensification effects listed)	Non-cultural products, total	0.0843** (0.0362)	0.1789*** (0.0453)
		Cultural products, total	0.1783*** (0.0445)	0.1417* (0.0731)
		Core cultural products	0.1128** (0.0474)	0.0893 (0.0752)
		Cultural heritage products	0.6262*** (0.2013)	0.4366*** (0.1444)
		Printed matter	−0.0358 (0.0509)	0.4224*** (0.1149)
		Music and the performing arts	0.2657*** (0.0974)	0.4252** (0.1841)
		Visual arts	0.7871*** (0.1257)	0.1472 (0.1011)
		Audio and audiovisual media	1.1799*** (0.1586)	0.162 (0.2125)
		Related cultural products	0.1943*** (0.0473)	0.3196*** (0.1048)
		Music	0.3355*** (0.0688)	0.2516* (0.1405)
		Cinema and photography	0.086 (0.0761)	0.4502** (0.198)
		Television and radio	0.1911*** (0.0615)	0.7607*** (0.1812)
		New media	0.1852*** (0.0691)	0.5827*** (0.2046)

Note:
For all estimated elasticities shown, the explanatory variable to which the estimated elasticities corresponds was the total immigrant stock: ln IM_{ijt}.
***, **, *, denote statistical significance at the 1 per cent, 5 per cent and 10 per cent levels, respectively.

immigrants' stays in the US and the corresponding squared term (included to capture non-linearity) are positive and negative as anticipated. This suggests that the pro-trade influences of immigrants diminish over time, a finding that is consistent with the estimated influences of immigrants from pre-1968 home countries being significantly weaker in magnitude as compared to the influences of immigrants from post-1968 home countries.

As noted above in the discussion of the second hypothesis (that is, the range of coefficient values), the influences of refugees and asylum-seekers on US trade with their home countries, although still positive and significant from zero, are significantly weaker as compared to the influences of other immigrants. This would correspond with refugees and asylum-seekers being likely to have more tenuous connections to social and business networks in their home countries and weaker preferences for home country products, perhaps the result of having spent time in third countries prior to their arrival in the US.

The seventh to tenth hypotheses relate to the implications of (dis)similarities between the US and immigrants' home countries for the immigrant–trade link. Chapters 4 and 5 reviewed the history of US immigration and illustrated that home countries whose citizens were afforded entry preference prior to the July 1968 implementation of the Immigration Act of 1965 are more culturally similar to the US than are the home countries of immigrants who were discouraged or restricted from entering the US prior to this policy change. The correlation coefficient between classification as a post-1968 home country and our measure of US–home country cultural distance is equal to -0.51. This essentially confirms the seventh hypothesis which posited that immigration policy can affect the extent to which immigrants influence US–home country trade if it is sufficiently influential as to affect the population's demographic composition and, hence, its cultural diversity. In the US case, the decades-long policy of preference for immigrants from countries in northern and western Europe (and to a lesser extent from southern European countries) led the US to evolve to become culturally more similar to Europe, Canada, Australia and New Zealand.

The relative influences of immigrants from home countries classified as part of the pre-1968 or post-1968 cohorts are summarized in Table 11.1. Three separate methods were employed to categorize home countries based on whether or not they were afforded preference historically by US immigration policy. These methods can be thought of as offering narrow-to-broad definitions of the pre-1968 home country cohort and, correspondingly, broad-to-narrow definitions of the post-1968 cohort. The discussion of trade-facilitating infrastructure provided in Chapter 6 indicates that, relative to the group of post-1968 home countries, pre-1968 home countries are, on average, institutionally more similar to the US. Each pair of coefficient estimates, regardless of the composition of the pre- and post-1968 groupings or the choice of aggregate exports or imports as the dependent variables, reveals significantly larger proportional pro-trade influences for immigrants from post-1968 home countries as compared to their counterparts from pre-1968 home countries. Even so, immigrants from both groupings are found to exert positive influences on US exports to and imports from their home countries.

Countries that are lacking in terms of the presence and quality of their trade-facilitating infrastructure are thought to face higher trade-related transaction costs. Similarly, home countries which are more culturally distant from the US are thought to face greater asymmetry of information relating to products and markets. This too would be expected to correspond with higher transaction costs and thus to inhibit trade flows. Given the strength of the correlation between classification as a post-1968 (or pre-1968) home country and US–home country cultural distance, as well as the relationship between classification as a post-1968 home country and poor infrastructure, it is not surprising that the US trades less with relatively more culturally-distant countries. This negative relationship between cultural distance and trade is indicated in a number of tables in Chapters 9 and 10. Results presented in Table 9.4, however, indicate that while cultural distance inhibits US–home country trade flows, immigrants act to increase trade, and their pro-trade influences are stronger if the corresponding home country is more culturally-distant.

Finally, having established a positive relationship between immigrants and US–home country trade and acknowledging that this relationship varies across the pre-1968 and post-1968 home country cohorts, absolute per-immigrant effects on US exports to and imports from each home country were estimated. These effects were produced using cohort-specific trade elasticities and observed bilateral trade flows. Thus, they are not country-specific and should be considered estimates in a strong sense of the word. That caveat in place, for all home countries the average estimated annual per-immigrant effects on US exports to and imports from their home country are $471 and $623, respectively. Across the two home country cohorts, we see significant differences in the average effects. Immigrants from pre-1968 home countries contribute an average of $657 annually to US exports and $939 to imports. By comparison, immigrants from post-1968 home countries contribute significantly less: $365 to US exports and $442 to imports.

Given the depiction of the US immigrant–trade link provided here, the general policy implications may seem fairly straightforward: immigrants increase trade and trade is welfare-enhancing, so the policy prescription would be to increase the annual number of immigrant arrivals. It is important to acknowledge, however, that public preferences as they relate to immigration need to be considered prior to applying the lessons of the empirical analysis to public policy. Given the positive influence of immigrants on US–home country trade, the following section relates these preferences, as they were described in section 11.1, to the issue of optimal policy formulation.

11.3 MAXIMIZING THE NET SOCIAL BENEFIT OF IMMIGRATION

The total benefits and costs of immigration depend largely on the level of the annual immigrant inflow, the composition of the inflow in terms of its demographic attributes, and the characteristics of the source countries. We address the maximization of the net social benefit of immigration in two steps. First, we discuss the optimal number of immigrant arrivals under the assumption that immigrants are homogeneous with respect to benefits and costs. Second, allowing for heterogeneity across immigrants with respect to their influences on trade flows we discuss the implications for the composition of immigrant inflows.

The summation of marginal private benefits and costs (MPB_i and MPC_i), at any given inflow level (denoted, here, by the subscript i), represents the total private benefits and costs (TPB_i and TPC_i). That is, $\Sigma_{i=0}^{i=1}MPB_i = TPB_i$ and $\Sigma_{i=0}^{i=1}MPC_i = TPC_i$. Subtracting costs from benefits yields the net private benefit (or cost if negative): $NPB_i = TPB_i - TPC_i = \Sigma_{i=0}^{i=1}MPB_i - \Sigma_{i=0}^{i=1}MPC_i$. (In the absence of external benefits or costs, the net private benefit, NPB, is equal to the net social benefit, NSB.) Identifying the socially optimal level of the annual immigrant inflow requires finding the level at which the marginal social benefit of immigration is equal to the corresponding marginal social cost. Several possibilities are illustrated in Figure 11.2. The total social benefit of immigration (that is, the area under the curve identified as MSB^R at a given inflow level) is illustrated as increasing at a decreasing rate, while the total social cost (that is, the area under the MSC^R curve at a given inflow level) is shown as increasing at an increasing rate. Another way of stating this is to say that it is assumed that there are diminishing net returns to immigration. Alternative depictions that involve either benefits increasing at a constant rate while costs increase at an increasing rate or that has costs increasing at a constant rate while benefits increase at a decreasing rate yield the same outcomes in terms of relative immigrant inflow levels.

Individual opinions regarding immigration are likely to be based on subjective (that is, perceived) benefits and costs. As has been noted, public opinion regarding immigration appears to be based on imperfect or incomplete information and, as a result, the perceived costs of immigration are likely to exceed the real costs and/or the perceived benefits fall short of the real benefits. Similarly, the public seems to exhibit risk-aversion with respect to immigration. Beginning with the case of a risk-neutral individual, such a person would formulate their opinion of the ideal level of immigrant inflows solely from the perceived benefits and costs. If we also ignore that immigrants exert pro-trade influences, which Gould (1994)

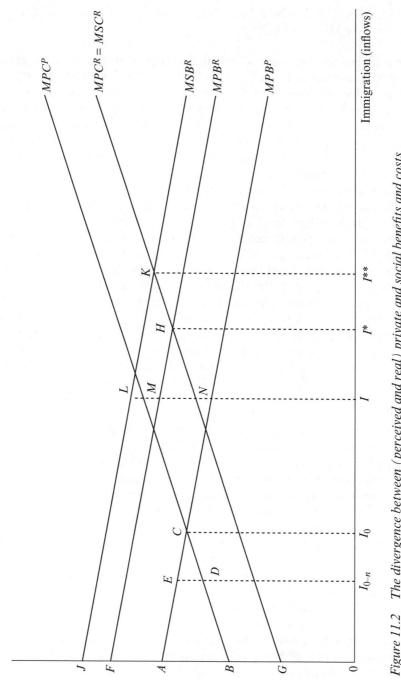

Figure 11.2   The divergence between (perceived and real) private and social benefits and costs

referred to as a positive human capital-type externality, private costs and benefits are equal to social costs and benefits, respectively. Thus, a risk-neutral individual would consider the inflow level at which the perceived marginal private cost is equal to the perceived marginal private benefit, $MPC^P = MPB^P$, as that which maximizes the net social benefit of immigration and, thus, that which is socially optimal. In Figure 11.2, this level is identified as I_0, and the corresponding value of the net social benefit is represented by the triangle ABC.

For risk-averse individuals, the preferred inflow would be less than the level identified as I_0. This is because risk-averse individuals require a side-payment of sorts, perhaps in the form of expected benefits that exceed expected costs, to accept exposure to the risk of experiencing a loss. Given the information provided, it is not possible to precisely identify a preferred inflow level for risk-averse individuals. Yet we can say that they would prefer a level that is less than that identified as I_0. An inflow level of I_{0-n} is identified in Figure 11.2 to illustrate the preference of risk-averse individuals relative to risk-neutral individuals. At this level, $MPB^P > MPC^P$. This compensates for the exposure to risk, but the $NSB(I_{0-n}) = ABDE < NSB(I_0) = ABC$. Specifically, the area identified by the triangle CDE represents the decrease in social welfare that results from risk-averse preferences for immigration. This implies that, even if perceived benefits and costs are equal to real benefits and costs and if there are no external benefits (such as those conferred by the immigrant–trade relationship), a risk-averse public will prefer fewer than the socially-optimal level of immigrant arrivals.

Again, allowing for risk-neutral preferences, if public opinion regarding immigration is based on incomplete or incorrect information and the perceived costs of immigration exceed the real costs while the perceived benefits are less than the real benefits, then an inflow equal to I_0 is lower than the level that would maximize social welfare. The inflow level noted as I^* in Figure 11.2 is that at which the real marginal private benefit of immigration is equal to the real marginal private cost ($MPB^R = MPC^R$). At this level, the $NSB(I^*) = FHG$. However, even this inflow level falls short of the socially-optimal level of immigrant inflows due to the presence of external benefits that are conferred by the immigrant–trade link. This means that the total social benefits (and, hence, the marginal social benefits) of immigration are greater than the total (and marginal) private benefits: $MSB^R > MPB^R$. In the absence of negative externalities, marginal social costs are equal to marginal private costs ($MSC^R = MPC^R$). The optimal inflow level would again be determined by equating marginal benefits and costs; however, as indicated, maximizing social welfare requires finding the immigrant inflow level at which marginal social benefits are equal to marginal social costs: $MSB^R = MSC^R$. This corresponds with the immigrant inflow level noted in Figure 11.2 as I^{**}, at which $NSB(I^{**}) = GJK$.

If policymakers fail to acknowledge the positive influences of immigrants on US trade with their home countries as an external benefit then it is quite likely that the actual immigrant inflow (I) is less than the socially-optimal level (I^{**}). Further, if policymakers base immigration policy (in terms of the level of inflows) on risk-averse preferences and/or on the imperfect information regarding benefits and costs that seems to characterize public opinion then it is also likely that $I < I^*$. That the public expresses a preference for fewer immigrant arrivals suggests that the actual inflow level is greater than I_{0-n}; thus, while we cannot accurately identify the level of I, we can say that because $I_{0-n} < I < I^* < I^{**}$, the $NSB(I_{0-n}) < NSB(I) < NSB(I^*) < NSB(I^{**})$. This would indicate that current policy (an inflow level equal to I) is a third-best outcome and that social welfare can be enhanced by increasing the level of immigrant inflows towards I^{**}. In fact, at a level of I as indicated in Figure 11.2, the social cost (in the form of forgone benefits) incurred by maintaining a sub-optimal level of immigrant arrivals is represented by the area KLN.

The external benefits of the immigrant–trade link are illustrated in Figure 11.2 as the vertical distance between the MSB^R and MPB^R curves. As has been mentioned, risk-averse individuals require compensation to accept exposure to risk. This could be in the form of expected benefits that exceed expected costs. Adding the external benefit of the immigrant–trade link to the upper-right quadrant of the cross plot in Figure 11.1 increases the expected change in an individual's utility conditional on 1) an increase in immigrant inflows and 2) individual welfare being determined, in part, by social welfare. Figure 11.3 illustrates. Consideration of these external benefits reduces the required benefit–cost differential and/or the amount by which the likelihood that benefits will be received must exceed the probability that costs will be incurred in order for a risk-averse individual to support higher immigrant inflows. In addition to the incomplete and/or incorrect information that produces a divergence between perceived and real private benefits and costs, the presence of external benefits offered by the immigrant–trade link is a form of incomplete information that policymakers can attempt to remedy.

11.4 IDENTIFYING AND ENGINEERING OPPORTUNITIES FOR WELFARE-ENHANCEMENT

Having illustrated that the level of immigrant inflows preferred by a large share of the public appears to fall short of the socially-optimal level, we

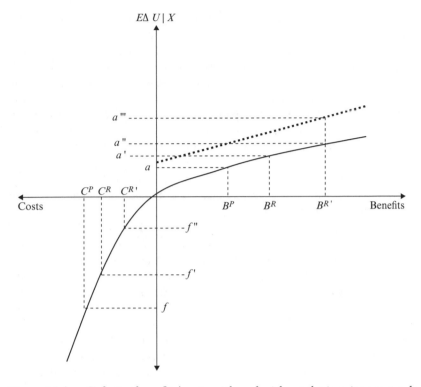

Figure 11.3:   Relative benefits/costs with and without the immigrant–trade externality

turn our attention to the issue of the ideal composition of immigrant inflows. The US experience since the end of World War II shows that immigration policy is important for a number of reasons. First, the decrease in birth rates that occurred during the twentieth century coupled with increased immigrant inflows in recent decades has led US immigrant inflows to comprise a larger share of total population growth. Thus, the composition of immigrant inflows is an important determinant of US culture. Second, immigration allows for the filling of vacancies in the US labor market. This occurs for low- or semi-skilled professions as well as for skilled trades and highly-skilled professions. Third, immigration policy is an important facet of US foreign policy. These are all important aspects of immigration that need to be considered when devising policy; however, as mentioned earlier, we forgo attempts to prescribe detailed modifications to the current immigration policy and instead limit our discussion to the offering of broad suggestions.

Given a desire to maximize the net social benefit of immigration, an important question to consider is whether there is variation in the costs attributable to immigrants across home countries or across the pre-1968 and post-1968 home country classifications. The analysis presented here focuses on the influence of immigrants on bilateral trade and, accordingly, offers no answer to this question. The discussion provided in sections 11.1 and 11.3 assumes that, in this respect, immigrants are homogeneous. While it may be that the public perceives variation in costs – for example, the costs of immigrants from post-1968 home countries may be perceived by the public, in general, to be greater than the costs of immigrants from pre-1968 home countries – additional research would need to be undertaken to determine if differences exist in terms of real costs. Lacking a basis to assume differences in real costs, we proceed by placing emphasis on relative differences in benefits.

The most prominent distinctions we have documented in terms of immigrant–trade links are that immigrants from countries that are relatively lacking in terms of trade-facilitating infrastructure and/or that are more culturally and institutionally dissimilar from the US exert stronger proportional effects on US–home country trade. Specifically, the influences of immigrants from post-1968 home countries tend to be stronger than those estimated for their counterparts from pre-1968 home countries. This is thought to reflect greater opportunities in the form of higher trade-related transaction costs faced by immigrants from post-1968 home countries. Since greater US–home country cultural distance is thought to correspond with greater product- and market-related information asymmetries, which also would increase transaction costs and afford greater opportunities for immigrants to exert pro-trade influences, increasing immigrant inflows from infrastructure-poor and/or culturally-distant countries or, more simply, from those countries in the post-1968 cohort may be desirable.

While stronger proportional trade effects are reported for immigrants from post-1968 home countries, estimated absolute per-immigrant trade effects are greater, on average, for immigrants from pre-1968 home countries. Even though there is considerable overlap in the distributions (see Table 10.2), this could be taken to indicate that immigrants from pre-1968 home countries are more influential in terms of generating US trade. It is important to remember, however, that these effects are calculated using existing trade flows and cohort-specific (rather than country-specific) trade elasticity estimates. As is shown in our estimation results, a number of factors other than immigrant stocks determine levels of bilateral trade. The fact that the US trades more with the typical pre-1968 home country as compared to the average post-1968 home country, if due to a factor(s) other than the influence of immigrants, would inflate estimated per-immigrant effects for the former group while deflating estimated effects for the latter. Thus, deriving policy recommendations on the basis of estimated absolute per-immigrant effects involves considerable risk.

While our analysis suggests that there may be greater external benefits to increased immigration from post-1968 home countries, it is not the case that immigrants from pre-1968 home countries fail to offer benefits. In fact, regardless of home country cohort, a more highly-skilled immigrant stock is estimated to exert stronger influences on US–home country trade as compared to a lower-skilled immigrant population. Thus, we would anticipate that a skilled immigrant from a pre-1968 home country may confer greater benefits than would an unskilled immigrant from a post-1968 home country. Likewise, we find that refugees and asylum-seekers exert weaker, although still positive, influences on US–home country trade flows as compared to their non-refugee/non-asylum-seeking counterparts. The skill composition of immigrant population stocks and whether or not they are refugees or asylum-seekers would matter for the immigrant–trade relationship in terms of the strength and scope of ties that the immigrants would be likely to maintain with social and business networks in their home countries. Generally speaking, skilled immigrants and immigrants who are neither refugees nor asylum-seekers would be expected to arrive in the US with more extensive connections to networks in their home countries, and this may assist in the facilitation of increased trade. Similarly, we would expect that the typical refugee or asylum-seeker might exert weaker preference effects on US imports from their home countries simply because their ties to the home country may be weaker, particularly so if they spent time in a third country after leaving their home country and prior to arrival in the US.

Before proceeding, it should be noted that when comparing the influences of individual immigrants, it may be the case that an unskilled refugee or asylum-seeker from a pre-1968 home country exerts stronger effects on US trade with their home country than does any skilled non-refugee/non-asylum-seeking immigrant from the cohort of post-1968 home countries. This certainly cannot be ruled out as a possibility; however, generally speaking, based on the empirical results presented here, we would expect that skilled immigrants who are neither refugees nor asylum-seekers and who are from countries that have been categorized as part of the post-1968 cohort would be likely to convey the greatest external benefits. The implication from this is that entry of immigrants who are described by these basic characteristics may contribute more to social welfare and, if maximization of social welfare is the goal of US policymakers, then immigration policy should be amended accordingly.

If one considers the reasons why individuals choose to migrate or, in the cases of refugees and asylum-seekers, find it necessary to leave their homelands, the policy prescription stated in the preceding paragraph may appear too strong, insensitive or, perhaps, even wrong-headed. The basis for the statement is that greater cultural and institutional differences lead to larger proportional pro-trade effects and, hence, greater benefits. This corresponds with a policy that affords entry preference based on the relative cultural and institutional dissimilarity between the US and the home country. Further, while societal differences are important for providing immigrants with opportunities to positively influence US–home country trade flows, it is also important for immigrants to have the means and the abilities to act in such a manner as to increase trade flows and, by doing so, deliver the corresponding benefits.

Having justified placing emphasis on the pro-trade influences of immigrants when setting immigration policy, it is important to note that these influences are but one of many that should be considered when formulating immigration policy. A revised US immigration policy could consider entry of refugees and asylum-seekers based solely on humanitarian grounds, absent of any embellishment of inflow numbers that results from consideration of immigrant–trade effects. Similarly, the longstanding policies of admission on the basis of family reunification and the filling of vacancies in the US labor market could also be maintained. Admission of refugees and asylum-seekers and admission based on family reunification is desirable as a matter of human decency and is advisable when one considers immigration policy as an aspect of foreign policy. Likewise, continuation of the current policy of admissions to fill vacancies in the domestic labor market is advisable on economic grounds.

Given a policy prescription of increased immigrant inflows where the relative pro-trade influences of immigrant types are considered when determining entry preference, the issue remains of how such a policy change could be implemented. It seems that there are four options that policymakers face. First, there is the default option of doing nothing. A great deal of discussion has been provided here regarding consideration of relative benefits and costs. Policymakers would not be immune to such considerations and, in the event that they perceive the costs they will be likely to incur (perhaps in the form of voter backlash) of acting to modify immigration policy to be greater than the corresponding benefits they expect to receive, leaving immigration policy unchanged may be their preferred course of action even though current policy is sub-optimal. A second related option involves amending immigration policy such that inflows are decreased and the public is appeased. This, of course, would not only fail to enhance social welfare; a movement towards a more restrictive immigration policy (in terms of fewer arrivals) would diminish social welfare.

Although it may seem that the options of maintaining current policy and of reducing immigrant inflows characterize much of the recent US policy debate regarding immigration, there are other choices facing policymakers. The two remaining options are similar. The first involves modifying policy as described in the preceding paragraphs and then explaining to the public that the change was necessary on the basis that it improves overall social welfare. The second option would be to attempt changing public opinion prior to embarking on a policy change in hopes of minimizing any related backlash. Both scenarios involve modifications to current policy wherein annual immigrant inflows are increased and entry preference is determined, in part, by the attributes of immigrants and their home countries as they relate to the immigrant–trade link. The specific mechanism by which such a policy is implemented is a detail that policymakers would need to negotiate when crafting legislation; however, a separate entry classification for 'trade-enhancing' immigrants that employs some form of points-based system to rank potential immigrants would accommodate such a policy change.

In addition to the incomplete/incorrect information held by the public with respect to the expected benefits and costs of immigration and trade, an additional challenge policymakers would face if attempting to garner support for policy reform is that the public seems to have risk-averse preferences for immigration. Recanting a lesson from recent history may be beneficial for this discussion. In the post-World War II period, efforts were undertaken by the US and other developed countries to reduce barriers to international trade that, largely, had been erected in the 1920s and 1930s. The GATT was particularly instrumental in facilitating multilateral reductions; however, in the late 1950s the pace of trade liberalization began to slow. The Kennedy administration, seeking to launch a new round of multilateral negotiations, asked Congress to pass legislation that would permit the White House to negotiate tariff reductions of up to 50 per cent. There was considerable opposition to the removal of trade barriers, particularly from organized labor. To garner the support of labor, the Kennedy administration proposed the creation of the Trade Adjustment Assistance (TAA) program. The TAA program offers a variety of benefits to workers who have lost their jobs or have seen their hours worked or wages/salaries decreased due to import competition. Nearly a half-century after its inception, the TAA program remains in place. In fact, a separate program, NAFTA-TAA, was implemented in 1994 alongside the North American Free Trade Agreement and, in 2002, TAA and NAFTA-TAA were combined and augmented with a program named Alternative TAA (and more commonly known as 'wage insurance'), which provides wage subsidies to trade-displaced workers.

Evidence of the effectiveness of these programs, in terms of aiding workers who have experienced detrimental trade-related labor market outcomes, is mixed. The effectiveness of the programs in aiding trade-displaced workers, however, is to a large degree irrelevant. The creation of the TAA program led organized labor to support the Trade Expansion Act of 1962 and this, subsequently, allowed for the Kennedy Round of GATT negotiations. In essence, the fact that workers were promised TAA benefits in the event they incurred costs due to trade was sufficient to reduce opposition to trade. This afforded the US government the opportunity to pursue welfare-enhancing trade liberalization. Thus, one could argue that the TAA program has been a success more because its implementation led to the removal of trade barriers than because of any benefits that have been provided to trade-displaced workers, simply because the benefits of trade liberalization are far-reaching while effects of imports (in terms of making workers eligible for TAA benefits) are limited.

The lesson for immigration policy is that, as part of a larger effort to alter the public's perceptions of benefits and costs, offering to provide benefits – perhaps in forms similar to those provided under the TAA framework – in the event that workers experience negative immigration-related labor market outcomes would be likely to reduce opposition to policy changes that would increase immigrant inflows. Incurring the cost of implementing and administering such a program would make sense if it is necessary to garner support for policy reform and as long as the program costs less than the external benefits garnered from the immigrant–trade link. Returning to Figure 11.2, such a program would have the effect of reducing the external benefit (shifting the MSB^R curve towards the MPB^R curve) while shifting down the perceived marginal private cost (MPC^P), real marginal private cost (MPC^R) and (its equivalent) real marginal social cost (MSC^R) curves. While this would result in an inflow level that falls short of the optimal inflow identified as I^{**}, it would represent an improvement on the current policy that delivers a level of I.

12.   Summing-up: concluding thoughts and (yet) unanswered questions

In this work, we have examined the US immigrant–trade link in considerable detail and have verified a positive influence of immigrants on US exports to and imports from their home countries. Immigrants exert pro-trade influences when trade between the US and their home countries is already occurring and also raise the likelihood that trade will occur when no trade is taking place. The former effect can be thought of as a trade-intensification effect while the latter may be described as a trade-initiation effect. Estimates of the proportional influence of immigrants on trade that were obtained when considering variation in the relationship across different measures of trade flows, home country cohorts, product types, and immigrants' attributes are consistent with expectations based on the channels by which immigrants are thought to influence trade. Taken collectively, the information presented here provides for a deeper understanding of the US immigrant–trade relationship and offers insights that may prove useful for public policy formulation.

Although the introductory chapter discusses the broad topic of globalization and the often contentious related public debate, subsequent chapters focus on the narrower topic of the US immigrant–trade link. These chapters provide a general overview of the relationship and discuss factors that are thought to affect the operability of the US immigrant–trade link and, hence, that contribute to the presence and magnitudes of pro-trade influences. A quantitative analysis of the link provides results that are evaluated with the corresponding implications for public policy in mind. This, in turn, leads to suggestions for the alteration of US immigration policy such that social welfare may be enhanced through the capture of positive external benefits that stem from the immigrant–trade link.

While developing a detailed understanding of the relationship between immigrants and trade is useful for the formulation of public policy, it is also important in a more general sense as understanding this relationship allows for a greater understanding of the broader topics of globalization and its effects. How the public and policymakers view global processes in terms of expected benefits and costs affects the formulation of public policies that govern various facets of the globalization process. Because the benefits afforded by greater global integration are sufficiently large to guarantee that many governments and international institutions will work to achieve greater integration, an informed understanding of global processes and linkages is essential. Acknowledging that the globalization process will continue still leaves the pace at which it should progress and how the related benefits and costs should be distributed as unresolved issues. Uncertainty regarding these issues often manifests in the form of anti-globalization sentiment and, at times, more vocal expressions of a backlash against globalization.

Illustrative of the extent to which disagreement exists, across and within countries, in terms of the desired pace of globalization and as to whether gains and losses are shared equitably, a recent BBC World Service poll (2008) found that one-half of all respondents believe 'economic globalization, including trade and investment' is occurring at too rapid a pace while slightly more than one-third (35 per cent) of respondents feel the process is moving too slowly.[1] Further there are stark contrasts in public opinion that largely correspond with variation in economic development across countries. On average, 57 per cent of respondents in the G-7 countries (Canada, France, Germany, Italy, Japan, the UK and the US) hold the opinion that the pace of economic globalization is too fast. That the overall mean is 50 per cent reflects that a smaller proportion of respondents, on average, in the remaining 27 countries (that are not G-7 members and, thus, are relatively lesser-developed) feels that the pace is too fast. The same poll asked respondents whether the benefits and costs resulting from 'the economic developments of the last few years' have been allocated fairly. In 27 of the 34 countries, a sizeable majority of respondents (64 per cent on average) believed that benefits and costs had not been fairly distributed.

Although it would seem unreasonable to expect the public, either across or within societies, to exhibit an overwhelming consensus on these topics, the high percentages of respondents who believe globalization is occurring too quickly and that the corresponding benefits and costs have not been equitably shared suggests a considerable lack of support for globalization in general. As we have discussed at length, individual opinions may be characterized by imperfect or incomplete information. Opinions may also reflect that individuals are risk-averse with respect to the issue of globalization. The findings presented here allow for a better understanding of the immigrant–trade link and, by doing so, may lead the public and policy-makers to more accurately quantify the benefits and costs of immigration as a facet of a more broadly-defined process of global integration.

To provide a theoretical basis for the empirical analysis, we reviewed trade theory as it relates to the expected effects of factor migration on trade flows. Whether the relationship between immigrants and trade is predicted to be one of complements or that of substitutes depends on each model's underlying assumptions. Standard factor-endowment models (that is, the Heckscher–Ohlin model and the Specific-Factors model) predict that migration and trade are substitutes; however, relaxation of certain assumptions allows models of this variety to predict a complementary relationship. Models based on New Trade Theory also suggest that migration and trade are complementary activities. The empirical literature consistently reports a positive relationship between migration and trade; however, because a positive relationship would be agnostic in terms of the direction of causality, our review of trade theory was followed with a discussion of the channels by which immigrants are thought to influence host–home country trade.

Having established a theoretical basis that supports the notion of an immigrant–trade link, the related literature was canvassed to formulate a series of hypotheses that are addressed in our analysis. While the literature provides abundant information regarding the extent to which immigrants affect trade flows and the channels through which these effects are thought to occur, a detailed explanation of the factors that enable the immigrant–trade link to be operable is lacking. Because immigrants are thought to exert pro-trade influences by reducing related transaction costs and/or through consumption preferences that are distinct from those of residents in their host country, host–home country cultural and institutional dissimilarity and the presence and quality of trade-facilitating infrastructure were considered as factors that contribute to variation in preferences or increase trade-related transaction costs and, hence, that may determine whether conditions are conducive for immigrants to exert pro-trade influences. Similarly, because immigrants would be likely to vary in their abilities to exert pro-trade influences if provided the opportunity, we also considered immigrants' attributes as potential determinants of trade flows.

A review of the history of US immigration led to the categorization of the countries included in the analysis as either pre-1968 or post-1968 home countries. The pre-1968 grouping consists of Canada, Australia, New Zealand and countries located in northern, southern and western Europe, and the post-1968 cohort is comprised of countries located elsewhere. Because entry preference was afforded, prior to the July 1968 implementation of the Immigration Act of 1965, to immigrants from pre-1968 home countries, the US evolved to be more culturally- and institutionally-akin to these countries than to the remainder of the world. Since greater cultural and institutional dissimilarity may correspond with greater variation in preferences and greater asymmetry of information regarding products and/or markets (which would lead to higher transaction costs), the notion of primacy effects and recency effects was introduced. It was assumed that because immigrants from post-1968 home countries potentially faced greater opportunities to exert pro-trade influences, their pro-trade effects (that is, the recency effect) would be proportionally stronger than those of their counterparts from pre-1968 home countries (that is, the primacy effect). Variation across the home country cohorts in terms of the existence and quality of trade-facilitating infrastructure was also examined. A lack of infrastructure or, if present, infrastructure that is of poor quality would be expected to correlate with higher trade-related transaction costs and, as with the case of asymmetric information, provide opportunities for immigrants to exert pro-trade influences.

We find that greater cultural and institutional differences correspond with larger proportional pro-trade effects and, hence, greater benefits. Yet while societal differences are important for providing immigrants with opportunities to influence trade flows positively, it is also important for immigrants to have the ability to increase trade flows and deliver the corresponding benefits. Generally speaking, the results presented here suggest that skilled immigrants who are neither refugees nor asylum-seekers and who are from post-1968 home countries are expected, on average, to convey the greatest benefits via their influences on US–home country trade flows. The implication, therefore, is that the entry of such immigrants would be expected to contribute more, on average, to US social welfare than would the entry of other immigrants.

If policymakers are influenced by public opinion, which may be based on incomplete or imperfect information, and/or are influenced by the public's seeming risk-averse preferences for immigration, then the current immigrant inflow level falls short of the socially-optimal level. Similarly, the fact that current policy does not consider the pro-trade influences of immigrants when determining entry preferences suggests that not only is the annual inflow of immigrants too low, it is also likely to include a sub-optimal mix of immigrants in terms of their countries of origin and individual characteristics. If maximization of social welfare is the goal of US policymakers, then immigration policy should be amended to allow for a larger number of immigrant arrivals and to consider immigrant–trade influences as a factor when determining entry preference. Although a movement towards a more socially-beneficial immigration policy would increase inflows and consider immigrants' pro-trade influences as a basis for entry, it is not the case that other factors should not be considered. A revised US immigration policy could include the current provisions that allow for admission on the basis of family reunification, the filling of vacancies in the domestic labor market and the entry of refugees and asylum-seekers. There are valid reasons, ranging from foreign policy considerations to economic efficiency to humanitarian concerns, to include these provisions. Consideration of immigrant–trade effects would be an additional basis that determines entry preference rather than a substitute criterion.

The US population currently consists of about 304 million individuals. It is projected that this figure will increase to 438 million by the middle of the current century (Passel and Cohn, 2008). It is also estimated that 82 per cent of this increase will be due to immigrants (57.5 per cent) and their US-born children or grandchildren (42.5 per cent). This implies that the US foreign-born population will rise from its current level of roughly 40 million (13 per cent of the total population) to slightly more than 100 million (23 per cent of the population) in fewer than five decades. Given this expected population increase, maximizing social welfare will require an immigration policy that adequately accounts for the benefits and costs of immigration. The work here attempts to provide information that is useful in this regard.

Finally, a caveat of sorts is in order. The results presented here are by no means the final word on the immigrant–trade link. Just as prior studies have offered insights into the relationship, the findings reported here offer additional information but are not intended to be taken as exhaustive. While any study may prove illuminating, no single analysis is definitive. Empirical research in economics requires numerous examinations involving different data (for example, various time periods and sample cohorts) before theoretical predictions can be confirmed or refuted. Each study offers information that contributes to a broad set of conclusions and, even when conclusions can be drawn, findings must be presented as general relationships rather than any sort of precise measurement of the relationships between variables. Thus far, a large body of literature has identified a positive statistical relationship between immigrants and host–home country trade flows. A theoretical basis is in place for this complementary relationship, and the results of studies that examine various aspects of the immigrant–trade link are consistent with the channels through which immigrants are thought to affect trade flows. Researchers continue to add to a more intricate understanding of the immigrant–trade link; however, additional study is necessary.

While the immigrant–trade literature has increased in volume in recent years, data limitations continue to hinder research efforts. Evaluation of data representing additional host countries, for example, would allow for the determination of whether the immigrant–trade link is universal or whether it is dependent on specific conditions to be operable. Somewhat similarly, prior studies have largely focused on individual host countries (or, at times, collections of host countries) and the related effects of immigrants on trade between these hosts and their respective home countries. Little has been done on the topic of emigrant–trade links. By focusing on the effects of immigrants on a host country's exports to and imports from their home countries, the resulting estimates of immigrants' pro-trade influences are treated as being common across all home countries. Evaluating the relationship from the perspective of individual home countries would provide additional information regarding the presence and relative magnitudes of immigrant–trade links.

As data for additional host and home countries become available, the scope of analysis will broaden. Likewise, examination of lengthier time periods (for which data currently are largely unavailable) will permit examination of how the immigrant–trade relationship evolves. So far, with few exceptions, prior studies have been limited to the past two or three decades. More accurate data on immigrant population stocks will yield more conclusive and more reliable results. Similarly, more complete information on immigrants' characteristics and better measures for variables that represent factors such as cultural and/or institutional dissimilarities or that reflect differences in the presence and quality of trade-facilitating infrastructure will permit future studies to offer more conclusive and more comprehensive results. This, in turn, will prove useful in terms of further informing both members of the public and the policymaking process.

NOTE

1. The poll was administered to 34528 individuals in 34 countries between October 2007 and January 2008.

References

Altonji, J.G. and D. Card (1991), 'The effect of immigration on the labor market outcomes of less-skilled natives', in J.M. Abowd and R.B. Freeman (eds), *Immigration, Trade and the Labor Market*, Chicago, IL: University of Chicago Press.

Anderson, J.E. (1979), 'A theoretical foundation for the gravity equation', *American Economic Review*, **69**, 106–16.

Anderson, J.E. and E. van Wincoop (2003), 'Gravity with gravitas: a solution to the border puzzle', *American Economic Review*, **93**, 190–92.

Bacarreza, C., G. Javier and L. Ehrlich (2006), 'The impact of migration on foreign trade: a developing country approach', MPRA paper no. 1090, accessed at http://mpra.ub.uni-muenchen.de/1090/.

Balassa, B. (1986), 'Determinants of intra-industry specialization in United States trade', *Oxford Economic Papers*, **38**, 220–33.

Baldwin, R. and P. Martin (1999), 'Two waves of globalization: superficial similarities, fundamental differences', National Bureau of Economic Research working paper no. 6904.

Bandyopadhyay, S., C.C. Coughlin and H.J. Wall (2008), 'Ethnic networks and US exports', *Review of International Economics*, **16**, 199–213.

Bardhan, A.D. and S. Guhathakurta (2004), 'Global linkages of sub-national regions: coastal exports and international networks', *Contemporary Economic Policy*, **22**, 225–36.

Batalova, J. and D. Dixon (2005), 'Foreign-born self-employed in the United States', accessed at www.migrationinformation.org/USFocus/display.cfm?ID=301, accessed August 2009.

BBC World Service (2008), 'Widespread unease about economy and globalization', accessed August 2009 at www.worldpublicopinion.org/pipa/pdf/feb08/BBCEcon_Feb08_rpt.pdf.

Bergstrand, J.H. (1985), 'The gravity equation in international trade: some microeconomic foundations and empirical evidence', *Review of Economics and Statistics*, **67**, 474–81.

Blanes, J.V. (2003), 'The link between immigration and trade in Spain', Universidad Pablo de Olavide paper presented at XXVIII Simposio de Analisis Economico, 11-13 December, Seville.

Blanes, J.V. (2005), 'Does immigration help to explain intra-industry trade?

Evidence for Spain', *Review of World Economics (Weltwirtschaftliches Archiv)*, **141**(2), 244–70.

Blanes, J.V. (2006), 'Immigrants' characteristics and their different effects on bilateral trade. Evidence from Spain', Universidad Pablo de Olavide Departamento de Economía working papers 06.08.

Blanes, J.V. and J.A. Martín-Montaner (2006), 'Migration flows and intra-industry trade adjustments', *Review of World Economics (Weltwirtschaftliches Archive)*, **127**, 567–84.

Boisso, D. and M. Ferrantino (1997), 'Economic distance, cultural distance, and openness in international trade: empirical puzzles', *Journal of Economic Integration*, **12**, 456–84.

Borjas, G.J. (1999), *Heaven's Door: Immigration Policy and the American Economy*, Princeton, NJ: Princeton University Press.

Borjas, G.J. (2003), 'The labor demand curve is downward sloping: re-examining the impact of immigration on the labor market', *Quarterly Journal of Economics*, **118**, 1335–76.

Borjas, G.J. and L. Hilton (1996), 'Immigration and the welfare state: immigrant participation in means-tested entitlement programs', *Quarterly Journal of Economics*, **111**, 575–604.

Borjas, G.J., R.B. Freeman and L.F. Katz (1997), 'How much do immigration and trade affect labor market outcomes?', *Brookings Papers on Economic Activity*, **1**, 1–90.

Bouscaren, A.T. (1963), *International Migrations Since 1945*, New York: Frederick A. Praeger.

Briggs, V.M. (2003), *Mass Immigration and the National Interest: Policy Directions for the New Century*, New York: M.E. Sharpe.

Brooks, D.H. (2008), 'Infrastructure and Asia's trade costs', *Asian Development Bank Policy Brief No. 27* (June), accessed December at http://www.adbi.org/research-policy-brief/2008/06/25/2598.infrastructure.asia.trade.costs/.

Brown, A. (1995), *Organizational Culture*, London: Pitman.

Bryant, J., M. Genc and D. Law (2004), 'Trade and migration to New Zealand', New Zealand Treasury working paper 04/18, Wellington.

Cano, A., G.M. del Corral and G. Poussin, United Nations Educational, Scientific and Cultural Organization (UNESCO) (2000), 'Culture, trade and globalisation: 25 questions and answers', Paris: UNESCO Publishing.

Card, D. (2001), 'Immigrant inflows, native outflows, and the local labor market impacts of higher immigration', *Journal of Labor Economics*, **19**, 22–64.

Castles, S. (2000), *Ethnicity and Globalization*, London: Sage.

Ching, H.S. and L. Chen (2000), 'Links between emigrants and the home country: the case of trade between Taiwan and China', in H. Kohno, P. Nijkamp and J. Poot (eds), *Regional Cohesion and Competition in the Age of Globalization*, Cheltenham, UK and Northampton, MA, USA: Edward Elgar.

Co, C.Y., P. Euzent and T. Martin (2004), 'The export effect of immigration into the USA', *Applied Economics*, **36**, 573–83.

Combes, P., M. Lafourcade and T. Mayer (2005), 'The trade creating effects of business and social networks: evidence from France', *Journal of International Economics*, **66**, 1–29.

Crafts, N. (2000), 'Globalization and growth in the twentieth century', International Monetary Fund working paper 2000/44.

Daniels, R. (2002), *Coming to America, A History of Immigration and Ethnicity in American Life*, New York: HarperCollins.

Daniels, R. (2003), *Guarding the Door: American Immigrants and Immigration Policy since 1882*, New York: Hill and Wang.

Davis, D. (1995), 'Intra-industry trade: a Heckscher-Ohlin-Ricardo approach', *Journal of International Economics*, **39**, 201–26.

Deardorff, A.V. (1998), 'Determinants of bilateral trade: does gravity work in a neoclassical world?', in J. Frankel (ed.), *The Regionalization of the World Economy*, Chicago, IL: University of Chicago Press.

Dolman, B. (2008), 'Migration, trade and investment', Australian Government Productivity Commission staff working paper, Canberra, February.

Doz, Y.L. and G. Hamel (1998), *Alliance Advantage: The Art of Creating Value through Partnering*, Boston, MA: Harvard Business School Press.

Dunlevy, J.A. (2006), 'The impact of corruption and language on the pro-trade effect of immigrants: evidence from the American states', *Review of Economics and Statistics*, **88**(1).

Dunlevy, J.A. and W.K. Hutchinson (1999), 'The impact of immigration on American import trade in the late nineteenth and early twentieth centuries', *The Journal of Economic History*, **59**(4), 1043–62, December.

Dunlevy, J.A. and W.K. Hutchinson (2001), 'The pro-trade effect of immigration on American exports during the late nineteenth and early twentieth centuries', Forschungs institute zur Zukunft der Arbeit Discussion paper no. 375, October.

Eaton, J. and S. Kortum (2002), 'Technology, geography and trade', *Econometrica*, **70**, 1741–79.

Eaton, J. and A. Tamura (1994), 'Bilateralism and regionalism in Japanese and US trade and foreign direct investment patterns', *Journal of the Japanese and International Economies*, **8**, 478–510.

Eichengreen, B. and D.A. Irwin (1996), 'The role of history in bilateral trade flows', National Bureau of Economic Research working paper no. 5565, Cambridge, MA.

Elsass, P.M. and J.F. Viega (1994), 'Acculturation in acquired organizations: a force-field perspective', *Human Relations*, **47**(4), 431–53.

Ethier, W.J. and L.E.O. Svensson (1986), 'The theorems of international trade with factor mobility', *Journal of International Economics*, **20**, 21–42.

Faustino, H. and N.C. Leitão (2008), 'Using the gravity equation to explain the Portuguese immigration–trade link', Technical University of Lisbon School of Economics and Management working paper no. 12/2008/DE/SOCIUS.

Federal Reserve Bank of St Louis (FRBSL) (2009a), 'Real exports of goods & services, Series ID: EXPGSCA', accessed January at http://research.stlouisfed.org/fred2/data/EXPGSCA.txt.

FRBSL (2009b), 'Real imports of goods & services, Series ID: IMPGSCA', accessed January at http://research.stlouisfed.org/fred2/data/IMPGSCA.txt.

FRBSL (2009c), 'Real gross domestic product, Series ID: GDPCA', accessed January at http://research.stlouisfed.org/fred2/data/GDPCA.txt.

Feenstra, R.C. (ed.) (2000), *The Impact of International Trade on Wages*, Chicago, IL: University of Chicago Press.

Feenstra, R.C., J. Markusen and A. Rose (2001), 'Using the gravity equation to differentiate among alternative theories of trade', *Canadian Journal of Economics*, **34**(2), 430–47.

Fix, M. and J. Passell (2002), 'The scope and impact of welfare reform's immigration provisions', Urban Institute discussion paper 02-03, Washington, DC.

Francois, J.F. and M. Manchin (2007), 'Institutions, infrastructure and trade', Centro Studi Luca d'Agliano Development Studies working paper no. 224, accessed at http://ssrn.com/abstract=964209.

Ghosh, S. and S. Yamarik (2004), 'Are regional trading arrangements trade creating? An application of extreme bounds analysis', *Journal of International Economics*, **63**(2), 369–95.

Gibson, C. and E. Lennon (1999), 'Historical census statistics on the foreign-born population of the United States, 1980–1990', US Census Bureau Population Division working paper no. 29.

Gilje, P.A. (1996), *Rioting in America*, Bloomington, IN and Indianapolis, IN: Indiana University Press.

Girma, S. and Z. Yu (2002), 'The link between immigration and trade: evidence from the UK', *Review of World Economics (Weltwirtschaftliches Archiv)*, **138**, 115–30.

Gould, D.M. (1994), 'Immigration links to the home nation: empirical implications for US bilateral trade flows', *Review of Economics and Statistics*, **76**, 302–16.

Graham, E.M. and P.R. Krugman (1995), *Foreign Direct Investment in the United States*, Washington, DC: Institute for International Economics.

Greenaway, D., P.A. Mahabir and C. Milner (2008), 'Has China displaced other Asian Countries' Exports?', *China Economic Review*, **19**, 152–69.

Grubel, H.G. and P.J. Lloyd (1975), *Intra-Industry Trade*, London: The Macmillan Press.

Guiso, L., P. Sapienza and L. Zingales (2005), 'Cultural biases in economic exchange', National Bureau of Economic Research working paper no. 11005, Cambridge, MA.

Hagenaars, J., L. Kalman and G. Moors (2003), 'Exploring Europe's basic values map', in Wil Arts, Jacques Hagenaars and Loek Halman (eds), *The Cultural Diversity of European Unity*, Boston, MA: Koninklijke Brill.

Hanson, G.H. (2005), *Why Does Immigration Divide America? Public Finance and Political Opposition to Open Borders*, Washington, DC: Institute for International Economics.

Haveman, J. and D. Hummels (1997), 'What can we learn from bilateral trade? Gravity and beyond', Purdue University, Krannert School of Management – Center for International Business Education and Research (CIBER) papers 97-002.

Haveman, J., A. Ardelean and C. Thornberg (2009), 'Trade infrastructure and trade costs: a study of selected Asian ports, in D.H. Brooks and D. Hummels (eds), *Infrastructure's Role in Lowering Asia's Trade Costs: Building for Trade*, Cheltenham, UK, and Northampton, MA, USA: Edward Elgar.

Head, K. and T. Mayer (2000), 'Non-Europe: the magnitude and causes of market fragmentation in Europe', *Weltwirtschaftliches Archiv*, **136**(2), 285–314.

Head, K. and J. Ries (1998), 'Immigration and trade creation: econometric evidence from Canada', *Canadian Journal of Economics*, **31**, 47–62.

Heer, D.M. (1996), *Immigration in America's Future: Social Science Findings and the Policy Debate*, Boulder, CO: Westview Press.

Helliwell, J.F. (1997), 'National borders, trade and migration', *Pacific Economic Review*, **3**(3), 165–85.

Helpman, E. and P.R. Krugman (1985), *Market Structure and Foreign Trade: Increasing Returns, Imperfect Competition, and the International Economy*, Cambridge, MA: MIT Press.

Herander, M.G. and L.A. Saavedra (2005), 'Exports and the structure of immigrant-based networks: the role of geographic proximity', *Review of Economics and Statistics*, **87**(2), 323–35.

Hofstede, G. (1980), *Culture's Consequences: International Difference in Work Related Values*, Beverly Hills, CA: Sage Publications.

Hofstede, G. (1981), 'Culture and organizations', *International Studies of Management and Organization*, **10**(4), 15–41.

Hong, T.C. and A.S. Santhapparaj (2006), 'Skilled labor immigration and external trade in Malaysia: a pooled data analysis', *Perspectives on Global Development and Technology*, **5**(4), 351–66, November.

Hutchinson, W.K. (2002), 'Does ease of communication increase trade? Commonality of language and bilateral trade', *Scottish Journal of Political Economy*, **49**(5), 544–56.

Inglehart, R., M. Basanez, J. Diez-Medrano, L. Halman and R. Luijkx (eds) (2004), *Human Beliefs and Values: A Cross-cultural Sourcebook based on the 1999–2002 Values Surveys*, Mexico City: Siglo Veintiuno Editores, S.A. de C.V.

International Monetary Fund (IMF) (2008), 'International Financial Statistics' computer file, Washington, DC.

International Organization for Migration (IOM) (2008), *World Migration 2008: Managing Labour Mobility in the Evolving Global Economy*, Geneva: IOM.

Ivanov, A.V. (2008), 'Informational effects of migration on trade', University of Mannheim Center for Doctoral Studies in Economics discussion paper no. 42, May.

Jiang, S. (2007), 'Immigration, information, and trade margins', University of Calgary Department of Economics working paper no. 2007-16.

Kandogan, Y. (2005), 'Is immigration necessary and sufficient? The Swiss case on the role of immigrants on international trade', working paper.

Kennedy, R.F. (1965), 'Statement by Robert F. Kennedy to the US Senate Subcommittee on Immigration', 4 March, Washington, DC.

Kennedy, T. (1965), 'Statement by Senator Ted Kennedy to the US Senate Subcommittee on Immigration and Naturalization of the Committee on the Judiciary', 10 February, Washington, DC.

Kletzer, L.G. (2001), *Job Loss from Imports: Measuring the Costs*, Washington, DC: Institute for International Economics.

Kletzer, L.G. (2002), *Imports, Exports and Jobs: What Does Trade Mean for Employment and Job Loss?*, Kalamazoo, MI: W.E. Upjohn Institute for Employment Research.

Kogut, B. and H. Singh (1988), 'The effect of national culture on the choice of entry mode', *Journal of International Business Studies*, **19**(3), 411–32, September.

Krugman, P.R. (1980), 'Scale economies, product differentiation, and the pattern of trade', *American Economic Review*, **70**, 950–59.

Larimo, J. (2003), 'Form of investment by Nordic firms in world markets', *Journal of Business Research*, **56**(10), 791–803, October.

Lazear, E.P. (1999), 'Culture and language', *Journal of Political Economy*, **107**, S95–S126.

League of Nations (1945), *Industrialization and Foreign Trade*, Geneva: League of Nations, Economic, Financial and Transit Department.

Lepore, J. (2002), *A is for American: Letters and Other Characters in the Newly United States*, New York: Knopf.

Lewer, J.J. (2006), 'The impact of immigration on bilateral trade: OECD results from 1991–2000', *Southwestern Economic Review*, **33**(1) (Spring), 9–22.

Light, I. (1985), 'Ethnicity and business enterprise', in M. Mark Stolarik and Murray Friedman (eds), *Making it in America*, Lewisburg, PA: Bucknell University.

Light, I. and E. Bonacich (1988), *Emigrant Entrepreneurs*, Berkeley and Los Angeles, CA: University of California Press.

Limao, N. and A.J. Venables (2001), 'Infrastructure, geographical disadvantage, transport costs and trade', *World Bank Economic Review*, **15**, 451–79.

Linders, G.J., A. Slangen, H.L.F. de Groot, and S. Beugelsdijk (2005), 'Cultural and institutional determinants of bilateral trade', Tinbergen Institute discussion paper-TI-2005-074/3, the Netherlands.

Markusen, J.R. (1983), 'Factor movements and commodity trade as complements', *Journal of International Economics*, **14**, 341–56.

Markusen, J.R. and L.E.O. Svensson (1985), 'Trade in goods and factors with international differences in technology', *International Economic Review*, **26**, 175–92.

Martin, P. and E. Midgley (1999), 'Immigration to the United States', *Population Bulletin*, **54**(2), June.

McCallum, J. (1995), 'National borders matter: Canada–US regional trade patterns', *American Economic Review*, **85**(3), 615–23, June.

McDonald, J.F. and R.A. Moffitt (1980), 'The uses of Tobit analysis', *The Review of Economics and Statistics*, **62**(2), 318–21.

Migration Policy Institute (MPI) (2003), 'Remittances from the United States in context', accessed January 2009 at www.migrationinformation.org/USFocus/display.cfm?ID=138.

Milanovic, B. (2002), 'Unexpected convergence: disintegration of world economy 1919–1939, and income convergence among rich countries', working paper.

Min, P.G. (1990), 'Korean immigrants in Los Angeles', Institute of Social

Sciences Research working paper **2**(2), University of California, Los Angeles.

Mitchell, S.A. (1840), *Mitchell's Geographical Reader: A System of Modern Geography, Comprising a Description of the World, with its Grand Divisions, America, Europe, Asia, Africa and Oceanica*, Philadelphia, PA: Thomas, Cowperthwait and Co.

Morgenroth, E. and M. O'Brien (2008), 'Some further results of the impact of migrants on trade', Dynamic Regions in a Knowledge-Driven Global Economy (DYNREG) working paper no. 26, Dublin.

Mundell, R. (1957), 'International trade and factor mobility', *American Economic Review*, **47**, 321–35.

Mundra, K. (2005), 'Immigration and international trade: a semiparametric empirical investigation', *Journal of International Trade & Economic Development*, **14**(1), 65–91, March.

Murat, M. and B. Pistoresi (2006), 'Migration and bilateral trade flows: evidence from Italy', Università di Modena e Reggio Emilia Dipartimento di Economia Politica working paper, October.

Nordas, H.K. and R. Piermartini (2004), 'Infrastructure and trade', World Trade Organization Staff working paper ERSD-2004-04.

OANDA (2008), *FXHistory Database*, accessed December at www.oanda. com/convert/fxhistory.

Parsons, C. (2005), 'Quantifying the trade-migration nexus of the enlarged EU: a comedy of errors or much ado about nothing?', Sussex Centre for Migration Research, Sussex Migration working paper no. 27.

Passel, J.S. and D. Cohn (2008), 'US population projections: 2005–2050', Pew Research Center Report, accessed August 2009 at http://pewhispanic.org/files/reports/85.pdf.

Piperakis, A.S., C. Milner and P.W. Wright (2003), 'Immigration, trade costs and trade: gravity evidence for Greece', *Journal of Economic Integration*, **18**, 750–62.

Polling Report (2009a), 'Immigration', accessed January at www.pollingreport.com/immigration.htm.

Polling Report (2009b), 'International trade/global economy', accessed January at www.pollingreport.com/trade.htm.

Price, C. (1996), 'Ethnic intermixture of migrants and indigenous peoples in Australia', *People and Place*, **4**(4).

Price, C. (1999), 'Australian population: ethnic origins', *People and Place*, **7**(4).

Purvis, T.L. (1997), *A Dictionary of American History*, Malden, MA: Blackwell Publishers Ltd.

Qian, M. (2008), 'The economic relationship between trade and immigration in New Zealand', Massey University – Albany Integration of Immigrants Programme working paper no. 1., November.

Ranjan, P. and J. Tobias (2005), 'Bayes and gravity', Iowa State University working paper no. 05026, Ames, IA.

Rauch, J. (1999), 'Networks versus markets in international trade', *Journal of International Economics*, **48**, 7–35.

Rauch, J. (2001), 'Business and social networks in international trade', *Journal of Economic Literature*, **39**, 1177–203.

Rauch, J. and V. Trindade (2002), 'Ethnic Chinese networks in international trade, *Review of Economics and Statistics*, **84**(1), 116–30.

Rauch, J. and J. Watson (2002), 'Entrepreneurship in international trade', National Bureau of Economic Research working paper no. 8708, Cambridge, MA.

Razin, E. (1990), 'Immigrant entrepreneurs in Israel, Canada, and California', University of California Los Angeles Institute of Social Sciences Research working papers **5**(15).

Ruiz, V. and V.S. Korrol (eds) (2006), *Latinas in the United States: A Historical Encyclopedia (Volume 1)*, Bloomington, IN and Indianapolis, IN: University of Indiana Press.

Sassen, S. (1990), 'US immigration policy toward Mexico in a global economy', *Journal of International Affairs*, **43** (Winter), 471–80.

Sassen, S. (1992), 'Why immigration?', *Report on the Americas*, **26**, 14–19.

Scheve, K.F. and M.J. Slaughter (2001), *Globalization and the Perceptions of American Workers*, Washington, DC: Institute for International Economics.

Schwartz, A.P. (1964), 'Foreign and domestic implications of US immigration laws', speech presented at St Olaf's College, Northfield, MN, 3 April.

Smith, J.P. and B. Edmonston (eds) (1997), *The New Americans: Economic, Demographic and Fiscal Effects of Immigration*, Washington, DC: National Academies Press.

Sum, A., N. Fog and P. Harrington (2002), *Immigrant Workers and the Great American Job Machine: The Contributions of New Foreign Immigrants to National and Regional Labor Force Growth in the 1990s*, Boston, MA: Northeastern University Center for Labor Market Studies.

Svensson, L.E.O. (1984), 'Factor trade and goods trade', *Journal of International Economics*, **16**, 365–78.

Tadesse, B. and R. White (2010a), 'Cultural distance as a determinant of bilateral trade flows: do immigrants counter the effect of cultural differences?', *Applied Economic Letters*, **17**(2), 147–52.

Tadesse, B. and R. White (2010b), 'Does cultural distance hinder trade?

A comparative study of nine OECD member nations', *Open Economies Review*, (February).

Tadesse, B. and R. White (2009), 'Do immigrants enhance international trade in services? The case of US tourism services exports', working paper.

Tadesse, B. and R. White (2008), 'Do immigrants counter the effect of cultural distance on trade? Evidence from US state-level exports', *Journal of Socio-Economics*, **37**(6), 2304–18, (December).

Tadesse, B. and R. White (2007), 'Does home country economic development matter for the immigrant–trade link? Evidence from Australia', working paper.

Tai, S.H. (2007), 'Immigration and trade: what is the difference between exportations and importations', working paper.

Taylor, T.L. (ed.) (2002), *Minority Families in the United States: A Multicultural Perspective*, 3rd edn, Upper Saddle River, NJ: Prentice Hall.

Tichenor, D. (2002), *Dividing Lines: The Politics of Immigration Control in America*, Princeton, NJ: Princeton University Press.

Tinbergen, J. (1962), *The World Economy. Suggestions for an International Economic Policy*, New York: Twentieth Century Fund.

United Nations (2005), *International Flows of Selected Cultural Goods and Services, 1994–2003: Defining and Capturing the Flows of Global Cultural Trade*, Montreal: UNESCO Institute for Statistics, UNESCO Sector for Culture.

United Nations Conference on Trade and Development (UNCTAD) (2008), *World Investment Report: Transnational Corporations, and the Infrastructure Challenge*, New York and Geneva: United Nations Publications.

United States Bureau of Economic Analysis (US BEA) (2008a), *US International Transactions, 1960–present*, accessed December at www.bea.gov/international/xls/table1.xls.

United States Bureau of Economic Analysis (US BEA) (2008b), 'Current-dollar and "real" GDP', accessed December at www.bea.gov/national/xls/gdplev.xls.

US Census (2001), *Profile of the Foreign-Born Population of the United States: 2000*, Washington, DC:

US Census (2003), *The Foreign-born Population: 2000*, Census 2000 brief, accessed December 2008 at www.census.gov/prod/2003puibs/c2kbr-34.pdf.

US Census (2006), 'Foreign-Born Profiles STP-159', accessed December 2008 at www.census.gov/population/www/socdemo/foreign/STP-159-2000tl.html.

US Census (2008), *Region of Birth of the Foreign-Born Population: 1850 to 1930 and 1960-1990*, accessed December at www.census.gov/population/www/documentation/twps0029/tab02.html.

US Census (2009), *American Community Survey*, accessed January at http://factfinder.census.gov.

US DHS (2004), *Yearbook of Immigration Statistics: 2003*, Washington, DC: Office of Immigration Statistics, US Government Printing Office.

United States Department of Homeland Security (US DHS) (2007a), *Estimates of Unauthorized Immigrant Population Residing in the United States: January 2006*, Washington, DC: Office of Immigration Statistics, US Government Printing Office.

US DHS (2007b), *Yearbook of Immigration Statistics: 2006*, Washington, DC: Office of Immigration Statistics, US Government Printing Office.

United States Department of Justice, Immigration and Naturalization Service (US INS) (1990–2001), *Statistical Yearbook of the Immigration and Naturalization Service*, Washington, DC: US Government Printing Office.

United States International Trade Commission (USITC) (2008), '*US imports/exports data (DataWeb)*, accessed December at http://dataweb.usitc.gov/.

University of California – Berkeley (2009), 'The Chinese in California, 1850–1925', compilation involving materials from The Bancroft Library and the Ethnic Studies Library of the University of California Berkeley and The California Historical Society, accessed May at http://memory.loc.gov/ammem/award99/cubhtml/cichome.html.

Venables, A. (1999), 'Trade liberalization and factor mobility: an overview', in R. Faini, J. de Melo and K. Zimmermann (eds), *Migration: The Controversies and the Evidence*, Cambridge: Cambridge University Press and CEPR.

Wagner, D., K. Head and J. Ries (2002), 'Immigration and the trade of provinces', *Scottish Journal of Political Economy*, **49**(5), 507–25.

White, R. (2007a), 'Immigrant–trade links, transplanted home bias and network effects', *Applied Economics*, **39**(7) (April), 839–52.

White, R. (2007b), 'An examination of the Danish immigrant–trade link', *International Migration*, **45**(5) (December), 61–86.

White, R. (2008), 'Exploring a US immigrant–intra-industry trade link', *Eastern Economic Journal*, **34**(2) (Spring), 252–62.

White, R. (2009a), 'Immigration, trade and product differentiation', *Economic Issues*, **14**(1) (March), 43–63.

White, R. (2009b), 'Immigration, trade and home country development:

state-level variation in the US immigrant–export link', *Journal of International Migration and Integration*, **10**(2) (May), 121–43.

White, R. and B. Tadesse (2007), 'Immigration policy, cultural pluralism and trade: evidence from the white Australia policy', *Pacific Economic Review*, **12**(4) (October), 489–509.

White, R. and B. Tadesse (2008a), 'Cultural distance and the US immigrant–trade link', *The World Economy*, **31**(8) (August), 1078–96.

White, R. and B. Tadesse (2008b), 'Immigrants, cultural distance and US state-level exports of cultural products', *North American Journal of Economics and Finance*, **19**(3) (December), 331–48.

White, R. and B. Tadesse (2009a), 'East–West migration and the immigrant–trade link: evidence from Italy', *The Romanian Journal of European Studies*, **5–6/2007** (April), 67–84.

White, R. and B. Tadesse (2009b), 'Immigration, cultural distance and trade: a study of nine OECD host countries', in L.B. Kerwin (ed.), *Cultural Diversity: Issues, Challenges and Perspectives*, Hauppauge, NY: Nova Science Publishers.

White, R. and B. Tadesse (2010), 'Refugee and non-refugee immigrants, cultural distance and US trade with immigrant home countries', *Journal of International Trade & Economic Development*, (Spring).

Wong, K. (1986), 'Are international trade and factor mobility substitutes?', *Journal of International Economics*, **21**, 21–43.

World Bank (2009a), *World Development Indicators*, Washington, DC: Development Data Group of the World Bank's International Economics Department, accessed January at http://go.worldbank.org/6HAYAHG8H0.

World Bank (2009b), 'Globalization', accessed May at http://youthink.worldbank.org/issues/globalization/.

World Bank (2009c), *World Governance Indicators, 1996–2008*, accessed January at http://info.worldbank.org/governance/wgi/index.asp.

Zimmerman, W. and K.C. Tumlin (1999), 'Patchwork policies: state assistance for immigrants under welfare reform', Urban Institute occasional paper 21, Washington, DC.

Zolberg, A.R. (2006), *A Nation by Design: Immigration Policy and the Fashioning of America*, New York: Russell Sage Foundation with Harvard University Press.

Index

Afghanistan 6, 70
Africa 75, 76, 80, 81
Albania 88, 107, 109, 112, 141, 142, 160, 174
Algeria 88, 107, 109, 112, 141, 142, 160
Alien and Sedition Acts 66
Altonji, J.G. 178
Anderson, J.E. 117
Anti–Coolie Act 67
Arabia 6, 70
Argentina 4, 88, 107, 109, 112, 142, 160, 174
Armenia 88, 107, 109, 113, 141, 142, 144, 160
Articles of Confederation 65
Asia 6, 9, 18, 51, 52, 63, 65, 68, 70–72, 74–6, 79–82, 84, 86, 158, 177
Asia–Pacific Triangle 72, 158
Asiatic Barred Zone 6, 70, 72, 84, 158
assimilate 31, 48
assimilation 31, 144
asylee 50, 123, 125, 126, 128, 129, 147, 185
asylum 8, 50, 58, 75, 119, 123, 147, 148, 152, 184, 189, 197, 198
asymmetric information 18, 29, 32–4, 41, 46, 47, 52, 61, 79, 86, 102, 105, 110, 162, 166, 184, 190, 196
Australia 4, 8, 9, 44, 47, 51–3, 59, 63, 71, 76, 86, 88, 105, 107, 109, 112, 114, 142, 160, 174, 189
Austria 60, 74, 83, 88, 107, 109, 112, 114, 142, 160, 174
Azerbaijan 88, 107, 109, 113, 142, 160

Bacarreza, C. 42, 43, 45
Balassa, B. 42
Baldwin, R. 5
Bandyopadhyay, S. 40
Bangladesh 9, 88, 107, 109, 112, 142, 160, 174

Bardhan, A.D. 39, 53, 144
Batalova, J. 14
BBC World Service 202
Belgium 74, 88, 107, 109, 112, 142, 160, 174
Bergstrand, J.H. 37, 117
Bermuda 64, 71
Blanes, J.V. 42, 43, 45, 49, 50
Bloomberg 12
Bohemia 83
Boisso, D. 33, 104
Bolivia 42, 43, 45
Bolshevik Revolution 82
Bonacich, E. 38
Borjas, G.J. 13, 178
Bouscaren, A.T. 52
Brazil 88, 107, 109, 113, 142, 160, 174
Bretton Woods Conference 8
Breusch–Godfrey test 119
Briggs, V.M. 6, 7, 9, 71, 77, 81, 84, 180
British Isles 66
Brooks, D.H. 89, 91, 92
Brown, A. 102
Bryant, J. 36, 43, 47
Bulgaria 88, 107, 109, 113, 142, 160, 174
Bureau of Security and Consular Affairs 73

California 66, 68, 69
California Gold Rush 6, 67
Cambodia 82
Canada 9, 43–5, 49–51, 54, 59, 63, 71, 73, 74, 76, 83, 84, 86, 88, 105, 107, 109, 112, 114, 141, 142, 153, 158, 160, 174, 189
Cano, A. 121
Card, D. 178
Caribbean Basin 9, 18, 35, 63, 71, 76, 79, 80, 81, 82, 84, 86, 177